# Lecture Notes in Computer Science 3427

Commenced Publication in 1973
Founding and Former Series Editors:
Gerhard Goos, Juris Hartmanis, and Jan van Leeuwen

T0223548

Gabriele Kotsis   Otto Spaniol (Eds.)

# Wireless Systems and Mobility in Next Generation Internet

First International Workshop
of the EURO-NGI Network of Excellence
Dagstuhl Castle, Germany, June 7-9, 2004
Revised Selected Papers

 Springer

Volume Editors

Gabriele Kotsis
Johannes Kepler Universität Linz, Telecooperation Department
Altenberger Straße 69, 4040 Linz, Austria
E-mail: gabriele.kotsis@jku.ac.at

Otto Spaniol
RWTH Aachen University, Department of Computer Science
Ahornstr. 55, 52074 Aachen, Germany
E-mail: spaniol@informatik.rwth-aachen.de

Library of Congress Control Number: 2005922179

CR Subject Classification (1998): C.2, H.4, H.3

ISSN 0302-9743
ISBN 3-540-25329-7 Springer Berlin Heidelberg New York

Springer is a part of Springer Science+Business Media

springeronline.com

© Springer-Verlag Berlin Heidelberg 2005
Printed in Germany

Typesetting: Camera-ready by author, data conversion by Markus Richter, Heidelberg
Printed on acid-free paper      SPIN: 11407492      06/3142      5 4 3 2 1 0

# Preface

The Internet is subject to permanent modifications and to continuous restructuring. This is primarily due to the tremendous rise in demand for bandwidth by the ever increasing number of users. When compared to the early years of the Internet the quality of the services offered had to be significantly improved in different respects (delay, network and service availability, jitter, ...) in order to satisfy the needs of many new applications.

Within the last decade two new developments have contributed to many new opportunities, as well as to a need for intensive research and development:

- the increased mobility of users together with the desire for ubiquitous high-quality access to all offered services, at reasonable cost;
- the use of wireless communication.

Despite their relatively low capacity (when compared with fixed backbone networks) the use of radio links supports the ubiquitous availability of Internet services in a quasiperfect way.

A considerable amount of research and development activities are currently going on worldwide in order to adapt Internet services to the particular needs of mobile users and of wireless communication links. These questions were intensively discussed at the first workshop organized by the EURO-NGI Network of Excellence ('Next Generation Internet'), which has been funded by the European Union since January 2004 under their IST programme. The workshop brought together more than 20 out of the almost 60 research groups from all over Europe which co-operate in EURO-NGI towards a restructuring of the Internet, with a particular emphasis on the European situation. The workshop on 'Mobile and Wireless Systems' was held in June 2004 at the International Conference and Research Centre for Computer Science (Schloss Dagstuhl, Germany; http://www.dagstuhl.de). The absolutely great and inspiring environment, as well as the technical and non-technical facilities which are provided by this centre contributed very much to very intensive discussions, to a common understanding, and to significant progress concerning the research topics discussed.

This workshop proceedings contains a selection of 16 research contributions, which were extended to incorporate the numerous suggestions made by the international reviewers. The editors are convinced that this book provides a most relevant and highly up-to-date summary of problems of, and of suitable solutions for, the next-generation Internet in the area of wireless communication for mobile users.

Aachen and Linz, January 2005                                    Gabriele Kotsis
                                                                  Otto Spaniol

# Reviewers

Blondia, Chris
Borcoci, Eugen
Boxma, Onno
Casaca, Augusto
Casares-Giner, Vicente
Courcoubetis, Costas
Czachorski, Tadeusz
De Meer, Hermann
Emstad, Peder
Fidler, Markus
Fiedler, Markus
Frata, Luigi
Garcia, Jorge
Georgiadis, Leonidas
Giordano, Stefano
Hackbarth, Klaus
Haring, Guenter
Hasslinger, Gerhard
Italiano, Giuseppe
Iversen, Villy Baek
Jajszczyk, Andrzej
Koehler, Stefan
Kouvatsos, Demetres
Levy, Hanoch
Mitrani, Isi
Nino-Mora, Jose
Norros, Ilkka
Pacheco, Antonio
Persaud, Rajendra
Pioro, Michal
Rieder, Ulrich
Roberts, James
Sabella, Roberto
Tutschku, Kurt
Villen-Altamirano, Manuel
Virtamo, Jorma
Wittevrongel, Sabine

# Table of Contents

## Network (Inter)connection and Resource Access

## Author Index

# Introduction

Gabriele Kotsis

Johannes Kepler University Linz, Institute for Telecooperation
Altenberger Strasse 69, A-4040 Linz, Austria
gabriele.kotsis@jku.ac.at
http://www.tk.uni-linz.ac.at

## 1   The Need for Mobile and Wireless Networks

Europe is in a transition from a low value manufacturing area into a "brainware region" producing high value added products and services. A key factor of success is the optimal usage of the most valuable resource in the information society, namely the human resources. Considering the need for specialisation along with the observable shortage of highly-qualified personnel, new forms of business organisations have been developed, migrating from a division oriented organisation to a task oriented organisation, bringing together the experts within an organisation in dynamically established teams. This trend is expected to continue and virtual organisations are evolving, in which expertise (and experts) are shared not only within a business organisation, but among the business organisations constituting the virtual enterprise. To efficiently support those types of business to business relations, support from information and communication technology is needed.

The major challenges from a technical point of view are to provide access to information sources and computation power, and to provide channels and media for cooperation and collaboration in a time and space independent way. This new paradigm in computing is referred to as mobile computing, or emphasising the idea of ubiquity of communication and computing resources, is called pervasive computing or ubiquitous computing.

The key underlying technologies for mobility are wireless networks and mobile computing/communication devices, including smart phones, PDAs, or (Ultra)portables. Wireless technologies are deployed in global and wide area networks, (GSM, GPRS and future UMTS, wireless ATM backbone networks, GEO and LEO satellite systems), in local area networks (WLAN, mobile IP), but also in even smaller regional units such as a campus or a room (Java/Jini, Bluetooth, Piano). Those technologies have enabled many different aspects of mobility which will be briefly discussed in the following three subsections.

### 1.1   Mobility in the Networking Infrastructure

For decades, computer network architectures and protocols have been designed assuming fixed, wired connections. Major design objectives are to characterise

G. Kotsis and O. Spaniol (Eds.): Mobile and Wireless Systems, LNCS 3427, pp. 1–6, 2005.

and handle traffic demands meeting pre-defined quality of service (QoS) requirements and to efficiently use the available resources in doing so.

Mobility and wireless connections are opening up new challenges. On the one hand, communication networks nowadays have to support a plethora of services whose traffic demands are not fully studied yet. Mobility of users, applications and services (see also the next two subsections) adds to this complexity. On the other hand, new mechanisms and protocols are needed in order to efficiently consider the scarcity and high cost of the radio resource. The capacity of wireless networks cannot be expressed in a simple way, like link bandwidth in wire-line networks, but is a complicated function of the time-varying channel quality of each active user and of the way radio resources, e.g. power and bandwidth, are shared.

From a performance point of view congestion control, traffic management and traffic engineering need to be reconsidered in the specific context of wireless networks. The design and analysis of corresponding mechanisms is extremely challenging due to the complexity but also the variety of the underlying wireless technology (e.g. CDMA, WLAN (802.11x), Bluetooth).

## 1.2   Mobility of Users

A fundamental necessity for mobile and wireless information delivery is to understand the behavior and needs of the users, i.e. of the people. Understanding user behaviour, both, from a qualitative as well as from a quantitative point of view, will help to design and dimension mobile and wireless network architectures and services.

Recent research issues include efficient mechanisms for the prediction of user behavior (e.g. location of users in cellular systems) in order to allow for proactive management of the underlying networks. Besides this quantitative evaluation user behavior can also be studied from a quantitative point of view (how well is the user able to do her or his job, what is the level of user satisfaction, etc.). Keeping in mind the need for privacy of users, the goal is not to identify the behaviour of an individual user (as this would be of interest for example in marketing studies), but to identify classes of users with similar behaviour in order to adapt applications and services according to their needs.

## 1.3   Mobility of Applications and Services

Mobile applications are based on a computational paradigm, which is quite different from the traditional model, in which programs are executed on a stationary single computer. In mobile computing, processes may migrate (with users) according to the tasks they perform, providing the user with his or her particular work environment wherever he or she is. To accomplish this goal of ubiquitous access, key requirements are platform independence but also automatic adaptation of applications to (1) the processing capabilities that the current execution platform is able to offer and (2) the connectivity that is currently provided by the network.

Mobile services and applications differ with respect to the quality of service delivered (in terms of reliability and performance) and the degree of mobility they support, ranging from stationary, to walking, to even faster movements in cars, trains, or airplanes. A particular challenge is imposed by (interactive) multimedia applications, which are characterized by high QoS demands. New methods and techniques for characterizing the workload and for QoS modeling are needed to adequately capture the characteristics of mobile commerce applications and services.

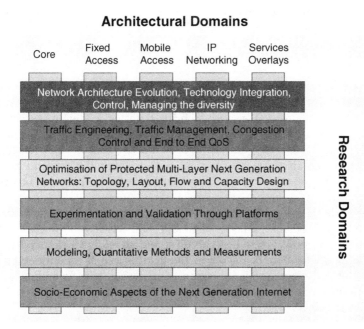

**Fig. 1.** Joint Research Program of EuroNGI

## 2   The EuroNGI Project

The main objective of the Euro NGI Network of Excellence is to create and maintain the most prominent European center of excellence in Next Generation Internet design and engineering, acting as a *Collective Intelligence Think Tank*, representing a major support for the European Information Society industry and leading towards a European leadership in this domain.

In this context, the main topics addressed by the NoE are: (1) Mastering the technology diversity (vertical and horizontal integration) for the design of efficient and flexible NGI architectures, and (2) Providing required innovative traffic engineering architectures adapted to the new requirements and developing the corresponding appropriate quantitative methods.

The present programme for jointly executed research activities is depicted in Figure 1. The architectural domains are defined to take into account the whole network architecture: the access, the core, the IP networking covering and hiding the transport technology diversity and the overlays for service infrastructure (CDNs, per-to-peer, etc.). The Research Domains are defined to face the various problems arising when integrating the various architectural domains to provide flexible network architectures. The research activities are accompanied by integration activities aimed at uniting the research efforts of the participating groups and spreading of excellence activities aimed at disseminating the research results and promoting knowledge transfer.

## 3    About This Book

In June 2004, a workshop on Wireless and Mobility in NGI was organised as an integration activity by the EuroNGI consortium at Schloss Dagstuhl, Germany. The objectives of the workshop were to bring together leading researchers from the NoE in this field of research in order to identify the fundamental challenges and future perspective of this important area. Participants of the workshop have been invited to submit their contributions for possible publication in this book. After a review by external experts, 16 papers have been chosen to be accepted for publication.

In line with the objectives of the EuroNGI project, the contributions discuss different performance aspects of mobile and wireless networks, including 3G cellular networks, WLANs or MANETs, and should give the reader a good understanding of the state of the art in the field as well as an outlook on topics subject to future research. The selection of papers in this volume also clearly indicates that mobile access cuts across all different EuroNGI research domains as shown in Figure 1.

The first five papers address the topic of network and capacity planning. Iversen et al. study the efficient utilisation of radio resources in 3G cellular networks in their paper on *Performance of Hierarchical Cellular Networks with Overlapping Cells*. The presented models are a generalization of the Erlang-B formula. Using Monte Carlo Simulation, Hossfeld and Staehle present a technique for evaluating the (web) capacity of an UMTS network. In their paper entitled *A Hybrid Model of the UMTS Downlink Capacity with WWW Traffic on Dedicated Channels* they argue that web traffic is expected to be a major application for packet switched services and thus study the applicability of existing planning methods to web traffic. Another study on UMTS networks is *Performance of Different Proxy Concepts in UMTS Networks* by Necker et al. The authors demonstrate that a combination of TCP and HTTP proxies can significantly improve end-to-end performance in UMTS networks. Optimisation models for positioning of access points in IEEE 802.11 based networks are presented by Amaldi et al. in *Algorithms for WLAN Coverage Planning*. Computational results are provided to show that the suggested heuristics provide near-optimal solutions within reasonable time. Optimisation models are also the method of choice for Van Quickenborne et al. in their work on *Designing Aggregation Networks to Support Fast Moving Users*. Distinguishing between access network related issues (where individual users are considered) and aggregation network issues (where groups of users are considered) the authors have designed and implemented protocols for tunnel configuration and activation.

Medium access and admission control are discussed in the next four contributions. In *Some Game-theoretic problems in wireless ad hoc networks* Altman et al. successfully apply game theory and stochastic approximation algorithms to the problem of finding optimum channel access rates in wireless ad hoc networks. Garroppo et al. use simulation techniques to evaluate the *Admission Region of Multimedia Services for EDCA in IEEE 802.11e Access Networks*. Voice over IP, videoconferencing and TCP traffic are considered in the study. Results show on the one hand the efficiency in traffic differentiation of the ECDA algorithm but also reveal the access point as bottleneck when services producing symmetrical traffic are conveyed. In *Admission Control Policies in Multiservice Cellular Networks: Optimum Configuration and Sensitivity* Garcia et al. evaluate different CAC policies for multiservice cellular networks. An optimization method is presented to find optimum configurations for most policies. A new CAC algorithm is proposed by Elayoubi et al. in *Admission Control in the downlink of WCDMA/UMTS*. Based on bandwidth expressions for different calls as a function of position in the cell and traffic class (voice or data), a mobility-based CAC is derived and analytically studied using Markovian modelling.

Methods to study and ensure QoS in wireless networks are the central focus of the next three papers. Hlavacs et al. study the *Effects of WLAN QoS Degradation on Streamed MPEG4 Video Quality*. Specifically, the effects of packet loss on the quality of streamed (MPEG-4) video are investigated. Extended Gilbert models are suggested as a model framework. Micro/macro mobility management and QoS control aspects are the primary focus of Axente-Stan and Borcoci in their work on *Integrating MPLS and Policy Based Management Technologies in Mobile Environment*. Variants for deploying the policy-based management approach in mobile environments are investigated. QoS reservation mechanisms are studied by Cerda et al. in their paper on *A Reservation Scheme Satisfying Bandwidth QoS Constraints for Ad-hoc Networks*. The given simulation results demonstrate the advantages of this reservation scheme.

The last group of papers discusses aspects of network (inter)connection and resource access. Hamidian et al. present an *Performance of Internet Access Solutions in Mobile Ad Hoc Networks*. A MANET routing protocol is extended and approaches for gateway discovery are presented to achieve interconnection between a MANET and the (fixed) Internet. The methods are compared by simulation. Many personal communication services rely on mechanism to identify the location of mobile terminals in order to correctly route incoming calls. Casares-Giner and Garciá-Escalle study such location management mechanisms in their paper *On the fractional movement-distance based scheme for PCS location management with selective paging*. Markovian modeling is used to analyse the suggested scheme. Access to data resources is the topic of *Enabling Mobile*

*Peer-to-Peer Networking* by Andersen et al. The authors present a file-sharing architecture that is designed and optimized for mobile 2.5/3G networks. One of the problems addressed is to reconcile the network operators interest in centralized traffic control versus the decentralized nature of file sharing systems. Ensuring connectivity within MANETs is the topic of the paper *A family of Encounter-based broadcast Protocols for Mobile Ad-hoc Networks* authored by Cooper et al. The suggested protocols for message propagation are studied analytically and by simulation to evaluate the relation between achievable coverage and the total number of broadcasts.

# Performance of Hierarchical Cellular Networks with Overlapping Cells

Villy B. Iversen, Vilius Benetis, and Peter D. Hansen

Research Center COM, Building 345v
Technical University of Denmark,
DK–2800 Kongens Lyngby, {vbi,vb}@com.dtu.dk

**Abstract.** An efficient utilisation of the radio resources in mobile communications is of a great importance. If the capacity is split into many independent small groups, then for a given blocking probability the utilization becomes low. In this paper we describe the basic principles and strategies for obtaining maximum utilisation as given by Erlang's B-formula. The models described are analytical models and generalisations of the Erlang-B formula, including general arrival processes and multi-rate (multi-media) traffic for second and third generation systems. A transformation from cell-based network to direct routing network model is used to carry out the calculations. By numerical examples we study the statistical multiplexing advantages of cell breathing, overlapping cells and hierarchical cell structures.

**Keywords:** blocking, cell breathing, cellular networks, direct routing, Erlang-B formula, hierarchical cellular networks, multi-rate services

## 1 Introduction

Cellular communication systems are designed to have an overlap between cells in order to provide better quality of communications, seamless hand-overs and capacity management. By a cell we denote a geographical area served by one transceiver (transmitter and receiver) station, such as base stations (BS) in Global System for Mobile Communications (GSM) and Node-B in the Universal Mobile Telecommunication System (UMTS).

Cell overlapping basically serves two purposes: (1) it provides continuous service by permitting smooth hand-over between cells and (2) customers in overlapped areas are ensured better connectivity by allowing access to resources of all cells in the overlapping area.

The latter case is analyzed in this paper, and it is shown by analytical modelling how it allows for improving the network performance by reducing blocking probabilities in both second and third generation mobile communication systems.

The purpose of this paper is to establish an analytical model which for a given cellular network structure with known overlap areas and hierarchical structure enables us to calculate the blocking probability for each type of traffic in each area. The traffic is modelled by mean offered traffic, peakedness, and slot-size.

G. Kotsis and O. Spaniol (Eds.): Mobile and Wireless Systems, LNCS 3427, pp. 7–19, 2005.

The model allows for allocation of a minimum number of channels to each traffic stream and also an upper limit to the number of calls from this stream. All models considered are insensitive to the service time distribution. The examples given are used to illustrate the ideas. The software developed [4] allows numerical calculations for any parameter values. The results can be used to develop simplified traffic engineering tools for dimensioning cellular systems.

The paper is organized as follows. At first related studies are over viewed, then cell overlap modelling is analyzed, followed by overview of modelling of hierarchical cell structures. Finally, evaluation methods and numerical examples are given to illustrate the theory along with a summary.

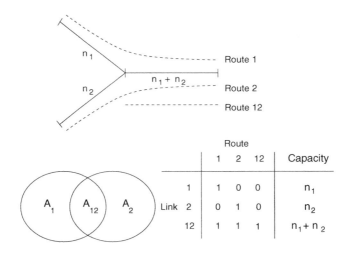

**Fig. 1.** Example of two overlapping cells and the equivalent circuit-switched network with direct routing

## 2    Related Studies

The subject of traffic modelling of cell overlap has been dealt with in few papers. In a recent paper [9] state-of-the-art is presented. One of the first papers are [2] which presents the product-form of the problem. Most papers consider the system as an overflow system and use the classical overflow theory for evaluation (e.g. [8]). They have for example dealt with overflow from micro-cell to macro-cell, but not take-back (also named call packing or rearrangement) from macro-cell to micro-cell.

A few papers (e.g. [1]) have set up the state transition diagram and solved the large set of linear equations. The convolution algorithm [5] was only applied in [6]. In this papers we will deal with both rearrangement of calls at the same hierarchical level, and rearrangement of calls between different levels of the hierarchy.

# 3    Overlapping Cell Boundaries

This section presents mathematical models used for modelling cell interaction and overlap capacity. As mentioned above, a cell is considered a geographical area served by one base station.

Let us consider an overlap between two cells in a cellular system as shown in Fig. 1 (left). The whole coverage zone is made out of three areas, area $A_1$ with access to $n_1$ channels of cell 1, area $A_2$ with access to $n_2$ channels of cell 2, and area $A_{12}$ with access to all $n_{12} = n_1 + n_2$ channels of both cells. Therefore, subscribers in $A_{12}$ will experience a smaller blocking probability than subscribers in the other areas. In an intelligent system we can freely rearrange (hand-over) calls in area $A_{12}$ between the two cells. We can formulate this as a set of restrictions on the number of calls of each type in this cellular system.

Denoting the number of existing connections in the area $A_i$ by $x_i$ we notice that we have the following restrictions:

$$0 \leq x_1 \leq n_1 \tag{1}$$
$$0 \leq x_2 \leq n_2 \tag{2}$$
$$0 \leq x_1 + x_2 + x_{12} \leq n_1 + n_2 \tag{3}$$

The above restrictions are equivalent to the restrictions in a circuit switched communication network with direct routing shown in the Fig. 1 (top). In general, for an arbitrary cellular network we may formulate restrictions upon the number of simultaneous calls of each type, for each restriction define a link, and transform the problem to an equivalent circuit switched network as shown in the following.

## 3.1    Direct Routing Network Model

A network with direct routing is described by *routes* $R_i$, *links* $L_j$, and the *number of channels* $d_{i,j}$ route $R_i$ utilises on link $j$. The models are valid for multi-slot systems with individual slot size $d_{i,j}$ for each route on each link.

## 3.2    Mapping Between Cellular and Direct Routing Network Models

The mapping between cellular networks and network with direct routing is done as follows. A route $R_i$ corresponds to a distinct area $A_i$ in the cellular model. Route index $i$ marks which cells are covering this area.

*Example 1.* According to the Fig. 1 (left), we can identify three routes. $R_1$ corresponds to the area $A_1$ (the serving area of cell 1 without overlapping parts). $R_2$ corresponds to the area $A_2$ (the serving area of cell 2 without overlapping parts). $R_{12}$ corresponds to the common overlapping area $A_{12}$ between cell 1 and cell 2.

A link $L_j$ corresponds to a territory which is the union of the areas covered by one or more cells. The link index $j$ indicates the cells included in the territory and numerically shows which routes are using the link.

| Link $j$ | Route $i$ | | | | Number of channels |
|---|---|---|---|---|---|
| | $R_1$ | $R_2$ | $\cdots$ | $R_N$ | |
| 1 | $d_{1,1}$ | $d_{2,1}$ | $\cdots$ | $d_{N,1}$ | $n_1$ |
| 2 | $d_{1,2}$ | $d_{2,2}$ | $\cdots$ | $d_{N,2}$ | $n_2$ |
| . | . | . | | . | . |
| $\cdots$ | $\cdots$ | $\cdots$ | | $\cdots$ | $\cdots$ |
| . | . | . | | . | . |
| K | $d_{1,K}$ | $d_{2,K}$ | $\cdots$ | $d_{N,K}$ | $n_K$ |

**Table 1.** In a circuit switched telecommunication network with direct routing, $d_{i,j}$ denotes the slot-size (bandwidth demand) of route $i$ upon link $j$.

*Example 2.* According to the Fig. 1 (left), we can identify three links. $L_1$ denotes the territory of $A_1$. $L_2$ denotes the territory of $A_2$. $L_{12}$ denotes the linked territory made of $A_1$ and $A_2$. In this way $L_{12}$ covers the whole network.

A link corresponds to a restriction. The number of routes $N$ becomes equal to the number of separate areas, whereas the number of links $K$ becomes equal to the number of restrictions, which is the number of connected areas (paths) we can built up from the distinguishable areas. If all $N$ cells are partially overlapping the number of links becomes equal to $K = 2^N - 1$, as we exclude the empty set. For the case considered in Fig. 2 both the number of routes and the number of links become 7. A maximum number of accessible resources (in units called channels) $n_j$ is associated with each link $L_j$. The sum of channels used by of all routes using this link $j$ is thus limited by $n_j$.

*Example 3.* According to the Fig. 1 (left), $n_j$ is given as follows: $n_1$ equals to the capacity $n_1$ of cell 1, $n_2$ equals to the capacity $n_2$ of cell 2, and $n_{12} equals n_1 + n_2$.

Another example is shown in Fig. 3. It may model part of as highway covered by cells. Due to the structure, the equivalent circuit switched network has 7 routes and 10 links.

### 3.3   Global Intelligence in the Network

We notice that if for example all channels are busy in cell one in Fig. 1, then if there are any connections in cell $A_{12}$ using channels of cell one we may rearrange (hand-over) one or more of these connections from cell one to idle channels in cell two and thus release channels in cell one. Thus we assume optimal rearrangement. In multi-cell systems this rearrangement may be necessary at several levels. Therefore we assume that the system has global optimal intelligence.

In Code Division Multiple Access (CDMA) networks, users in a cell interfere with each other as they use the same frequencies. Therefore, by adding a user in

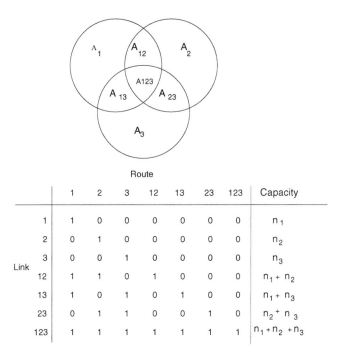

| | Route | | | | | | | |
|---|---|---|---|---|---|---|---|---|
| | 1 | 2 | 3 | 12 | 13 | 23 | 123 | Capacity |
| 1 | 1 | 0 | 0 | 0 | 0 | 0 | 0 | $n_1$ |
| 2 | 0 | 1 | 0 | 0 | 0 | 0 | 0 | $n_2$ |
| 3 | 0 | 0 | 1 | 0 | 0 | 0 | 0 | $n_3$ |
| Link     12 | 1 | 1 | 0 | 1 | 0 | 0 | 0 | $n_1 + n_2$ |
| 13 | 1 | 0 | 1 | 0 | 1 | 0 | 0 | $n_1 + n_3$ |
| 23 | 0 | 1 | 1 | 0 | 0 | 1 | 0 | $n_2 + n_3$ |
| 123 | 1 | 1 | 1 | 1 | 1 | 1 | 1 | $n_1 + n_2 + n_3$ |

**Fig. 2.** Example of three overlapping cells and the corresponding equivalent circuit-switched network with direct routing.

the serving cell, the total noise level increases and the cell size shrinks. Avoiding shrinking of cell size to zero and providing necessary coverage is done by limiting allowed load (power budget) for the cell. For macro coverage a smaller load is set, for micro/urban coverage a higher load is allowed.

Such cell shrinking behaviour in CDMA pushes calls from the actual Node-B to a less loaded neighbouring Node-B and in such way automatically implements call rearrangement as described below for GSM systems. From a traffic point of view rearrangement in GSM systems is equivalent to cell breathing in CDMA systems.

## 3.4   Decentralized Intelligence

In the above models we have assumed that the call packing is optimal. We may thus need to perform many successive rearrangements to move one idle channel from one cell to another.

In GSM networks with directed retry blocked calls are automatically retried in another cells after failure of getting channels in current cell. This corresponds to decentralized intelligence and calls are only redirected at call setup. Of course, this can only be done in the overlapping areas.

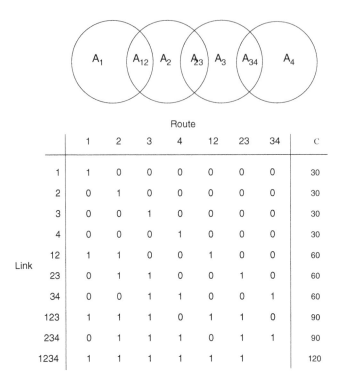

**Fig. 3.** Example of four overlapping cells and the equivalent circuit-switched network with direct routing.

|  |  | Route |  |  |  |  |  |  |  |
|---|---|---|---|---|---|---|---|---|---|
|  |  | 1 | 2 | 3 | 4 | 12 | 23 | 34 | C |
|  | 1 | 1 | 0 | 0 | 0 | 0 | 0 | 0 | 30 |
|  | 2 | 0 | 1 | 0 | 0 | 0 | 0 | 0 | 30 |
|  | 3 | 0 | 0 | 1 | 0 | 0 | 0 | 0 | 30 |
|  | 4 | 0 | 0 | 0 | 1 | 0 | 0 | 0 | 30 |
| Link | 12 | 1 | 1 | 0 | 0 | 1 | 0 | 0 | 60 |
|  | 23 | 0 | 1 | 1 | 0 | 0 | 1 | 0 | 60 |
|  | 34 | 0 | 0 | 1 | 1 | 0 | 0 | 1 | 60 |
|  | 123 | 1 | 1 | 1 | 0 | 1 | 1 | 0 | 90 |
|  | 234 | 0 | 1 | 1 | 1 | 0 | 1 | 1 | 90 |
|  | 1234 | 1 | 1 | 1 | 1 | 1 | 1 |  | 120 |

In e.g. Digital Enhanced Cordless Telecommunications (DECT) systems the intelligence is distributed to the individual handsets. Thus it is possible to let the handset, which knows the state of the channels at the local base station in the area, make local decisions based on the local information. A handset may hand-over a call from a cell with all channels busy to a cell with idle channels. However, this strategy will in general not be globally optimal (but we know the optimal reference value). These models with local intelligence can in practice only be evaluated by simulation because they don't have product form. Simulations show that the decentralized strategy is close to the optimal strategy. Thus from a traffic point of view systems with global intelligence are much simpler to model due to the product form than systems with local intelligence. In this paper we only present examples with global intelligence.

## 4  Overlay and Underlay Structure

Mathematical model of overlap cells is easily extended to hierarchical mobile networks. The performance of cellular mobile communication systems can be improved significantly by introducing macro cells. If a call (either a new or a hand over call) attempts to establish a connection in a micro-cell but all the channels of that cell are busy, it may try to establish the connection in an overlaid macro-cell. Fig. 4 shows a two-level system with $N$ micro-cells and one macro-cell. Micro-cell number $i$ has $n_i$ channels of its own. The macro-cell has a total of $m$ channels, but micro-cell number $i$ may at most borrow $m_i$ channels in the macro-cell at a given point of time (class limitation). In comparison with the previous section this corresponds to overlapping cells with full overlap.

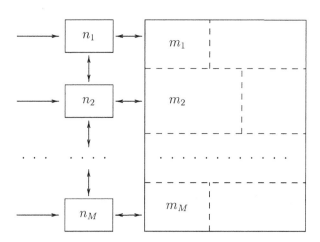

**Fig. 4.** Model of a cellular system with $M$ micro-cells and one macro-cell corresponding to a link model offered more traffic streams with minimum and maximum allocation. The model has product form when there is rearrangement (take-back) of calls between from macro-cell to micro-cell.

Thus the subscribers in a given micro-cell has a minimum allocation of $n_i$ channels and a maximum allocation of $n_i + m_i$. This allows us to guarantee a certain grade of service. The macro-cell is common to a number of micro-cells, i.e. it acts as a shared resource for a number of micro-cells. The multilayer structure is equivalent to that of a classical overflow system. Two call management strategies for operating macro-cells exist:

- *Without rearrangement (no call packing)*, i.e. once a call has established a connection in a channel in a macro-cell, it continues to utilize the channel until the call is terminated.
- *With rearrangement (call packing)*, if a call is using a channel in a macro-cell it will rearrange to the micro-cell (where the call is located) when a channel in that particular micro-cell becomes idle.

The rearrangement strategy increases the number of hand-over operations and requires that the system keeps information about which micro-cell a call belongs to.

## 5    Evaluation Methods

The performance of multi-layer systems are calculated in the following way. Systems without rearrangement are similar to classical overflow systems and can be evaluated by well-known methods as Wilkinson's Equivalent Random Traffic (ERT) method or the Interrupted Poisson Process (IPP) method. If the rearrangement strategy is applied, the state transition diagram is reversible and has product form. Blocking probabilities, utilisation, etc. are obtained exploiting the product form, for instance by using the *convolution algorithm* [5].

For smaller networks we have exact algorithms for evaluating the end to end blocking probability for each route, i.e. for each area. The convolution algorithm [5] allows calculation of both time congestion, call congestion, and traffic congestion for Multi-slot BPP (Binomial – Poisson - Pascal) traffic, which is used for modelling traffic in the cells. The state of the system is specified by the number of calls on each route $p(x_1, x_2, \ldots, x_N)$, where $x_i$ is the number of busy channels on route $i$. When the system has product form we have:

$$p(x_1, x_2, \ldots, x_N) = p(x_1) \cdot p(x_2) \cdot \ldots \cdot p(x_N).$$

Thus the routes are independent, and we may use the convolution algorithm to aggregate the states of any two routes to one route, and thus successively reduce the system to one route. We we assume all $N$ links have a capacity $n$, then the product form reduces the number of states on the system from the order $n^N$ to $n \cdot N$ and by aggregation using convolution finally to $n$. This is a enormous simplification of the problem.

As the number of routes and links for realistic systems (e.g. GSM networks) becomes very large, the exact methods are not applicable. Then numerical simulation or approximate methods as the Erlang reduced load (Erlang fixed point) methods have to be used. However for large networks, where a typical route may use a very large number of links, these methods are not very good.

## 6    Numerical Examples

In the following we present an example of overlapping cells and an example with hierarchical cell structure. Also an example with multi-rate traffic is presented.

### 6.1    Example of Overlapping Cell Structure

To get an idea of the increased capacity obtained by exploiting the overlap of cells, we may consider a cellular system where every cell has 20 traffic channels. Also let us assume that the offered traffic per cell is 15 erlang. The worst case (maximum) blocking is obtained when the cells are completely separate, and from Erlang's B-formula we find a blocking probability $E = 4.56$ %.

Now we consider the cellular system shown in Fig. 1. Each base station is again supposed to have 20 channels, and we assume the offered traffic in each of the two separate areas is 12 erlang, and in the overlap area 6 erlang. Thus the total traffic is again 30 erlang. This corresponds to that 6 out of 30 erlang are in overlap area, which is an overlap of 20 %.

By evaluating the equivalent circuit-switched network we find a blocking in the separate areas equal to 1.90 %, and in the overlap area a blocking probability equal to 1.24 %. The weighted overall blocking probability becomes 1.77 %. Worst case utilization is 2 separate systems as considered above. The optimal usage is a full accessible system with 40 channels offered 30 erlang, which by Erlang's B-formula will result in a blocking probability $E = 1.44$ %. Thus 20 % overlap results in almost the same utilization as in a full accessible system.

In Fig. 2 we consider a system with three cells, which are mutually overlapping, so that subscribers in some areas may have access to two cells. Therefore, subscribers in overlapping areas will experience a smaller blocking probability than subscribers in separate areas. In an intelligent system with optimal packing we can rearrange calls in the overlapping areas from one cell to another. Thus we assume that the system has global optimal intelligence. The model with restrictions on the number of simultaneous calls is equivalent to a circuit switched communication network with direct routing as shown in the table of Fig. 2.

For the case considered in Fig. 2 the blocking probability as a function of the overlapping is shown in Fig. 5. The offered average traffic is 25 erlang per cell and each cell has 30 channels. For example, we may have 20 erlang in every separate area and 5 erlang in each of the overlapping areas. This will correspond to 20% overlap. We notice that we have the same capacity as for full accessibility when the overlapping is greater than 30 %. This will be the case in most real systems. For separate cells without overlap the blocking probability is obtained from Erlang's B-formula $E_{30}(25) = 5.2603$ %. For full overlap the blocking probability is $E_{90}(75)= 1.0695$ %. The limiting value of the blocking probability in overlapping areas when the overlap decreases to zero is $E_{30}(25)^2 = 0.2767$ % as the cells become independent.

From the above examples we conclude that if cells have an overlap of at least 20 % with some other cells, then the blocking probability in this cell is close to the blocking of a full accessible system with a number of channels equal to all channels of the involved cells.

## 6.2   Example of Hierarchical Cell Structure

We now consider a network with 40 micro-cells and one macro-cell covering all the micro-cells. Each micro-cell has 40 channels. In order to reduce the blocking probability, a number of channels is allocated to the macro-cell.

Fig. 6 features a plot of the total carried traffic versus the number of channels in the macro-cell. If the call management strategy without rearrangement is applied the utilisation of the channels in the macro-cell is close to one. If the rearrangement strategy is applied, the increase in total carried traffic per additional channel in the macro-cell is *greater* than one erlang. This is due to the fact that when a call is blocked at the micro-cell and gets a channel in the macro-cell it will only remain in the macro-cell until a channel in the micro-cell

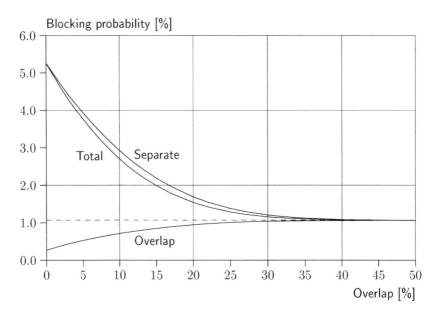

**Fig. 5.** System with three cells adjacent to each other (Fig. 2). $A = 25$ erlang per cell, $n = 30$ channels per cell. 10 % overlap means that 10 % of the traffic (users) are in an overlap area of two cells. There are no users with access to all three cells.

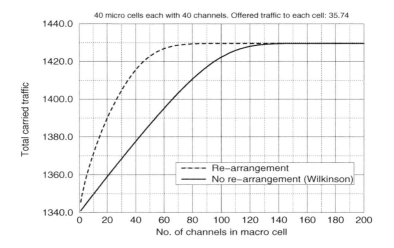

**Fig. 6.** The total carried traffic as a function of the number of channels in the macro-cell. By adding 20 channels in the macro-cell we notice that the total carried traffic increases by 50 erlang.

is released. On average this takes only 1/40 of a holding time (if only one call is waiting for a channel in the micro-cell). In this way the shared resource (the macro channel) is made available for new calls as soon as possible. Obtaining the same amount of carried traffic (or correspondingly the same blocking probabilities) without rearrangement requires a significantly higher number of channels in the macro-cell.

The increased utilisation of the micro-cells implies that a higher number of calls are blocked in the micro-cells but accepted in the macro-cell. Thus the total number of hand-overs (rearrangements) increases. If the number of channels in the macro-cell becomes large the system starts to make unnecessary rearrangements. A rearrangement of a call from the macro-cell to a-micro cell is unnecessary if no other micro-cell requests to use the released channel in the macro-cell. The upper limit of additional hand-overs is one hand-over per call. In this study we have not considered hand-over between neighbouring micro-cells.

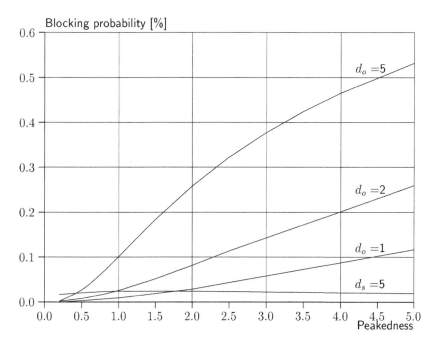

**Fig. 7.** Traffic congestion as a function of peakedness and slot-size for the system described in Section 6.3.

## 6.3    Example with Multi-rate Traffic

For multi-rate traffic the number of parameters increases. As an example, we again consider the network in Fig. 2 with 30 channels in each cell and 20 %

overlap. For separate areas, the offered traffic is Poisson-arrival single-slot traffic with mean value 20 erlang. For overlapping areas between two cells, the offered traffic is multi-rate traffic with 5 erlang measured in channels. So for single-slot traffic we offer 5 calls per mean holding time, whereas for 5-slot traffic we offer one call per mean holding time. No traffic is offered to the 3-overlap area. We consider three examples with slot-sizes $d_0 = 1$, 2 and 5, respectively. Furthermore, the arrival process is BPP–traffic (Binomial – Poisson – Pascal), and we consider peakedness-values from 0.2 to 5. The peakedness is the variance/mean ratio of state probabilities. The blocking probability is the traffic congestion which is the relevant performance measure [7].

Fig. 7 shows the resulting blocking probability for the traffic in overlap areas. It is observed that the blocking probability is almost proportional with both the peakedness and the slot-size.

The lower curve $d_s= 5$ is the blocking probability for traffic in separate areas when the multi-rate traffic has slot-size = 5. We notice that this is almost constant. It decreases a little, when the blocking probability of the multi-rate traffic increases. The two other curves for separate areas are almost overlapping with this curve.

## 7   Conclusions

By exploiting the intelligence of digital systems we are able to obtain a very high utilization of the radio channels. In particular systems with overlapping cells and overlaid cells are able to manage local overload and at the same time guarantee a certain grade-of-service by sharing resources. The strategy corresponds to a minimum and maximum allocation of radio resources (channels) to each class of users or services. If we are able to rearrange calls, then we have reversibility and product form, and we are able to evaluate the systems. All models considered becomes insensitive to the holding time distribution. Each traffic stream is modelled by mean value, peakedness, and slot-size. The examples show that this is valid for actual systems which have at least 20 channels per cell and an overlap which is much more than 20%. The methodology and tools developed are foreseen as powerful tools to investigate and engineer current and future cellular systems.

## References

1. Beraldi, R. & Marano, S.& Mastroianni, C.: Performance of a reversible hierarchical cellular system. International Journal of Wireless Information networks, Vol. 4 (1997) : 1, 43–54.
2. Everitt, D. (1991): Product form solutions in cellular mobile communication systems, Teletraffic and Datatraffic in a Period of Change, ITC–13, A. Jensen & V. B. Iversen (editors), North Holland, 1991, pp. 483–488.
3. Fitzpatrick, P. & Lee, C.S. & Warfield, B.: Teletraffic performance of mobile radio networks with hierarchical cells and overflow. IEEE Journal on Selected Areas in Communications, Vol. 15 (1997) : 8, 1549–1557.

4. Hansen, P. Damsgaard (2004) Dimensioning of multi-service networks (in Danish). Master thesis. Research Center COM, Technical University of Denmark, May 2004. 93 pp.
5. Iversen, V. B. (1987): The Exact Evaluation of Multi–Service Loss Systems with Access Control. Teleteknik, English ed., Vol. 31 (1987) : 2, 56–61.
6. Iversen, V.B. & Glenstrup, A.: Resource allocation in wireless systems. IFIP Conference on Personal Wireless Communications, Gdansk, Poland, September 14–15, 2000. J. Wosniak & J. Konorskipp, editors. Proceedings 123-132. Kluwer Academic Publishers, 2000, 270 pp.
7. Iversen, V.B. (2004): Teletraffic Engineering. Chapter 10: Multi-dimensional loss systems. Dpt. of Telecommunications, Technical University of Denmark, 2004. http://www.com.dtu.dk/teletraffic
8. Ko, K.T. & Cheung, C.C. (1992): Calculation of call congestion in multi-layer cellular networks with non-Poissonian traffic. ISTN–92, Second International Seminar on Teletraffic and Network Issues. Beijing, China, September 9-12, 1992. Beijing University of Posts and Telecommunications. Proceedings pp. 88–91.
9. Wu, X. & Mukherjee, B. & Ghosal, D.: Hierarchical architectures in the third-generation cellular network. IEEE Wireless communications, Vol. 11 (2004) : 3, 62–71.

# A Hybrid Model of the UMTS Downlink Capacity with WWW Traffic on Dedicated Channels

Tobias Hoßfeld and Dirk Staehle

University of Würzburg, Institute of Computer Science,
Department of Distributed Systems,
Am Hubland, 97074 Würzburg, Germany
{hossfeld,staehle}@informatik.uni-wuerzburg.de

**Abstract.** One of the main advances of 3G networks like UMTS is the ability to support a large variety of different services. These services are subdivided in two domains, circuit-switched services and packet-switched services. The main application expected for packet-switched services is the browsing of the World Wide Web. The web traffic is usually described by quite sophisticated source traffic models and the packet arrivals on IP layer are determined by TCP. On the other hand, the planning process for UMTS networks relies on analytic methods or Monte Carlo simulations that assume the number of users to be Poisson distributed. The intention of this work is to examine if it is possible to apply the existing planning methods to web traffic. We are able to show that the Poisson assumption holds for the number of web users that simultaneously transmit over the air interface and that the resulting NodeB transmit power distribution is valid. We use the Monte Carlo simulation technique to evaluate the web capacity of an example UMTS network.

## 1 Introduction

One of the main enhancements of third generation (3G) networks is that they allow for a service differentiation and offer a large variety of different services. In the *Universal Mobile Telecommunication System* (UMTS) [1] the services are subsumed in the categories conversational, streaming, interactive, and background that are distinguished by their QoS profiles. The conversational class guarantees a low delay and a low jitter. Typical applications of the conversational class are voice or video telephony that produce a symmetric data volume on the uplink and the downlink. The QoS requirements of the streaming class are less stringent. They sustain a larger delay and tolerate more jitter. The typical applications are audio or video streaming that produce asymmetric traffic. The QoS requirements of the conversational and streaming classes are expressed by the bit rate and the radio link quality, i.e. signal energy per bit / noise energy per bit ratio $E_b/N_0$, of the service. The characteristic of the interactive class is a request response pattern. The most prominent candidate application in the existing and future UMTS networks is the browsing of the world wide web (WWW) which was the dominant kind of Internet traffic for the last decades and only file sharing causes similar traffic volumes in the recent years. Web browsing is also the typical representative of the interactive class while the file sharing falls in the background class. The background class has practically

G. Kotsis and O. Spaniol (Eds.): Mobile and Wireless Systems, LNCS 3427, pp. 20–35, 2005.

no QoS requirements and uses the bandwidth only when it is available. The web traffic, as a representative of the interactive class, is somehow located between the streaming class and the background class. We distinguish the best-effort web traffic and the QoS web traffic. The best-effort web traffic is close to the background class and utilizes the capacity that remains from the higher classes, i.e. conversational, streaming, and QoS web traffic. On the downlink - which is the relevant link due to the asymmetry typical for web traffic - the best-effort web traffic is transmitted over the downlink shared channel (DSCH), the high-speed downlink shared channel (HS-DSCH), or in the initial phase of UMTS over a rate-controlled dedicated channel (DCH). Like for the background traffic there is no QoS guaranty for the best-effort web traffic. In contrast, the QoS web traffic is transmitted over a non-rate controlled dedicated channel that guarantees a certain QoS. Like for the conversational and streaming class the QoS requirements of the web service are expressed by the bit rate and the target $E_b/N_0$.

In this paper we focus on the QoS web service. In particular, we are interested in the number of QoS web users that a NodeB is able to handle in parallel. The capacity analysis of the uplink [16,6,10,8] and the downlink [4,9,11] of CDMA and WCMDA systems mainly assume a Poisson distributed number of users per cell and service and a service is defined by its bit rate, target $E_b/N_0$ and activity factor or mean activity during their sojourn time in the system.

The first objective of this paper is to show by means of a detailed simulations that it is possible to describe a QoS web service by these parameters. This detailed simulation includes a sophisticated web traffic model [15], the implementation of TCP [13,14] according to 4.4BSD-Lite, and the power control according to the 3GPP standard [3]. As a result of this simulation we obtain the distribution of the number of active web users, where "active" means actively transmitting on the UMTS downlink, and the distribution of the NodeB transmit power. We use a second simulation that does not consider power control to obtain the probability distribution of web session durations and web session activities. In the first instance, we use this distribution in an "activity" simulation to describe the web sessions and show that the results match with the detailed simulation. In a further step, we calculate an offered load from the web session duration and web activity distribution and use it in the Monte Carlo simulation from [11] to determine the NodeB transmit power distribution according to a certain offered web traffic load.

The rest of this paper is organized as follows: In Sec. 2 we formulate the objective of this paper more clearly and show how we model the web traffic. In Sec. 3 we describe the different simulation models that we use for computing the NodeB transmit power, namely the detailed ON/OFF, the activity, and the Monte Carlo simulation. The results from the three simulation types are compared in Sec. 4 where we also evaluate the web traffic capacity of an example scenario. In Sec. 5 we summarize our main results.

## 2    Problem Formulation

We consider a UMTS network that consists of $L$ NodeBs which provide a set of services to the mobile users. These services are either circuit-switched (CS) or packet-switched (PS). The CS service $s$ is defined by a bit rate $R_s$ and an $E_b/N_0$-target $\varepsilon_s$. The users of service $s$ arrive according to a Poisson process with rate $\lambda_s$ and have an exponential service time with mean $1/\mu_s$. The activity of the CS users is modeled by a Bernoulli random variable with mean $\nu_s$ which is referred to as the activity factor.

In the PS domain, a large variety of different protocols and applications is expected. The browsing of the World Wide Web is assumed to be the most important one. WWW traffic is complex to model, since the size and structure of web pages is very heterogeneous. Furthermore, the pages are transported over HTTP and TCP, that determine the packet arrival process on the UMTS air interface.

In the recent years, a lot of work considered the characterization of web traffic in wireless and wire-line environments. The authors of [15] give an overview of source traffic models that describe web traffic and other applications with some relevance to wireless networks. The web traffic model is mainly based on the measurements of [5].

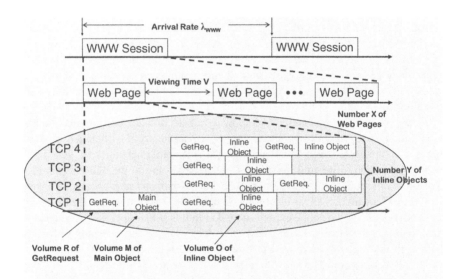

**Fig. 1.** Web traffic model is structured into session, page, and TCP layer

Figure 1 illustrates the web traffic model. We can recognize three layers: session layer, page layer, and TCP layer. On session layer, the users become active according to a Poisson process. In a web session, they download and view a number of web pages.

A web page consists of the main object and optional inline objects. The main object is the HTML code and an inline object is a file or script and referenced in the main object. HTTP opens a TCP connection and sends a getRequest for the main object. After receiving the main object, the inline objects are requested from the server and sent back in up to four parallel TCP connections. The actual number of TCP connections depends on the HTTP version and the web browsing client.

In our model, we describe the WWW traffic by the session arrival rate $\lambda_{WWW}$, the number $X$ of pages per session, and the viewing time $V$. A page consists of the getRequest size $R$, the volume $M$ of the main object, the number $Y$ of inline objects, and the size $O$ of an inline object. The size of a getRequest for an inline object is also $R$.

**Table 1.** Description of the parameter set of the WWW source traffic model

| RV | description | distribution | E[RV] | STD[RV] |
|----|-------------|--------------|-------|---------|
| I | time between two WWW sessions | exponential | $\lambda_{WWW}^{-1}$ | $\lambda_{WWW}^{-1}$ |
| X | number of web pages per session | lognormal | 25 | 100 |
| V | viewing time | geometric | 5.0 s | 30.0 s |
| M | volume of main object | lognormal | 10 kB | 25 kB |
| Y | number of inline objects per page | gamma | 5.55 | 11.4 |
| O | volume of inline object | lognormal | 7.7 kB | 126 kB |
| R | volume of GetRequest | lognormal | 360 B | 106 B |

All these values are iid random variables which follow distributions obtained through measurements, e.g. [5], and are listed in Table 1.

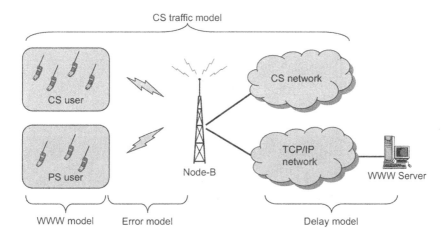

**Fig. 2.** UMTS scenario is described by a given CS traffic and a composed WWW traffic model

Figure 2 shows the CS and PS domain in a UMTS network. The CS traffic model considers only the air interface, as the behavior on the air interface is independent of the core network and frame errors on the air interface. On the other hand, the WWW traffic is transported over the Internet by TCP/IP. The flow control mechanism of TCP tries to adapt the bandwidth to the congestion in the network. That makes the effective bandwidth depend on the delay in the Internet and lost packets. We model the delay in the Internet by a random variable $D$ for the transmit time between the NodeB and a WWW server in the Internet. The delays for all packets belonging to the same web page are equal. TCP packets get lost with a probability $P_{loss}$ which is assumed to be independent of the system load.

We measured the delay within the GPRS network of a German operator. Therefore, we transmitted periodically ICMP packets from our mobile station to different WWW servers for 12 hours. Figure 3 shows the single delay from the mobile station to the servers. We obtained a mean delay about 400 ms. We simulate the delay time $D$ uniformly distributed between 350 ms and 450 ms.

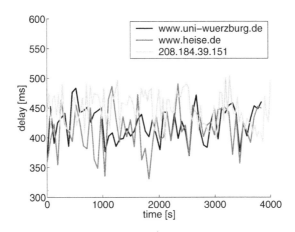

**Fig. 3.** Delay for the transmit time between the NodeB and a WWW server in the Internet

On the air interface, the CS and PS users compete for the existing resources. The air interface capacity of a UMTS network is on the uplink limited by the multiple access interference and on the downlink by the NodeB transmit power. We focus on the downlink as the traffic a web user produces on the downlink is a multiple of the traffic on the uplink. This shifts the bottleneck to the downlink as long as the users in the CS domain produce symmetric traffic. The 3GPP standard proposes three ways to transport web traffic: on dedicated channels, on shared channels, and in the future on high speed shared channels. We focus on WWW users with a guaranteed quality of service (QoS) that transmit over a dedicated channel with guaranteed bit-rate and $E_b/N_0$-target.

As the air interface is a scarce resource, power control is employed in order to maximize its capacity. In UMTS, the fast power control is applied on both, the uplink and the downlink. On the downlink, it minimizes the NodeB transmit power while ensuring acceptable service quality. We investigate stationary mobile stations. The power control consists of the inner loop and the outer loop. The inner loop power control adapts the NodeB transmit power in order to meet the $E_b/N_0$-target by sending one ''power-up" or ''power-down" command in each time slot. The outer loop power control adapts the $E_b/N_0$-target in order to maintain a certain frame error rate. We assume a constant $E_b/N_0$-target throughout the simulation and ignore the outer loop.

The fundamental relation between transmission power $\hat{T}_x$ of NodeB $x$, connection properties ($E_b/N_0$-target $\hat{\varepsilon}_k^*$, bit rate $R_k$, orthogonality factor $\alpha$), and radio channel conditions (path gain $\hat{d}_{x,k}$ from the mobile station $k$ to the base station $x$, thermal noise density $N_0 = -174$ dBm/Hz) is summarized in (1) which is derived by using the signal energy per bit / interference energy per bit ratio in the downlink direction for an MS $k$. The transmission power $\hat{S}_{x,k}$ of NodeB $x$ dedicated to MS $k$ is denoted as $\hat{S}_{x,k}$. $W = 3.84$ Mcps is the UMTS chip rate. Assuming perfect power control means that values fulfilling (1) have to be found.

$$\hat{\varepsilon}_k^* = \frac{E_k^{bit}}{\hat{I}_k} = \frac{\frac{\hat{S}_{x,k}^{rcvd}}{R_k}}{\hat{N}_0 + \hat{I}_{k,other}} = \frac{\frac{W}{R_k}\hat{S}_{x,k}\hat{d}_{x,k}}{W\hat{N}_0 + \alpha(\hat{T}_x - \hat{S}_{x,k})\hat{d}_{x,k} + \sum_{y \neq x}\hat{T}_y\hat{d}_{y,k}} \qquad (1)$$

The aim of this paper is to decide whether the UMTS system is stable for a given scenario. A UMTS system is considered as stable, if the transmit power of all NodeBs stays below a given maximum $\hat{T}_{max}$. If the transmit power exceeds this threshold, the NodeB cannot fulfill the $E_b/N_0$-target requirements and outage occurs. In order to determine the probability that outage occurs, we require the distribution of the NodeB transmit power for a given scenario.

In the following, we present three ways for evaluating this distribution: an ON/OFF simulation, an activity simulation, and an analysis. The ON/OFF simulation reproduces the packet transfer on TCP/IP layer in order to determine when a user is active on the air interface, i.e. a packet is transmitted over the air interface. The TCP layer models the interaction between TCP and HTTP. In our simulation TCP is implemented according to 4.4BSD-Lite. We use the HTTP1.1 version with 4 parallel and persistent TCP connections proposed in [12], too.

The idea of the activity simulation is to approximate the WWW user behavior on web page or session layer by using an activity factor instead of realizing the full TCP stack, as a UMTS user only interferes with other users when being active. For the same reason, an analytical evaluation of a UMTS system requires the approximation of a mobile station by means of activity. Thereby, the activity factor is derived for a given scenario by an ON/OFF simulation.

## 3   Simulation Description

We study web traffic on page and session layer. For the investigation on page layer, we generate $N$ web users. A web user obtains a location and starts downloading web pages. After one web page is completed, the user immediately requests the next web page such that there is actually no viewing time. We expect the number of active users to be binomial distributed with parameters $N$ and $p$, whereby $p$ depends on the user activity. We call this type of simulation as *web page simulation*.

In the *session simulation*, we start with no users in the system and then generate web session interarrival times according to the arrival rate $\lambda_{WWW}$ which we use to scale the traffic intensity. At each arrival event, we determine the location of the new user randomly. We consider a homogeneous spatial traffic distribution, so every position is selected with equal probability. The user keeps this location during the whole session. The web pages in a session are generated according to the model in Figure 2 with the parameters in Table 1.

We have implemented two different simulations how to determine the NodeB transmit power for the web page and the session scenario:

- The ON/OFF simulation has a full implementation of the TCP Reno stack and the WWW source traffic model up to the web page/session layer. We implement the ON/OFF simulation either with or without power control.
- The activity simulation performs snapshots due to the activity factors of the individual users. In order to determine the activity behavior of web users on the air interface for the activity simulation, we use the ON/OFF simulation without power control.

### 3.1  Implementation of Power Control in the ON/OFF Simulation

The ON/OFF simulation determines the packet arrivals on the air interface exactly according to the TCP/IP protocol stack. This means that for every time instant we know which users are actively transmitting on the downlink. This allows us to determine the NodeB transmit power according to the fast power control algorithm.

However, the fast power control works with a frequency of 1500 Hz, i.e. 15 power updates for each user within a frame of 10 ms. In the simulation, this is very time-consuming, so according to [7] we implement an approximative power control algorithm with only one power update per frame.

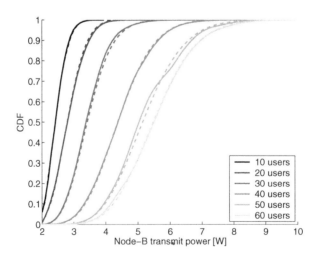

**Fig. 4.** Comparison of the approximative power control algorithm and the exact implementation of the UMTS power control mechanism

In Figure 4, we validate this approach against the exact implementation. We consider 10 to 60 users with fixed propagation gains. The dashed lines show the cumulative distribution function (CDF) of the NodeB transmit power for the approximative power control algorithm and the solid ones for the exact power control. We can see that the curves agree very well.

---

**Approximative Power Control (APC) Algorithm**

---

*Input:* set $\mathbb{MS}$ of mobile stations transmitting packets on air interface at time $t$

For each time frame $t$ do

1. Update transmission power and received $E_b/N_0$ for all mobile stations

$$\forall k \in \mathbb{MS} \quad \exists x = \mathrm{BS}(k) \in \mathbb{BS} :$$

$$\hat{S}_{x,k}(t) = \omega_k \frac{W\hat{N}_0 + \alpha\hat{T}_x(t)\hat{d}_{x,k} + \sum_{y \neq x} \hat{T}_y(t)\hat{d}_{y,k}}{\hat{d}_{x,k}} \quad \text{with } \omega_k = \frac{R_k\hat{\varepsilon}_k^*}{W + \alpha R_k\hat{\varepsilon}_k^*}$$

$$\hat{\varepsilon}_k(t) = \frac{\frac{W}{R_k}\hat{S}_{x,k}(t)\hat{d}_{x,k}}{W\hat{N}_0 + \alpha(\hat{T}_x(t) - \hat{S}_{x,k}(t))\hat{d}_{x,k} + \sum_{y \neq x} \hat{T}_y(t)\hat{d}_{y,k}}$$

2. Identify transmission power

$$\forall x \in \mathbb{BS} : \hat{T}_x^*(t) = \hat{T}_{CCH} + \sum_{k \in \mathbb{MS}} \hat{S}_{x,k}(t) \text{ , whereas } x \neq \mathrm{BS}(k) \Rightarrow \hat{S}_{x,k} = 0$$

$$\hat{T}_x(t + \Delta t_{frame}) = \begin{cases} \hat{T}_x^*(t) & \text{if } \hat{T}_x^*(t) \leq \hat{T}_{max} \\ \hat{T}_x(t) & \text{else outage} \end{cases}$$

---

### 3.2 Activity Simulation

In contrast to the ON/OFF TCP simulation, the activity simulation does not emulate TCP. It uses an activity factor describing if an user is active or not. The activity factor $\nu = \frac{t_{air}}{t_{total}}$ describes the ratio between the packet transmission time $t_{air}$ over the air interface and the total web page/session download time $t_{total}$. The web page/session download time is defined as the time between the request of the mobile station to open the first TCP connection and the arrival of the last packet for completing the web page/session.

From the ON/OFF simulation, we obtain a compound distribution for the web page/session download time and the downlink activity of a web page/session. Figure 5 shows this distribution for web pages. The brighter an area is illuminated, the higher is the probability for a web page with the given duration and activity. The structure of the compound distribution shows us that web page activity and download time are correlated.

In the activity simulation, we generate the arrival times of web pages/sessions as described above. We determine the download time and the activity factor according to the compound distribution. To determine the distribution of the NodeB transmit power,

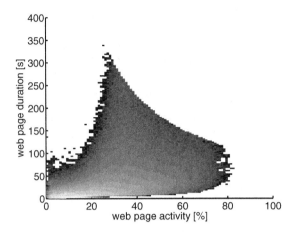

**Fig. 5.** Web page simulation – Compound distribution for download times and activity factors

we generate a system snapshot in regular time intervals. From the compound distribution, each user $k$ obtained an individual activity factor $\nu_k$. This means that at a certain time instant $t$ the user $k$ is active with probability $\nu_k$. The snapshot returns the set of active users. In the next section we describe how to determine the NodeB transmit power for such a snapshot.

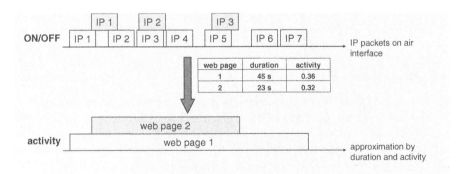

**Fig. 6.** Illustration of the activity simulation

## 3.3    Monte Carlo Simulation

With the activity simulation we present a possibility to separate the exact simulation of the web traffic model and the TCP/IP protocol stack and the simulation of the UMTS air interface with the fast power control. However, the simulation is still a time-dynamic simulation and requires the compound distribution of web page/session duration and web page/session activity as input. In contrast to the activity simulation, the Monte Carlo simulation evaluates system snapshots and has no time dynamic. In a snapshot, the number of active web users is described by a binomial distribution in a web page simulation and by a Poisson distribution in the web session simulation. In Section 4 we will validate that the active web users really follow these distribution and also discuss their parameters.

In this section we will describe how to evaluate the NodeB transmit power for a system snapshot. This method and also an entirely analytic method to approximate the NodeB are already published in [11] for general services that are described by their bit rate and target $E_b/N_0$ value. We formulate the Monte Carlo simulation for a general UMTS network operating with multiple QoS services and one of these is the QoS web service.

A snapshot consists of a set of mobiles with their service and position. The number of users follows from a predefined distribution, in case of the web users either the binomial or the Poisson distribution. The position of each mobile is determined according to the spatial traffic distribution. In our special scenario the traffic distribution is homogenous so every position inside the considered area is chosen with equal probability. The position of the mobile also determines the propagation gain to the different NodeBs.

Consider a mobile $k$ that belongs to NodeB $x$, or short $k \in x$. Then the transmit power $\hat{S}_{x,k}$ follows from (1) as:

$$\hat{S}_{k,x} = \left( \omega_{k,0} W \hat{N}_0 + \sum_{y \neq x} \omega_{k,y} \hat{S}_y + \omega_{k,x} \hat{S}_x \right) \tag{2}$$

We define the service dependent load of a mobile $k$ as

$$\omega_k = \frac{\hat{\varepsilon}_k^* R_k}{W + \alpha \hat{\varepsilon}_k^* R_k} \quad \text{and} \quad \omega_{k,y} = \begin{cases} \omega_k \frac{1}{\hat{d}_{x,k}} & \text{if } y = 0 \\ \omega_k \alpha & \text{if } y = x \\ \omega_k \frac{\hat{d}_{y,k}}{\hat{d}_{x,k}} & \text{if } y \neq x \end{cases} \tag{3}$$

is its service and location dependent load. The correspondent $y$ for the load is either the own NodeB, another NodeB or the thermal noise $N_0$. The location and service dependent load can be interpreted as the translator between the interference that $y$ causes at the mobile and the transmit power that NodeB $x$ has to spend to overcome this interference. The load of a NodeB similarly comprises the three different kinds of interference. If we sum over all mobiles belonging to NodeB $x$ we speak of the load $\eta_{x,y}$ for NodeB $x$ related to the interference origin $y$ and define this load as

$$\eta_{x,y} = \sum_{k \in x} \omega_{k,y} \quad \text{and abbreviate} \quad \eta_x = \frac{\eta_{x,x}}{\alpha} = \sum_{k \in x} \omega_k. \tag{4}$$

Again, $y$ is either the NodeB itself, another NodeB, or the thermal noise. The total transmit power $\hat{S}_x$ of NodeB $x$ consists of a constant part $\hat{S}_{x,C}$ required for common channels and the variable part spent for the dedicated channels to the mobiles belonging to $x$:

$$\hat{S}_x = \hat{S}_{x,C} + \eta_{x,0} W \hat{N}_0 + \sum_{y \in \mathcal{B}} \hat{S}_y \eta_{x,y} \tag{5}$$

These equations for the $L$ NodeBs are written as a matrix equation and solved for the vector $\bar{S} = (\hat{S}_1, ..., \hat{S}_L)^T$:

$$\bar{S} = \bar{S}_C + \bar{\eta}_0 W \hat{N}_0 + \tilde{\eta} \bar{S} \quad \Leftrightarrow \quad \bar{S} = \left(\tilde{\mathcal{I}} - \tilde{\eta}\right)^{-1} \left(\bar{S}_C + \bar{\eta}_0 W \hat{N}_0\right) \tag{6}$$

Note, that a variable $\bar{v}$ stands for a vector and a variable $\tilde{m}$ for a matrix. So $\bar{\eta}_0 = (\eta_{1,0}, ...\eta_{L,0})^T$, $\bar{S}_C = (\hat{S}_{1,C}, ..., \hat{S}_{L,C})^T$, $\tilde{\eta}$ is the $L \times L$-matrix with $\tilde{\eta}(x,y) = \eta_{x,y}$, and $\tilde{\mathcal{I}}$ is the $L \times L$-identity matrix. A reasonable solution exists if the inverse of the matrix $(\tilde{\mathcal{I}} - \tilde{\eta})$ is entirely positive. A sufficient condition for this is that the row sums of $\tilde{\eta}$ are strictly lower than 1.

This condition gives us the means to determine for a snapshot if a power allocation exists such that the $E_b/N_0$-requirements of all mobiles are met. If there is such a solution the NodeBs' total transmit powers follow from (6) and the power allocated to each mobile from (2). By generating a series of system snapshots we obtain the moments or the distribution of the transmit powers under the condition that a reasonable power allocation exists. The advantage of the Monte Carlo simulation is that we can easily consider different service combinations, spatial processes, slow fading, and imperfections of power control.

## 4  Numerical Results

We consider a UMTS network with 19 NodeBs with hexagonal cells that are arranged in two tiers around a central NodeB. The distance between two neighbored NodeBs is 2 km. The mobiles are homogeneously distributed on the considered cell area. For comparison with the ON/OFF simulation the considered area is restricted to the central cell as the simulation of the whole area is too time-consuming. Instead, the NodeBs of the first and second tier transmit with a constant power of 5 W. The parameters of the default scenario are summarized in Table 2.

**Table 2.** Simulation parameters

**UMTS network parameter**

| cell layout | hexagonal |
|---|---|
| NodeB distance | 2 km |
| number of tiers around the central NodeB | 2 |
| propagation gain from NodeB $x$ to MS $k$ according to [2] | $d_{x,k} = -129.4 - 35.2 \cdot \log_{10}(\text{dist}(x,k))$ |
| constant power for common channels | $\hat{T}_{CCH} = 2$ W |
| power of surrounding NodeBs | $\hat{T}_y = 5$ W |

**Web traffic parameter**

| bit rate of a WWW user | $R = 64$ kbps |
|---|---|
| target $E_b/N_0$ of a WWW user | $E_b/N_0 = 3$ dB |
| delay between WWW server and NodeB | $D = Uniform(350; 450)$ ms |
| packet loss probabilty | $P_{loss} = 3$ % |

In the following we first investigate the influence of the IP packet loss probability and the fixed network delay between NodeB and web server on the air interface activity of a web user. Afterwards we show that the number of active web users follows a binomial distribution in the web page scenario and a Poisson distribution in the web session scenario. Then, we consider the distribution of the NodeB transmit power and show that the ON/OFF simulation, the activity simulation, and the Monte Carlo simulation yield consistent results. At the end we use the Monte Carlo simulation to determine the probability that the NodeB transmit power exceeds a maximum of 10 W for different web users and web users arrival rates, respectively.

### 4.1 Factors Influencing the Air Interface Activity

For investigating the air interface activity while downloading a web page, we use the ON/OFF web page simulation without power control and simulate a single user for 100 hours. Figure 7(a) shows the influence of the packet loss on the web page activity. The larger the packet loss probability is, the smaller is the activity. The same relation holds for the delay time, illustrated in Figure 7(b). A higher delay results in a smaller activity.

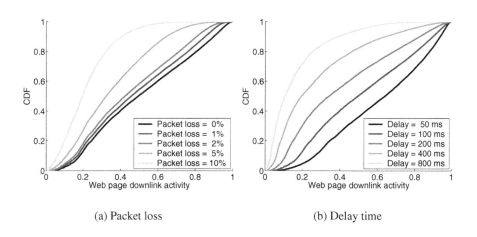

(a) Packet loss                    (b) Delay time

**Fig. 7.** Web page simulation – Influence factors on the activity factors of web pages

### 4.2 Distribution of the Number of Active Web Users

We first consider the web page scenario with a constant number $N$ of web users that continuously download web pages. Therefore, we use the ON/OFF simulation without power control and measure the number $N_{active}$ of active users on the air interface. We fit the distribution with a binomial distribution $N_{active} \sim binom(N, \nu)$. Figure 8(a) shows the probability function for $N = 10, 20, ..., 60$ users. The solid line indicates the ON/OFF simulation and the crosses mark the fitted binomial distribution. We can state a good agreement. The parameter of the fitted distribution is $\nu = 0.32$. If we however investigate the mean activity of a random web page, we find that it is only 0.2. The reason for this is that larger web pages with longer download times have larger activities. Therefore, we have to include this correlation in the computation of the parameter and obtain the mean weighted activity as $E[\nu_{weighted}] = \frac{\sum_{web\ page\ i} t_{air\ i}}{\sum_{web\ page\ i} t_{total\ i}}$.

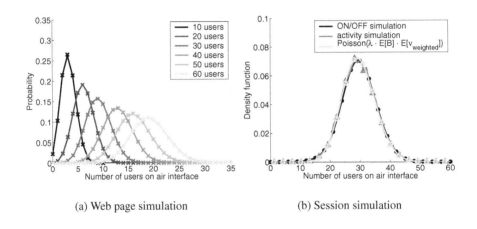

(a) Web page simulation                    (b) Session simulation

**Fig. 8.** Number of active users on the air interface

Next, we consider the web session scenario with a session interarrival time of $\lambda_{WWW}^{-1} = 6$ s. The session duration $B$ is a random variable with independent and identical distribution for each session. Thus, we can model the system by an $M/GI/\infty$ queue and obtain that the number of ongoing web sessions $N$ follows the Poisson distribution with parameter $\lambda \cdot E[B]$. If we look at a random time instant on the air interface, we see $N$ sessions and the number of active users on the air interface is $binom(N, \nu)$. We show that despite of the burstiness of the web traffic and the correlation between web page activity and web page download time, the number of user active on the air interface is Poisson distributed:

$$N_{active} \sim binom(N, \nu) = binom(Poiss(\lambda \cdot E[B]), \nu) = Poiss(\lambda \cdot E[B \cdot \nu]). \quad (7)$$

Figure 8(b) shows that the activity simulation and the ON/OFF simulation match very well. Furthermore, we compare both simulation types with a Poisson distribution. We derive the parameter by computing the weighted mean $E[\nu_{weighted}]$ of the activity factor of the session trace according to the computation of the weighted mean for web page simulations and obtain $E[B \cdot \nu] = E[\nu_{weighted}] \cdot E[B] = 0.267 \cdot 12.08$ min $= 3.22$ min.

### 4.3   NodeB Transmit Power

We now come to the actual objective of our paper and validate if the Monte Carlo simulation assuming a binomial/Poisson distributed number of users yields the same NodeB transmit power as the ON/OFF simulation. Therefore, we consider both scenarios, the web page scenario and the session scenario. In the web page scenario we consider 10 users located randomly in the central cell. In the ON/OFF simulation and the activity simulation, the users keep their position during the whole simulation period. In the Monte Carlo simulation we generate 10000 snapshots with a binomial distributed number of users that have random positions. In Figure 9(a), we compare the CDFs of the NodeB transmit power obtained from the different simulations. The activity simulation is marked with a triangle, the ON/OFF simulation with a circle, and the Monte Carlo simulation with an asterisk. We see that the activity simulation and the ON/OFF simulation match nearly completely. The Monte Carlo simulation differs as it averages over all possible user locations. In the web session scenario, every new user obtains a random location, so the ON/OFF simulation and the activity simulation are not restricted to a single location snapshot. The CDFs of the NodeB transmit power is shown in Figure 9(b) for a session arrival rate of $\frac{1}{6\,\mathrm{s}}$. As expected the three curves show only small differences.

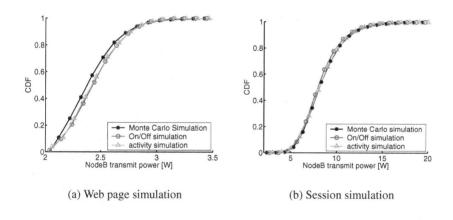

(a) Web page simulation                    (b) Session simulation

**Fig. 9.** Comparison of ON/OFF, activity, and Monte Carlo simulation

In a UMTS network, the transmit power of a NodeB is technically limited to a maximum $\hat{T}_{max}$ which is typical either 10 W or 20 W. In our scenario we choose $\hat{T}_{max} = 10$ W. If the demand for power exceeds this maximum, the NodeB cannot follow all power-up commands and the mobiles cannot maintain their desired QoS in terms of target $E_b/N_0$. This event is called outage and a mobile has to be removed if this situation continues for a longer period of time. One objective of radio network planning is therefore to keep the outage probability below a certain threshold. We obtain the outage probability directly from the CDF of the NodeB transmit power and can thus estimate if the network is capable of carrying the offered traffic or not.

We define the web page/session capacity of a UMTS network as the maximum number of web users/maximum web session arrival rate such that the outage probability stays below a predefined threshold $p_{stable}$. In the following example, we set $p_{stable} = 5\%$. We use the Monte Carlo simulation to determine the NodeB transmit power. Therefore, we generate system snapshots with mobiles in all 19 cells and evaluate the transmit power of the central NodeB. Figure 10(a) shows the CDF of the transmit power for 70 to 85 web users per cell. We mark the maximum transmit power by a vertical line and indicate the outage probabilities for the different user numbers by the corresponding horizontal lines. The outage probabilities are between 1% for 70 web users and 67% for 85 web users. The maximum tolerable outage probability $p_{stable} = 5\%$ is between the outage probabilities for 75 and 80 web users. So we can conclude that the web page capacity of the example UMTS network is equal to 75 web users.

Figure 10(b) shows the analogous curves for the web session scenario with mean web session interarrival times between 7 and 9 seconds. The web session capacity for $p_{stable} = 5\%$ is reached for an interarrival time in the range of 7.5 and 8 seconds.

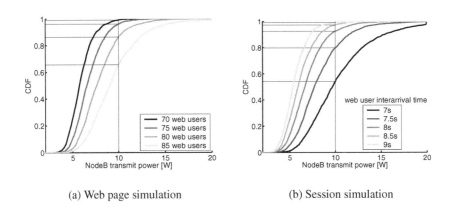

(a) Web page simulation          (b) Session simulation

**Fig. 10.** Outage occurs if the NodeB transmit power exceeds 10 W

## 5   Conclusion

The main intention of this paper was to show that we can use well-studied methods for analyzing the UMTS web traffic capacity. These methods are mostly analytic approaches or Monte Carlo simulation that rely on a Poisson distributed number of users per cell and service. By implementing a detailed ON/OFF simulation we could show that the number of web users concurrently transmitting on the UMTS downlink is binomial distributed for the web page scenario with a constant number of web users downloading web pages back-to-back. In the web session scenario where the web users arrive according to a Poisson process and download a random number of web pages the actively transmitting users are Poisson distributed. We also compared the ON/OFF simulation with power control, the simplified time-dynamic activity simulation, and the static Monte Carlo simulation and could state that they all lead to the same NodeB transmit power distribution. Finally, we showed how to use the Monte Carlo simulation to derive the web traffic capacity of a UMTS network with a certain spatial user distribution.

# References

1. 3GPP: Quality of service (QoS) concept and architecture. Technical Report TS 23.107 (2004)
2. 3GPP: Radio frequency (RF) system scenarios. Technical Report TR 25.942 (2004)
3. 3GPP: Physical layer procedures (FDD). Technical Report TR 25.214 (2004)
4. Choi, W., Kim, J.: Forward-link capacity of a DS/CDMA system with mixed multirate sources. IEEE Trans. on Veh. Tech. **50** (2001) 737–749
5. Choi, H., Limb, J.: A behavioral model of web traffic. In: Protocol 99' (ICNP 99'), International Conference of Networking (1999)
6. Evans, J., Everitt, D.: On the teletraffic capacity of CDMA cellular networks. IEEE Trans. on Veh. Tech. **48** (1999) 153–165
7. Leibnitz, K.: Analytical Modeling of Power Control and its Impact on WCDMA Capacity and Planning. PhD thesis, University of Würzburg (2003)
8. Mäder, A., Staehle, D.: Uplink blocking probabilities in heterogeneous WCDMA networks considering other-cell interference. In: Southern African Telecommunication Networks & Applications Conference, South Western Cape, South Africa (2004)
9. Schröder, B., Weller, A.: Prediction of the connection stability of UMTS-services in the downlink - an analytical approach. In: Proc. of IEEE VTC Fall, Vancouver, CA (2002)
10. Staehle, D., Leibnitz, K., Heck, K.: Fast prediction of the coverage area in UMTS networks. In: Proc. of IEEE Globecom, Taipei, Taiwan (2002)
11. Staehle, D., Mäder, A.: An analytic model for deriving the Node-B transmit power in heterogeneous UMTS networks. In: IEEE VTC Spring, Milano, Italy (2004)
12. Staehle, D., Leibnitz, K., Tran-Gia, P.: Source traffic modeling of wireless applications. Technical report, University of Würzburg (2000)
13. Stevens, W.R.: TCP/IP illustrated (vol. 1): the protocols. Addison-Wesley Longman Publishing Co., Inc. (1993)
14. Stevens, W.R., Wright, G.R.: TCP/IP illustrated (vol. 2): the implementation. Addison-Wesley Longman Publishing Co., Inc. (1995)
15. Tran-Gia, P., Staehle, D., Leibnitz, K.: Source traffic modeling of wireless applications. International Journal of Electronics and Communications (AEÜ) **55** (2001)
16. Viterbi, A., Viterbi, A.: Erlang capacity of a power controlled CDMA system. IEEE Journal on Selected Areas in Comm. **11** (1993) 892–900

# Performance of Different Proxy Concepts in UMTS Networks

Marc C. Necker[1], Michael Scharf[1], and Andreas Weber[2]

[1] Institute of Communication Networks and Computer Engineering
University of Stuttgart, Pfaffenwaldring 47, D-70569 Stuttgart
{necker,scharf}@ikr.uni-stuttgart.de

[2] Alcatel SEL AG, Research and Innovation
Lorenzstr. 10, D-70435 Stuttgart
Andreas.Weber@alcatel.de

**Abstract** It is well known that the large round trip time and the highly variable delay in a cellular network may degrade the performance of TCP. Many concepts have been proposed to improve this situation, including performance enhancing proxies (PEPs). One important class of PEPs are split connection proxies, which terminate a connection from a server in the Internet in a host close to the Radio Access Network (RAN) and establish a second connection towards the mobile User Equipment (UE). This connection splitting can be done either purely on the transport layer (TCP proxy) or on the application layer (HTTP proxy in the case of web traffic). While it is clear that an application layer proxy also infers the splitting of an underlying transport layer connection, the performance of applications may be essentially different for both approaches. In this paper, we first study the general impact of a split connection proxy on TCP bulk data transfer. We then focus on the case of web traffic and investigate the TCP connection behavior of the Mozilla web browser. Based on this, we study the performance of TCP and HTTP proxies in UMTS networks under different scenarios and for different HTTP configurations.

## 1 Introduction

The access to the World Wide Web is one of the most important applications in today's Internet. Since UMTS networks provide much higher data rates compared to GSM-based cellular networks, surfing the Web is expected to be a very promising service. The characteristics of mobile networks differ from fixed networks due to the error-prone radio channel and terminal mobility. Therefore, it is important to understand how wireless web access can be improved. This usually requires cross-layer optimization of all involved protocol layers, in particular including the transport layer.

There are two main approaches to address this issue: First, the performance can be optimized end-to-end by using well-tuned protocol mechanisms, i.e. by

G. Kotsis and O. Spaniol (Eds.): Mobile and Wireless Systems, LNCS 3427, pp. 36–51, 2005.

using optimized TCP versions. This typically requires modifications in the protocol stacks in the end-systems and is thus difficult to deploy in the global Internet. Alternatively, a performance enhancing proxy (PEP) [3] can be used between the radio access network and the Internet. These proxies can operate at different protocol layers. In the case of web traffic, the proxy can either operate at the transport layer (TCP proxy) or at the application layer (HTTP proxy). While HTTP proxies are already present in todays networks, TCP proxies have not been deployed yet. However, a number of approaches have been presented in literature, such as *Indirect TCP* [1] and *Multiple TCP* [20].

In [6], Chakravorty et al. evaluated the WWW performance in GPRS networks by means of measurements. A comprehensive discussion of proxies in general, and how TCP proxies can improve the throughput of a TCP download session can be found in [13]. After a brief study of the impact of PEPs on TCP bulk data transfer, we focus on the WWW as an application in this paper. Consequently, we do not limit ourselves to the transport layer only. Instead, we explicitly take into account the behavior of the WWW application, i.e. the way TCP connections are handled by web browsers. In particular, we study the behavior of the Mozilla web browser with different HTTP configurations and evaluate the performance gain of TCP and HTTP proxies compared to a non-proxied scenario by means of emulation.

This paper is organized as follows. In section 2, we give a brief survey of PEPs. In section 3, we describe the scenario and the emulation environment used for our studies. Next, we present and discuss the results for the case of FTP and WWW traffic in section 4 and section 5, respectively. Finally, we conclude the paper in section 6.

## 2   Performance Enhancing Proxies in Mobile Networks

The use of PEPs in mobile networks has been studied extensively. Most of the research has been motivated by the fact that TCP does not perform well in the presence of non congestion related packet loss. On the other hand, e.g. in UMTS, for PS traffic over DCH, the RLC layer can be configured to provide excellent reliability by using Forward Error Correction (FEC) and Automatic Repeat reQuest (ARQ). Furthermore, the UTRAN ensures in-order delivery. As a consequence, well-configured TCP connections [12] hardly benefit from PEPs which perform local error recovery and in-order delivery [13]. However, UTRAN error protection comes at the cost of higher latency and delay jitter [14].

High latencies and high bandwidth delay products are a challenge for TCP. First, the connection establishment takes longer. Second, if the bandwidth delay product is greater than the transmitter window size, the pipe between server and client cannot be fully utilized by the TCP connection. The transmitter window size is reduced at the start of a TCP connection (Slow Start), but also after a Retransmission Timeout (RTO), which causes the system to perform Slow Start followed by Congestion Avoidance. Furthermore, the transmitter window size may never exceed the advertised window size of the receiver which may be reduced, e.g. due to buffer problems in the receiver. Beside these issues, round trip delay jitters in the order of seconds can trigger spurious TCP timeouts, resulting in unnecessarily retransmitted data [17]. In the following, we will give a brief overview how these problems can be mitigated by different proxy concepts [3].

## 2.1   Protocol Helpers

Protocol helpers are able to add, manipulate, resort, duplicate, drop or delay messages. This includes data messages as well as acknowledgments. However, they neither terminate a connection, nor modify user data. The classical example for a protocol helper is the Berkeley Snoop Protocol [2], which buffers unacknowledged TCP segments and retransmits them locally in the RAN in case of a packet loss. Moreover, acknowledgments are filtered in order to hide packet losses from the TCP sender. However, e.g. for UMTS DCH channels, such a local recovery is done much more efficiently by the UMTS RLC layer.

Protocol helpers have also been proposed to improve TCP performance in the presence of spurious timeouts, either by filtering redundant segments [18], by buffering of acknowledgments [7] or by manipulating the receiver advertised window [4]. However, none of these approaches can mitigate problems caused by high bandwidth delay products.

## 2.2   TCP Proxies

A TCP proxy is an entity which, from the perspective of an Internet server, is located before the RAN. It splits the TCP connections into one connection in the fixed network part and one connection in the mobile network part. TCP proxies are a well-known approach to improve TCP performance in wireless networks [1,20] and have extensively been studied in literature. For instance, Meyer et al. [13] showed that a TCP proxy can significantly improve TCP throughput, especially in case of high data rates (i.e. 384kBit/s in UMTS).

TCP proxies shield the mobile network from potential problems in the Internet. Usually, the transmission delay in the fixed network part is much smaller compared to the delay in the mobile network. Hence, a TCP connection in the fixed network part recovers much faster from packet losses. Another advantage is the high flexibility, since TCP proxies can be modified without great effort. In particular, the PEP's TCP sender directed towards the wireless link can use optimized algorithms, which might not be suitable for the worldwide Internet.

## 2.3   HTTP Proxies

HTTP proxies are well understood and commonly used in wireline networks. Typically, the user can decide whether a proxy shall be used by configuring the web browser accordingly. As with all application layer proxies, HTTP proxies split the underlying transport layer connections. Additionally, they cache frequently accessed data and thus may reduce page loading times[3]. The proxy

---

[3] Note that this might not be possible for dynamic pages

reduces the number of DNS lookups over the wireless link as it can perform these lookups on behalf of the web browser. If the persistence feature in HTTP is activated, it may also reduce the number of TCP connections, since the user equipment usually accesses the same proxy for the duration of a session. It can then maintain one or several persistent TCP connections to that proxy, as compared to several shorter lasting connections when connecting to different servers in the Internet. This highly improves the performance as the overhead of connection setup is removed and the connections are less likely to be in slow start.

### 2.4  Implications of Using PEPs

All PEPs violate the end-to-end argument and the protocol layering, two fundamental architectural principles of the Internet [3]. They require additional processing and storage capacity and have limited scalability. Furthermore, a proxy is an additional error source, and end-systems might not be able to correct errors occurring within a proxy. The location of a PEP within the network architecture has to be chosen very thoroughly since it might be necessary to transfer state information if the route from the user equipment to the Internet changes. Finally, proxies are not compatible to encryption and digital signature on the IP-layer, i.e. IPsec. This implies that a PEP might also prevent the usage of Mobile IP.

Border et al. disadvise proxies that automatically intervene in all connections [3]. Instead, it is recommended that end users should be informed about the presence of a proxy and should have the choice whether to use it or not. Such a procedure would favor the deployment of application-specific proxies.

## 3  Scenario and Simulation/Emulation Environment

### 3.1  Network Scenario and Simulation Environment

The basic scenario is shown in Fig. 1 (top). We consider a single-cell environment, where the User Equipment (UE) on the left side connects to the Node B via a 256kBit/s dedicated channel (DCH) in the uplink and the downlink direction. The Node B is connected to the Radio Network Controller (RNC), which itself is connected to the Internet via the 3G-SGSN and 3G-GGSN of the cellular system's core network. Finally, the UE establishes the data connection with a web server in the Internet. The Internet and core network were assumed to introduce a constant delay $T_{\text{INet}}$ and randomly lose IP packets with a probability of $P_{\text{loss}}$. The UTRAN was modeled in detail with all its relevant protocols and parametrized according to the optimal parameters found in [14]. It was implemented using the event-driven simulation library *IKR SimLib* [9]. The loss probability for a MAC frame on the air interface was set to 0.2 and 0.1 in the down- and uplink, respectively. As indicated in Fig. 1 (bottom), we assume the TCP and HTTP proxy to be located somewhere within the core network, where the delay and IP loss probability from the proxy towards the UTRAN is zero.

## 3.2 Emulation Environment

The previously described scenario is mapped to the emulation setup shown in Fig. 2, which consists of four standard Linux-PCs. The heart of the emulation setup is the UTRAN emulation, which is based on the emulation library developed at the IKR [16]. IP packets are sent from the server-PC, which runs an Apache 1.3.29 web server, to the emulator. The emulator delays (and possibly drops) the IP packets according to the same Internet and core network model which is used for the simulation. Afterwards, the packets may be forwarded to the proxy-PC, which runs a Squid 2.5 HTTP proxy or a hand-written TCP proxy. Finally, the emulator delays the IP packets according to the UTRAN model and forwards them to the client-PC, which runs a Mozilla 1.6 web browser. Note that, in contrast to the model described in the previous section, there is a small delay due to the networking overhead between the proxy PC and the emulation PC. This is an acceptable circumstance, since the delay within the UTRAN is several orders of magnitude higher.

The Mozilla web browser was automated using an XUL-script, which automatically surfs a given list of web-pages. A new page was requested from the web server two seconds after a page and all its inline objects were completely loaded and displayed. The cache size of Mozilla was set to 1MByte, which is large enough to cache small images, such as arrows and bullet points, during one list cycle but too small to cache pictures belonging to any actual content.

To a large extend, Apache and Squid were run with its default configurations. Squid's *pipeline_prefetch* option, which supposedly improves the performance with pipelined requests, was turned on for all scenarios with activated HTTP pipelining. In a first trial, Squid was run in proxy-only mode, i.e. with deactivated

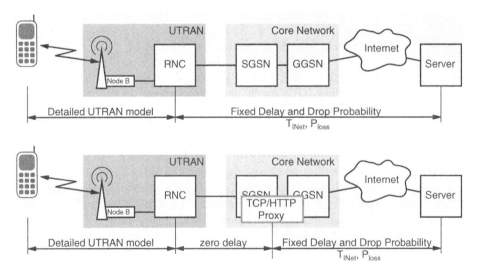

**Figure 1.** UMTS scenario without (top) and with TCP or HTTP proxy (bottom)

caching functionality. In a second trial, 1MByte of disc cache and 1MByte of memory cache were added, which again is large enough to cache small objects, but too small to cache actual content during one list cycle. Additionally, the Squid cache was forced to always use the objects from its cache, regardless of the expiry date reported from the web server. This implies that objects are only removed from the cache due to its limited storage capacity. We believe that this configuration quite well imitates the situation of a highly loaded proxy which has to serve millions of pages per day to many different users.

In contrast, the hand-written TCP proxy simply opens another TCP connection towards the server for each incoming connection from the client, and directly writes any data received from either side to the respective other socket.

Throughout our paper, we do not consider DNS lookups. On the one hand, DNS lookups can impose a significant waiting time at the beginning of a page load, especially if the network's Round Trip Time (RTT) is large (as it is in mobile networks). On the other hand, they have to be done only once upon the first access to a particular server within a session. Therefore, their frequency is hard to determine and model. We will therefore omit the effect of DNS lookups. As DNS lookups can be done by application layer proxies very efficiently, we have to keep in mind that this simplification favors scenarios with no proxy and with a TCP proxy.

### 3.3   FTP Service Scenario

In this paper, we investigate FTP traffic by means of simulation, where we only consider downlink bulk data transfer. The TCP flavor was *NewReno* with activated window scaling. For TCP bulk data transfer, it is sufficient to consider the TCP proxy case, since an application layer proxy (i.e. bulk data transfer over HTTP or FTP) would essentially yield the same results.

### 3.4   WWW Service Scenario

Since WWW traffic is very difficult to model for a simulative study, we chose to investigate it by means of emulation. For that purpose, we created a snapshot

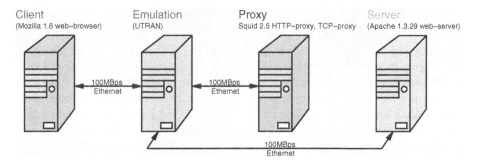

**Figure 2.** Emulation Setup

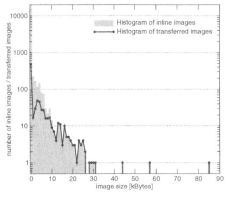 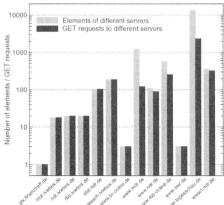

**Figure 3.** Histogram of inline images and transferred images

**Figure 4.** Histogram of elements of different servers and GET requests to different servers

of the web-site `www.tagesschau.de` and related sites on the local web server. Figure 3 shows the histogram of all inline images contained on all web-pages within one Mozilla list cycle. This histogram counts identical images on one particular web-page multiple times. Additionally, Fig. 3 contains the histogram of the number of actually transferred images, which are less due to the browser's internal cache. As it is the case with most web-sites, there is a strong tendency towards many small helper images, such as transparent pixels, bullet images and the like. Figure 4 shows the distribution of objects across the different involved domains. Additionally, the figure shows the distribution of the GET requests issued to the different domains within one list cycle. The majority of accesses goes to the main `tagesschau.de`-server. In addition, several web-pages and inline objects are fetched from related regional web-sites, such as `ndr.de` for news from northern Germany or `swr.de` for news from southern Germany. Moreover, there are several accesses to web-servers responsible for tracking access statistics (`ivwbox.de`, `stat.ndr.de`).

## 4   FTP Results

In this section, we evaluate the performance of a downlink bulk data transfer in dependence of the loss probability $P_{\text{loss}}$ and the delay $T_{\text{INet}}$ in the fixed network part. Figure 5 shows the total TCP throughput plotted over the delay $T_{\text{INet}}$ for different loss probabilities $P_{\text{loss}}$ and the two cases with and without proxy. Without a TCP proxy, the throughput dramatically decreases if the fixed network exhibits packet losses. Even for as few as 0.5% of lost packets in the fixed network, the throughput is reduced by more than 10%. If a TCP proxy is used, the situation is completely different. Now, the system can recover from packet losses in the fixed network part much quicker. Consequently, the TCP throughput remains at a high level for low to medium loss probabilities $P_{\text{loss}}$. Only for

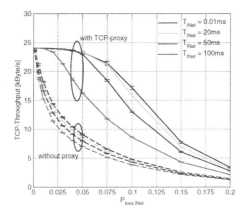

**Figure 5.** Performance of downlink bulk TCP traffic with and without TCP proxy

high loss probabilities or long delays $T_{\text{INet}}$ does the system throughput decrease again. This goes well along with the results presented in [13].

## 5  WWW Results

### 5.1  TCP Connection Behavior

We will first discuss Mozilla's TCP connection behavior for different system configurations. Figure 6 illustrates the TCP connection behavior for a direct connection to the web server with no proxy. The figure shows the duration of all TCP connections on their corresponding port numbers over the time[4]. No automated surfing was used here. Instead, the main page www.tagesschau.de was manually accessed at time t=0s, and subsequent subpages were accessed at times t=40s, t=60s and t=80s. The browser was terminated at t=100s. HTTP version was 1.1 with deactivated keep-alive and no pipelining. The browser's cache was cleared at the beginning of the measurement. This protocol configuration forces the web browser to open a separate TCP connection for each inline object which results in 414 TCP connections for loading all four pages. This implicates a considerable overhead with respect to delay and transmitted data, since each TCP connection needs one RTT to be established and at least one RTT to be torn down [19]. Especially in networks which exhibit a high RTT, the performance will suffer from this behavior.

The situation can be improved by activating the HTTP keep-alive feature [8] (persistent connections). Figure 7 shows the new pattern of TCP connections, with the destination server annotated for each TCP connection. The number of TCP connections reduces to only 16 in total. Note that TCP connections to the server hosting the main web-page are kept persistent for a long time, while

---

[4] Note that not all consecutive port numbers are used within the session.

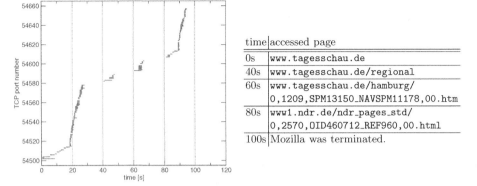

| time | accessed page |
|------|---------------|
| 0s | `www.tagesschau.de` |
| 40s | `www.tagesschau.de/regional` |
| 60s | `www.tagesschau.de/hamburg/` `0,1209,SPM13150_NAVSPM11178,00.htm` |
| 80s | `www1.ndr.de/ndr_pages_std/` `0,2570,OID460712_REF960,00.html` |
| 100s | Mozilla was terminated. |

**Figure 6.** Timeline of TCP connections with no proxy and no HTTP keep-alive

connections to servers serving inline objects are torn down much faster. However, this relatively fast connection teardown is not caused by the web browser, but by the web-server, i.e. the browser has no influence on it. Instead, it highly depends on the settings of the Apache web server, which provides two main parameters to control the teardown of persistent connections, namely *MaxKeepAliveRequests* and *KeepAliveTimeout*. The first parameter specifies the maximum number of objects that may be transmitted over a persistent connection before it is being closed, while the second parameter indicates the time after which a persistent connection is closed if it became idle. The default values of these parameters are 100 and 15 seconds, respectively. Since, most likely, there are many web-sites using the default values, we will use the same values for our studies. Figure 7 nicely reflects the value of *KeepAliveTimeout* for servers serving inline objects.

With HTTP keep-alive, the number of connections reduces, leading to less overhead with the potential of faster loading times. On the other hand, the client has to wait for the response from the server for each requested inline object before it can issue another request. This implies that there may be far fewer outstanding requests as compared to non-persistent connections, which is

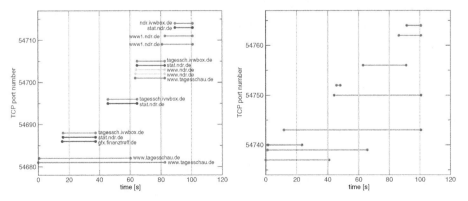

**Figure 7.** Timeline of TCP connections with no proxy and HTTP keep-alive

**Figure 8.** Timeline of TCP connections with HTTP proxy and HTTP keep-alive

a potential performance inhibitor in networks with large RTTs. This situation can be greatly improved by activating pipelining in HTTP 1.1, which allows the request of multiple inline objects over the same persistent connection without waiting for each response.

Finally, we will consider the connection behavior if an HTTP proxy is used. RFC 2616 [8] states that "talking to proxies is the most important use of persistent connections". The reason is that multiple different servers can be accessed via the same persistent client–proxy connection. The connection behavior in such a scenario is shown in Fig. 8. It is now no longer possible to associate a TCP connection with a particular server. The chart shows that the number of connections almost halfened to 9. Again, all but one of the connections that are closed before the end of the session are terminated by the WWW proxy.

We do not need to consider the case of a TCP proxy here, since it does not change the semantics of an HTTP connection.

## 5.2   Page Loading Times

In this section, we investigate the page loading times for ideal Internet conditions. In particular, we chose $T_{INet} = 20$ms and $P_{loss} = 0$. Table 1, Fig. 9 and Fig. 10 show the mean and median of the page loading times for all considered proxy scenarios and different HTTP 1.1 configurations. For the Squid scenario, we have provided two values per table cell. The first one was obtained with Squid acting as a proxy only, the second one with Squid additionally caching web objects. Since the difference is very small, Fig. 9 and Fig. 10 show only the values with caching enabled.

For the non-proxied scenario and the scenario with a TCP proxy, it is obvious that HTTP performs best when keep-alive and pipelining is activated, and performs worst if both is deactivated. In contrast, according to information in [11], Squid does not support pipelined requests towards servers very well. While it accepts pipelined requests from the client side, it transforms them into parallel requests, where no more than two requests from a pipeline can be fetched in parallel. This drawback is reflected in Table 1, since, with pipelining, performance does not improve compared to the non-pipelined case.

**Table 1.** Mean values and median of the loading time

|  | no keep-alive | | keep-alive | |  |
|---|---|---|---|---|---|
|  | Mean | Median | Mean | Median |  |
| no pipelining | 8.2s | 6.3s | 7.73s | 5.95s | no proxy |
| pipelining | — | — | 6.22s | 4.96s |  |
| no pipelining | 8.56s | 6.47s | 8.22s | 6.16s | TCP proxy |
| pipelining | — | — | 6.74s | 4.94s |  |
| no pipelining | 8.85s / 8.81s | 6.67s / 6.58s | 7.02s / 6.92s | 5.35s / 5.26s | Squid proxy |
| pipelining | — | — | 7.09s / 6.91 | 5.41s / 5.40s |  |

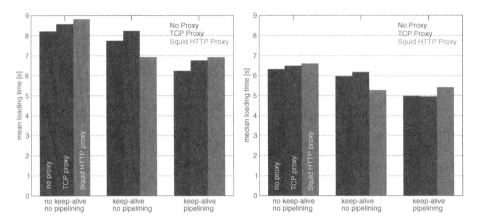

**Figure 9.** Mean page loading time      **Figure 10.** Median of page loading time

When comparing the different proxy scenarios, we can see that a proxy not necessarily improves the performance. For all considered HTTP configurations, the TCP proxy worsens the performance compared to the non-proxied case, which results from the overhead introduced by the proxy. However, the proxy could significantly increase the performance under two circumstances: First, if the fixed part of the connection was non-ideal, the TCP proxy could efficiently recover from lost packets within the fixed part of the network and also mitigate the effects of long RTTs in the fixed network (see section 5.3 and 5.4). The second circumstance is a proxy with an optimized TCP sender towards the UE. The most efficient and simple measure hereby certainly is an increase of the initial congestion window, since a small congestion window will prevent the full usage of the available bandwidth within the RAN for a relatively long time at the beginning of a TCP connection. This results from the long RTT in mobile networks (see [6] for measurements in GPRS networks on this issue).

The same can be said for the Squid scenario and non-persistent HTTP connections with no pipelining. If keep-alive is activated, we observe a significant performance increase compared to the non-proxied scenario. This goes well along with the observations made in section 5.1: The UE can now maintain persistent HTTP connections to the proxy, even if the requests are issued across different servers. This leads to fewer TCP connection establishments and teardowns across the RAN. If pipelining is activated, the performance in the non-proxied scenario significantly increases, whereas the performance with Squid remains about the same. The reason is again the lack of pipelining support in Squid.

Figures 11 and 12 show the complementary cumulative distribution function (CCDF) of the page loading time for the different proxy scenarios with deactivated and activated keep-alive, respectively. Pipelining was deactivated in both cases. In both diagrams, we can identify three groups of pages. About 40% of all pages are loaded within 5 seconds. 50% are loaded faster than 12 – 15 seconds, depending on the scenario. Only 10% or less of all pages take longer than 15 seconds to load. For the case of non-persistent connections, all CCDFs are very

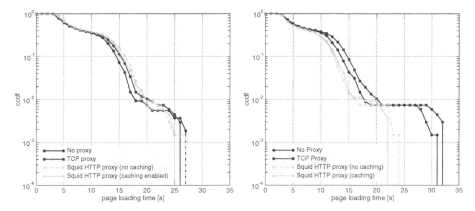

**Figure 11.** CCDF of page loading times, no HTTP keep-alive and no pipelining

**Figure 12.** CCDF of page loading times, HTTP keep-alive without pipelining

close together, whereas the performance gain with an HTTP proxy is well visible if persistent connections are allowed. In contrast, for the case of persistent connections, there is a noticable difference between the performance of the HTTP proxy and the other two scenarios. This again reflects the great advantage that HTTP proxies can take of persistent connections.

We already know that the mean and median of the page loading time becomes smaller if persistent connections are activated. However, when comparing Fig. 11 and 12, we can observe a much heavier tail in the CCDFs for persistent connections as compared to the non-persistent case. In other words, there are a few pages that have a significantly longer loading time if persistent connections are allowed. In fact, the heavy tail is caused by only one page, which is the main page www.tagesschau.de. This page is characterized by a number of inline objects well above average. It is a good example of where the more serialized issuing of HTTP requests with persistent connections reduces performance.

## 5.3 Internet Packet Losses

Studies of the Internet packet dynamics, such as in [15], and recent measurements [10] reveal that typical IP-packet loss probability on the Internet are on the order of 0 to 5 percent, or even more in very bad cases.

Figures 13 and 14 plot the mean and median of the page loading time over the Internet packet loss $P_{\text{loss}}$ if keep-alive is activated but pipelining is deactivated. Figure 15 and 16 shows the same but with activated pipelining. Squid is considered with caching enabled only. As it can be expected from previous studies (e.g. [13]), the mean and median of the page loading time increase in the non-proxy case as $P_{\text{loss}}$ increases. It is interesting to observe that this increase is approximately linear with $P_{\text{loss}}$.

A similar increase can be observed if a TCP proxy is used. However, the increase is much smaller. We already noted that the performance with TCP

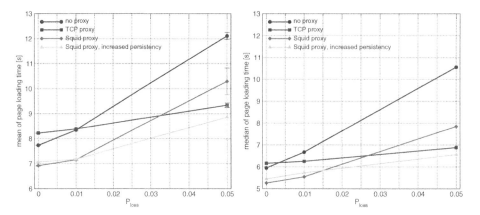

**Figure 13.** Mean of page loading times, HTTP keep-alive without pipelining

**Figure 14.** Median of page loading times, HTTP keep-alive without pipelining

proxy is worse compared to the non-proxied case if $P_{loss} = 0$. As $P_{loss}$ increases, the advantage of the proxy becomes obvious, as it outperforms the non-proxied case for $P_{loss} > 0.01$. We should expect a similar behavior for an HTTP proxy. However, we observe a strong performance decrease in the Squid scenario as $P_{loss}$ increases. For both HTTP configurations, the Squid performance eventually drops far below the performance of the TCP proxy. This behavior is not intuitive, since both proxies split the TCP connection and should be able to quickly recover from packet losses in the Internet.

The reason for this is the following. In the non-proxied case, for each displayed page, the web browser has to issue many GET requests to the web server. That means, persistent HTTP connections are usually busy. Hence, they will not be closed by the web server due to a timeout caused by the *KeepAliveTimeout* timer, but only due to reaching the maximum number of transmitted inline objects on a

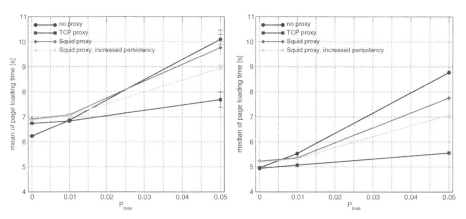

**Figure 15.** Mean of page loading times, HTTP keep-alive with pipelining

**Figure 16.** Median of page loading times, HTTP keep-alive with pipelining

connection. Consequently, the TCP connections will be in congestion avoidance most of the time, unless multiple TCP packets are lost per RTT. The same thing applies to the TCP proxy scenario. In contrast to this, the Squid proxy has an essentially different connection behavior towards the web server. Since it caches most of the web objects, the persistent connections towards the web server are mostly idle and frequently get closed by the web server. This implies that the connections towards the web server are in slow-start very often. That is, a TCP connection is more likely to be in slow-start when a packet loss occurs, which results in long recovery times[5]. The final consequence is that the link from the HTTP proxy to the web server may be idle for quite a long time, while the web browser is still waiting for objects to be served from the proxy. This eventually leads to the bad performance in the Squid scenario if packet losses in the Internet are present.

Squid performance can be improved by setting the Apache parameters *Max-KeepAliveRequests* and *KeepAliveTimeout* to higher values. Here, we set it to infinity and 150s, respectively. Now, Apache waits much longer before closing any persistent connections. Figures 13 through 16 contain the measured results obtained in the Squid scenario, labeled with *increased persistency*. Looking at the non-pipelined case, the Squid proxy now behaves as we expect it: the mean loading times are below or about equal to those of the TCP proxy, which is intuitive, since the HTTP proxy can cache content. The pipelined case shows some improvements, but the performance cannot match that of the TCP proxy due to the reasons discussed in section 5.2.

### 5.4   Internet Packet Delay

Finally, we will investigate the influence of the packet delay $T_{\text{INet}}$ in the fixed network part. Figures 17 through 19 plot the mean page loading time over the loss probability $P_{\text{loss}}$ for different delays $T_{\text{INet}}$ and the three considered proxy scenarios. It is obvious, that the mean page loading time must increase as $T_{\text{INet}}$ increases. It is more interesting to note that, for each scenario, the slope of the curves is independent of the delay $T_{\text{INet}}$. That is, the delay $T_{\text{INet}}$ has an additive impact on the loading times. This indicates that the persistent TCP connections are mostly in congestion avoidance.

As expected, the advantage of the proxy solutions becomes greater as the delay $T_{\text{INet}}$ increases. The reason is again the faster recovery from packet losses in the proxy case, especially if the delay is large. We can also see that an HTTP proxy can take more advantage of its caching functionality if the delay is large, as it takes longer to retrieve documents and objects from the actual web server.

## 6   Conclusion

We investigated the connection behavior of the Mozilla web browser and evaluated the performance of TCP and HTTP proxies under typical web traffic in

---

[5] We measured TCP timeout durations of 10s and more.

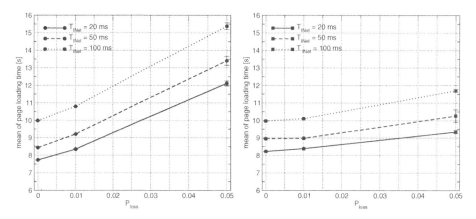

**Figure 17.** Mean of page loading times, no proxy, HTTP keep-alive without pipelining

**Figure 18.** Mean of page loading times, TCP proxy, HTTP keep-alive without pipelining

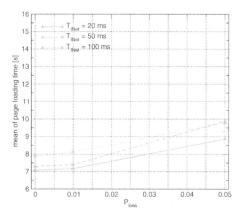

**Figure 19.** Mean of page loading times, Squid HTTP proxy with increased persistency, HTTP keep-alive without pipelining

an UMTS environment. Our studies show that proxies do not increase system performance by default. Instead, the proxy concept and the parameters of all involved devices must be carefully chosen under consideration of all network aspects. In the case of a good server connection, HTTP performs best with activated keep-alive and pipelining and without any proxy. If the connection towards the server is bad, the same HTTP configuration in combination with a TCP proxy delivers best results, whereas the Squid HTTP proxy does not perform well due to the lack of pipelining support.

# Acknowledgements

Michael Scharf is funded by the German Research Foundation (DFG) through the Center of Excellence (SFB) 627. The authors would like to thank Jochen Zwick for his valuable work on the automation of the Mozilla web browser.

# References

1. A. Bakre and B. R. Badrinath: "I-TCP: Indirect TCP for Mobile Hosts", in Proc. *Proc. 15th Int'l. Conf. on Distr. Comp. Sys.*, May 1995.
2. H. Balakrishnan, S. Seshan und R. H. Katz: "Improving Reliable Transport and Handoff Performance in Cellular Wireless Networks", *Wireless Networks* 1(4), pp. 469 – 481, Feb. 1995.
3. J. Border, M. Kojo, J. Griner, G. Montenegro and Z. Shelby: "Performance Enhancing Proxies Intended to Mitigate Link-Related Degradations", RFC 3135, June 2001.
4. K. Brown and S. Singh: "M-TCP: TCP for Mobile Cellular Networks": *ACM SIGCOMM Computer Communications Review*, 27(5), pp. 19 – 43, Oct. 1997.
5. R. Chakravorty and I. Pratt: "Rajiv Chakravorty and Ian Pratt, WWW Performance over GPRS", in *Proc. IEEE MWCN 2002*, Sep. 2002, Stockholm, Sweden.
6. R. Chakravorty, J. Cartwright and I. Pratt: "Practical Experience With TCP over GPRS", in *Proc. IEEE GLOBECOM*, Nov. 2002.
7. M. C. Chan and R. Ramjee: "TCP/IP Performance over 3G Wireless Links with Rate and Delay Variation", in Proc. *ACM MobiCom 2002*, Sept. 2002.
8. R. Fielding, J. Gettys, J. Mogul, H. Frystyk, L. Masinter, P. Leach and T. Berners-Lee: "Hypertext Transfer Protocol – HTTP/1.1", RFC 2616.
9. http://www.ikr.uni-stuttgart.de/IKRSimLib/
10. http://www.internettrafficreport.com, September 2004.
11. http://www.squid-cache.org, September 2004.
12. H. Inamura, G. Montenegro, R. Ludwig, A. Gurtov and F. Khafizov: "TCP over second (2.5G) and third (3G) generation wireless networks", RFC 3481, Feb. 2003.
13. M. Meyer, J. Sachs and M. Holzke: "Performance Evaluation of a TCP Proxy in WCDMA Networks", *IEEE Wireless Communications*, Vol. 10, Iss. 5, pp. 70–79, Oct. 2003
14. A. Mutter, M. C. Necker and S. Lück: "IP-Packet Service Time Distributions in UMTS Radio Access Networks", in *Proc. EUNICE 2004*, Tampere, Finland.
15. V. Paxson: "End-to-End Internet Packet Dynamics", *Trans. on Networking*, Vol. 7, No. 3, pp. 277–292, June 1999.
16. S. Reiser: "Development and Implementation of an Emulation Library", Project Report, University of Stuttgart, IKR, September 2004.
17. M. Scharf, M. C. Necker and B. Gloss: "The Sensitivity of TCP to Sudden Delay Variations in Mobile Networks", LNCS 3042, pp. 76 – 87, May 2004.
18. J. Schüler, S. Gruhl, T. Schwabe and M. Schwiegel: "Performance Improvements for TCP in Mobile Networks with high Packet Delay Variations", in Proc. *Int. Teletraffic Congress (ITC-17)*, Sept. 2001.
19. W. R. Stevens: "TCP/IP Illustrated, Volume 1", Addison-Wesley, 1994.
20. R. Yavatkar and N. Bhagawat: "Improving End-to-End-Performance of TCP over Mobile Internetworks", in *Proc. IEEE Workshop on Mobile Computing Systems and Applications*, Dec. 1994.

# Algorithms for WLAN Coverage Planning

E. Amaldi, A. Capone, M. Cesana, L. Fratta, and F. Malucelli

Politecnico di Milano - DEI
Piazza L. da Vinci 32, 20133, Milano,Italy
{amaldi, capone, cesana, fratta, malucell}@elet.polimi.it

**Abstract.** The impressive market spread of IEEE 802.11 based Wireless Local Area Networks (WLANs) is calling for quantitative approaches in the network planning procedure. It is common belief that such networks have the potentials to replace traditional indoor wired local networks and allow flexible access outdoor, eventually competing with classical cellular systems ($GSM$, $GPRS$, $UMTS$, etc.). The appropriate positioning of the Access Points (AP) is crucial to determine the network effectiveness. In a companion paper we argue that previously proposed approaches to coverage planning neglect the features of the IEEE 802.11 access mechanism, which limits system capacity when access points coverage areas overlap. In this paper we describe the optimization models with hyperbolic and quadratic objective functions that directly accounts for system capacity and we propose heuristics combining greedy and local search phases. Computational results show that our heuristics provide near-optimal solutions within a reasonable amount of time.

**Keywords** WLAN, radio planning, coverage problem, set covering problem, 802.11, wireless hot spots.

## 1  Introduction

WLAN technology is having a surprising diffusion in the market of telecommunications. WLAN hot spots are creeping up day by day and almost all portable devices like PDAs, laptops etc. come equipped with 802.11 network interface card and adapters. This amazing success is mainly due to the simplicity of the solution, its cost effectiveness, and, last but not least, the increasing demand for "anywhere, anytime" connectivity. A WLAN is basically constituted by one or more wireless Access Points (APs) connected to the backbone network which provide wireless connectivity to the covered area.

In many situations, the deployment of a single AP is not enough to provide the required connectivity. As an example, large facilities, such as an office complex, apartment buildings, hospitals, university campuses, or warehouses generally require many cooperating APs in order to provide the required services to the end users.

In order to access the network, a user terminal needs to receive the radio transmission of an AP at an adequate level of power. A simple way to plan radio

G. Kotsis and O. Spaniol (Eds.): Mobile and Wireless Systems, LNCS 3427, pp. 52–65, 2005.

coverage is to consider a set of possible positions of user terminals (Test Points, TPs) in the service area and a set of AP candidate sites (CSs). A subset of CSs in which to install APs has then to be selected so as to guarantee a high enough signal level at all TPs. The problem of minimizing the number of candidate AP sites that are able to cover all TPs amounts to a well-known combinatorial optimization problem, namely the minimum cardinality set covering problem [2]. This problem is $NP$-hard and heuristics are usually adopted to obtain sub-optimal solutions.

However, not all feasible solutions (subsets of AP candidate sites that are able to cover all TPs) provide the same system capacity and level of service. Due to the WLAN medium access mechanism, if a user terminal is covered by more than one AP and is transmitting/receiving to/from one of them, the other APs are prevented to transmit/receive to/from other users [5]. Therefore, the overlaps between the subsets of TPs covered by different APs should be taken into account during the radio planning phase.

Classical methods for coverage planning based on random search heuristics can be applied to the problem [4]. In [6] the authors propose a formulation driven jointly by the maximization of the signal quality in the service area and by the minimization of the areas with a poor signal quality. The objective function comes from a combination of the above objectives. Rodrigues et al. [8] propose an integer linear programming (ILP) formulation in which the signal quality at the test points is maximized. This formulation, which does not require full coverage, is solved by using the state-of-the-art CPLEX ILP commercial solver. In [7] a traffic intensity is assigned to each TP and a formulation aimed at maximizing the channel utilization of each AP is proposed. This formulation turns out to be a special case of the capacitated facility location problem. In general, all the above-mentioned works focus on the problem of achieving high coverage level in terms of received signal quality. Very few of them consider network capacity as an optimization objective.

In [1] we proposed novel mathematical programming formulations for the WLAN planning problem which take into account the coverage overlap between APs and its impact on the network capacity. In particular, we formalized the planning problem by using hyperbolic and quadratic objective functions. Since the proposed formulations are hard to ($NP$-hard) tackle, in this paper we show how the special underlying structure makes it possible to devise effective heuristics based on combined greedy and local search procedures to provide near-optimal solutions within a reasonable amount of time. After briefly describing the formulations, the heuristics are presented in Section 3. Computational results are reported and discussed in Section 4, and concluding remarks are contained in Section 5.

## 2   Planning Problem Formulations

The access mechanism of IEEE 802.11 WLANs is based on the "listen before talk" approach, i.e., each station willing to use the shared resource listens to the channel for ongoing communications before attempting its own access. If the channel is sensed busy the station refrains from transmitting (*Carrier Sensing Multiple Access*, CSMA).

The peculiar characteristics of the 802.11b access mechanism affect the coverage planning process and the planning procedure should take into account the incidence of overlapping regions, beside all the other optimization parameters.

In [1] the planning problem is formalized as follows. Let $J = \{1, \ldots, n\}$ denote the set of the indices of the candidate sites to host access points and $I = \{1, \ldots, m\}$ be the set of users' indices. For each $j \in J$ a subset of users $I_j \subseteq I$ is given. This subset represents the users which can use the access point $j$. A second family of subsets $I'_j$, $j \in J$, representing the users affected by the interference of access point $j$, can be also defined. As a matter of fact, the IEEE 802.11-powered devices work with two thresholds on the received power: a carrier sensing threshold, which is used in the channel sensing phase, and the receive threshold, which defines the correct reception of a packet on the wireless channel. Namely, if the power on the channel is above the carrier sensing threshold, any device refrains from transmitting,and if a self-destined transmission is received with a power level above the receive threshold, the transmission can be correctly captured by the receiver. The value of the carrier sensing threshold is generally lower than the one of the receiving threshold. $I'_j$ represent the set devices which whose transmissions are received by device $j$ with a power level above the carrier sensing threshold, whereas $I_j$ is the set of devices whose transmissions are received by $j$ at a power level above the receive threshold value. Clearly $I_j \subseteq I'_j$. In the following we consider $I_j \equiv I'_j$ in order to ease the formulation of the planning problem, i.e., we assume that the carrier sensing threshold coincides with the receive threshold. The proposed formulations still hold two separate thresholds are considered.

Further, we assume that each user is connected to a single AP whose capacity is shared by all users within its coverage range. Without loss of generality, we assume that the overall capacity of an AP is equal to 1. However, due to the multiple access mechanism of the IEEE 802.11 standard, a user that is in the interfering range of a set of AP blocks the transmissions to/from all APs in this set. Therefore, we can assume that the fraction of the AP capacity available to each user is equal to the reciprocal of the number of users in the interference range of the set of APs the considered user can interfere with. The focus of our work is not on the accuracy of the capacity of a WLAN, since this rather complete and out the scope of this paper. On the other hand, we try to define a qualitative measure of the network efficiency to be used in the planning problem definition which captures some of the features of the IEEE 802.11 access mechanism.

Thus, assuming uniform traffic for all users, the network capacity can be estimated by the following expression:

$$c(S) = \sum_{i \in I(S)} \frac{1}{|\cup_{j \in S : i \in I_j} I'_j|}, \tag{1}$$

where $S \subseteq J$ is the subset of CSs in which APs are installed and $I(S)$ the subset of users covered that is included in some $I_j, j \in S$.

As in any covering problem, the basic decision variables indicate which subsets are included in the solution:

$$x_j = \begin{cases} 1 \text{ if an AP is installed in } j \\ 0 \text{ otherwise} \end{cases}$$

To measure the cardinality of the union of subsets containing each element, we also need the following variables which clearly depend on $S$ (and hence on $x$'s):

$$y_{ih} = \begin{cases} 1 \text{ if elements } i \text{ and } h \text{ appear together in some } I_j \\ \quad \text{with } j \in S \\ 0 \text{ otherwise} \end{cases}$$

Consider the usual elements-subsets incidence matrix $A$ where $a_{ij} = 1$ if element $i$ belongs to subset $j$, and 0 otherwise, for each $i \in I$ and $j \in J$. The hyperbolic formulation of the problem aiming at maximizing the capacity (Planning Capacity with Hyperbolic formulation, PCH) is:

$$PCH : \max \quad \sum_{i \in I} \frac{1}{\sum_{h \in I} y_{ih}} \tag{2}$$

$$subject\ to:$$

$$\sum_j a_{ij} x_j \geq 1 \qquad\qquad i \in I \tag{3}$$

$$a_{ij} a_{hj} x_j \leq y_{ih} \qquad j \in J, i, h \in I \tag{4}$$

$$x_j \in \{0, 1\} \qquad\qquad j \in J \tag{5}$$

$$y_{ih} \geq 0 \qquad\qquad i, h \in I \tag{6}$$

where (3) imposes the complete coverage and (4) defines the variables $y_{ih}$.

Since even small-size mathematical programs with hyperbolic objective functions are very challenging (see [3]), the AP location problem can be approximated in terms of quadratic programming. Consider an arbitrary subset $I_j$ in a given solution $S \subseteq J$. If $I_j$ does not intersect any other subset in the solution (or is the only subset in $S$), its contribution to the network capacity amounts to $1/|I_j|$ for each element of $I_j$, which gives a total contribution over all TPs in $I_j$ equal to 1. If a solution contains two subsets $I_j$ and $I_\ell$ with an empty intersection, the contribution to the network capacity due to $I_j$ and $I_\ell$ is equal to $c_j + c_\ell$. Conversely, if $I_j$ and $I_\ell$ do intersect, the above contribution must be decreased by an amount which depends on the cardinality of their intersection. In particular, the contribution of the intersection must be subtracted from the capacity of the two subsets and a new evaluation of the contribution of the intersection considering the union of the two subsets must be added to the capacity measure. To estimate the decrease in network capacity due to the overlapping between a pair of selected subsets $I_j$ and $I_\ell$, we define the coefficients:

$$q_{j\ell} = -\frac{|I_j \cap I_\ell|}{|I_j|} - \frac{|I_j \cap I_\ell|}{|I_\ell|} + \frac{|I_j \cap I_\ell|}{|I_j \cup I_\ell|}. \tag{7}$$

Note that these coefficients assume values between -1 (when $I_j \subseteq I_\ell$ or $I_\ell \subseteq I_j$) and 0 (when the two subsets are disjoint) and are symmetric, that is $q_{j\ell} = q_{\ell j}$.

The problem of locating APs so as to guarantee full coverage can then be approximated by the following quadratic program:

$$QPC : \max \quad \frac{1}{2} \sum_{j \in J} \sum_{\ell \in J, \ell \neq j} q_{j\ell} x_j x_\ell + \sum_{j \in J} x_j \tag{8}$$

$$subject\ to:$$

$$\sum_j a_{ij} x_j \geq 1 \qquad\qquad i \in I \tag{9}$$

$$x_j \in \{0, 1\} \qquad\qquad j \in J \tag{10}$$

which turns out to be an interesting Quadratic set Covering Problem. It is worth noting that this formulation contains a substantially smaller number of variables than the hyperbolic one. Moreover, it is easy to verify that the objective function coincides with the network capacity if each TP belongs at most to two different selected subsets $I_j$ and it provides a lower bound if $l$-tuples ($l > 2$) of selected subsets have a non-empty intersection. Figure 1 shows a case where the quadratic objective function provides lower network capacity than the hyperbolic one. Three access point are installed, each one serving one test point. Furthermore, a test point point falls in the transmission range of all the three access points. The value of the hyperbolic objective function is $1/2 + 1/2 + 1/2 + 1/4 = 7/4$, where $1/2$ is the contribution to network capacity of the test point covered by one access point only, and $1/4$ is the contribution due to the test point in the overlapping region.

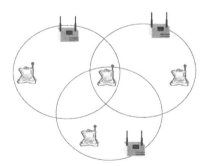

**Fig. 1.** Network configuration with multiple overlaps

On the other hand, the value of the coefficients $q_{j\ell}$ defined in Equation 7 is $-4/9$ for each $j$ and $\ell$, thus the quadratic objective function (see Equation 8) is $3\mathrm{x}(1 - 2/3) = 1$.

# 3   Heuristics

Since the two above formulations are hard to tackle even for small instances, we developed effective heuristics able to provide near-optimal solutions in a reasonable amount of time.

All proposed algorithms are composed of two phases: in the first one a greedy approach is used to build a feasible solution and in the second one the resulting solution is improved through local search. The greedy phase starts from a empty solution and iteratively adds to the current solution the candidate site which maximizes a certain benefit function. This function measures the benefit achieved when adding a candidate site to a current partial solution. The benefit function is adaptively computed for each candidate site that is not yet included in the current solution.

The general structure of the proposed heuristics can be summarized as follows:

```
PROCEDURE Heuristic(A)
   S = ∅;
   BuildUpSolution(A, S);
   LocalSearch(S);
   RETURN(S)
END Heuristic
```

where $S$ is the set of candidate sites in which APs are installed and $A$ is the incidence matrix defined in Section 2. Function *BuildUpSolution* implements the greedy phase of the heuristic which iteratively converges to a feasible solution $S$. Function *LocalSearch* refines the solution $S$ through a local search.

## 3.1   Greedy Phase

The greedy phase of the proposed heuristics starts off from a NULL solution $(S = \emptyset)$ and keeps adding iteratively one CS at a time. The procedure stops when all the TPs are covered by the CS in set S. At each iteration, the CS which maximizes a greedy *benefit function* is added to the solution. A pseudo code implementation of the greedy procedure is reported hereafter:

```
PROCEDURE BuildUpSolution(A, S)
   Best_CS = PickBestCS(A);
   S = S ∪ Best_CS;
   Covered_TPs = Covered_TPs ∪ I_Best_CS;
   WHILE Covered_TPs != ALL_TPs
      GreedyStep(A, Covered_TPs,S);
END BuildUpSolution;
```

The function `PickBestCS` chooses the first CS to be added to the solution. The idea is to choose the AP whose coverage area has the smallest overlap with the coverage areas of all the other CS. The pseudo code of this function is not reported for the sake of brevity.

The GreedyStep function, which represents the core of the greedy phase, returns the next CS to be added to the solution set. The pseudo code of this function is the following:

```
PROCEDURE GreedyStep(A, Covered_TPs, S)
  MaxFunction = 0;
  DO FOR j ∉ S
    IF Benefit_function_j > MaxFunction;
      CS_ToAdd = j;
      MaxFunction=Benefit_function_j;
    FI
  OD
  S = S ∪ CS_ToAdd;
  Covered_TPs = Covered_TPs ∪ I_CS_ToAdd
END GreedyStep;
```

where I_CS_ToAdd following the notation of Section 2 is the set of TPs covered by the $j$-th CS.

The CS to be added to the solution is the one with the highest *benefit function* which is calculated as follows:

$$\texttt{Benefit\_Function\_j} = \frac{\Delta_{OF}}{ATP_j}$$

where $\Delta_{OF}$ denotes the increase in the objective function if an AP is added in CS $j$ and $ATP_j$ the corresponding increase in the total number of TPs covered. The greedy algorithm is adaptive since both $\Delta_{OF}$ and $ATP_j$ are re-calculated at each iteration.

Since each iteration adds to the solution a CS which covers one TP at least, the procedure *BuildUpSolution* requires $\min(n, m)$ steps to converge at most, where $n$ and $m$ are the TP number and the CS number respectively.

## 3.2   Local Search

The local search phase takes as input the solution $S$ provided by the greedy phase and tries to enhance it. In particular, the neighborhood of solution $S$ is explored to check for the presence of a better solution. In our case, starting from $S$ we eliminate first one, then two CS belonging to $S$ itself and we apply to the perturbed solution $S_p$ the *BuildUpSolution* procedure described in the previous section. The final solution $S^*$ is the one with the highest objective function, otherwise $S^* = S$.

The pseudo code of the local search is:

```
PROCEDURE LocalSearch(A,S)
  MaxOF=ComputeOF(A, S);
  DO
  Enhanced=FALSE;
  DO FOR j ∈ S
    S = S \ {j};
    Covered_TPs = Covered_TPs \ {I_j};
    BuildUpSolution(A,Covered_TPs,S);
    NewOF=ComputeOF(A,S);
    IF NewOF > MaxOF
      MaxSOL=S;
      MaxOF=NewOF
      Enhanced=TRUE;
    FI
    DO FOREACH i IN S AND i>j
      S = S \ {i,j};
      Covered_TPs=Covered_TPs \ {I_i, I_j};
      BuildUpSolution(A, Covered_TPs,S);
      NewOF=ComputeOF(A, S);
      IF NewOF > MaxOF
        MaxSOL=S;
        MaxOF=NewOF
        Enhanced=TRUE;
      FI
    OD
  OD
  IF Enhanced
    S=MaxSOL;
  FI
  WHILE Enhanced;
END LocalSearch;
```

Obviously the function ComputeOF has different implementations according to the formulation of the planning problem we are applying the heuristic to (hyperbolic, quadratic).

The same heuristic approach can be extended with slight modifications to hyperbolic and quadratic formulations of the planning problem without full coverage constraint. For the sake of brevity, the details of this extension are not described in this paper.

## 4   Computational Results

Firstly, we have tested the effectiveness of the above algorithms on synthetic instances representing WLANs in order to gather information on the quality of the models and the proposed heuristics. Secondly, we have used the proposed approach to plan the positions of 802.11 APs at the Telecommunications Section of the Department of Electronics and Information (DEI) of the Politecnico di Milano.

## 4.1    Analysis of Synthetic Instances

The synthetic instances generation software takes as input the following parameters:

- the edge of the square area to be simulated $(L)$
- the number of Candidate Sites $(CSNumber)$, i.e., the positions where a AP can be installed
- the number of Test Points $(TPNumber)$, i.e., the end users
- the value of each AP's coverage range, expressed in meters $(r)$.

Each AP is assumed to have a circular coverage region with radius $r$.

According to the above parameters, the generating tool randomly draws the positions for the $CSNumber$ candidate sites and of the $TPNumber$ test points. An instance is not feasible when no solution covering all the $TPs$ can be found. In order to generate feasible instances, the generator does the following: firstly, the positions of the $CS$ are randomly generated within the simulated area, secondly each $TP$ is forced to belong to the coverage range of one $CS$ at least.

Using the tool described above we have generated a set of "*uniform*" instances where all the APs to be installed have uniform value of coverage radius $r$. All the results in the following have been obtained averaging on 10 instances of the same type.

The first step of our analysis is to test the effectiveness of the proposed approaches by comparing their results with the optimum values of the two objective functions, hyperbolic and quadratic. Since the quadratic and hyperbolic problems are solved at optimum by enumeration, we are forced to limit the comparison to relatively small uniform instances with $CSNumber = 10, 20$.

Table 1 reports the comparison between the optimum values of the different objective functions and the ones obtained through the heuristics. The optimal values have been obtained through enumeration. The results have been compared when varying the number of CS (10, 20) and the value of the coverage radius $(r = 50, 100, 200m)$. The number of TP to be covered is set to 100.

The left hand part of the table, named $OPTIMUM$ reports the optimum values of the hyperbolic $(PCH)$ and quadratic $(QPC)$ objective functions. The other two parts on the right report the results obtained applying the heuristic approach to the hyperbolic and quadratic formulation respectively. The solution providing the heuristic optimum for one formulation is used to calculate the objective functions of all the other formulations. For example, referring to the part of the table named $HEURISTIC\ PCH$, the column with the terms in bold reports the value of the $PCH$ objective function when looking for a heuristic solution for the $PCH$ problem, while the column named $QPC$ reports the value

**Table 1.** TPNumber=100, uniform instances, randomly generated positions of CS and TPs within 1Km edge square area, comparison between the optimal values of the objective functions and the values calculated by the hyperbolic and quadratic heuristics

|  |  | OPTIMAL | | HEURISTIC PCH | | HEURISTIC QPC | |
|---|---|---|---|---|---|---|---|
|  |  | **PCH** | **QPC** | **PCH** | **QPC** | **PCH** | **QPC** |
|  | r=50m | 9.334 | 9.323 | **9.334** | 9.323 | 9.334 | **9.323** |
| **CS=10** | r=100m | 7.424 | 7.262 | **7.424** | 7.251 | 7.424 | **7.262** |
|  | r=200m | 4.344 | 4.06 | **4.344** | 3.708 | 4.338 | **4.06** |
|  | r=50m | 17.187 | 17.105 | **17.187** | 17.105 | 17.187 | **17.105** |
| **CS=20** | r=100m | 12.243 | 11.852 | **12.243** | 11.508 | 12.243 | **11.812** |
|  | r=200m | 5.494 | 5.238 | **5.47** | 4.71 | 5.407 | **5.192** |

of the $QPC$ objective function computed using the heuristic solution of the $PCH$ problem. Same thing for the part of the table named $HEURISTIC\ QPC$.

In most cases the heuristics come out with the optimum values of the objective function. A slight discrepancy from the optimum just happens for high sized instances $(CS = 20)$ and high coverage radius $(r = 200m)$. In these cases the number of feasible solutions is greater and the heuristic approach presents slight differences with respect to the optimum.

Once validated the effectiveness of the proposed heuristics in predicting the optimum values of the hyperbolic and quadratic objective functions, let's compare the results obtained with the heuristics themselves and the classical minimum cardinality set covering approach. The Set Covering Problem $(SCP)$ aims at minimizing the cost of installed CS with the full coverage constraint. In our case all the CS are supposed to have the same installation cost, thus the $SCP$ tend to install the smallest number of CS, without considering network capacity in the objective function definition.

Table 2 reports the values of the objective functions calculated with the optimum solution of a classical set covering problem. On the other hand, Tables 3 and 4 report the values of the objective functions when running the hyperbolic and quadratic heuristics respectively. All the three tables 2, 3 and 4 refer to the case where 300 Test Points are deployed within the simulation area. As in Table 1, the solution obtained solving one particular formulation is used to calculate the values of the objective functions of the other two formulations.

From the tables, the classical set covering approach does install a smaller number of Access Points than the heuristic approaches. On the other hand, the set covering solutions provide smaller values of capacity. The difference between the two planning approaches appears clear: on one side the set covering tends to optimize the installation costs, thus reducing the number of installed APs, on the other side our approach privileges solutions with higher network capacities.

**Table 2.** TPNumber=300, uniform instances, exact solution of the set covering problem

|        | Radius | PCH    | QPC    | SCP  |
|--------|--------|--------|--------|------|
|        | 50m    | 24.1   | 23.9   | 28.9 |
| CS=30  | 100m   | 14.196 | 12.63  | 23.1 |
|        | 200m   | 5.23   | 4.588  | 9.7  |
|        | 50m    | 29.799 | 29.372 | 38   |
| CS=40  | 100m   | 15.34  | 13.502 | 26.6 |
|        | 200m   | 5.368  | 4.86   | 9.5  |
|        | 50m    | 34.047 | 33.359 | 44.8 |
| CS=50  | 100m   | 16.49  | 14.945 | 27.8 |
|        | 200m   | 5.278  | 4.714  | 9.5  |

**Table 3.** TPNumber=300, uniform instances, values of the various objective functions calculated with the solution of the hyperbolic heuristic

|        | Radius | PCH    | QPC    | SCP  |
|--------|--------|--------|--------|------|
|        | 50m    | 24.2   | 24     | 29.1 |
| CS=30  | 100m   | 14.3   | 12.548 | 24.1 |
|        | 200m   | 5.7    | 4.089  | 11.4 |
|        | 50m    | 29.943 | 29.49  | 38.3 |
| CS=40  | 100m   | 15.76  | 13.639 | 27.9 |
|        | 200m   | 5.995  | 4.509  | 11.8 |
|        | 50m    | 34.216 | 33.233 | 46.1 |
| CS=50  | 100m   | 17.1   | 14.642 | 30.1 |
|        | 200m   | 6.286  | 4.765  | 12.3 |

## 4.2   Planning a Real Environment

Once acquired a feeling on the quality of the proposed planning models and heuristics, we show hereafter the results of the WLAN planning procedure of the Telecommunications Section at the Department of Electronics and Information of the Politecnico di Milano.

Figure 2 reports the area to be covered with the feasible CS positions and their correspondent coverage radii ($R$). That area is composed of 18 offices occupied by faculties and PhD students, and a square Open Space area with several workstations dedicated to master students. As in the previous section, we assume a simplified propagation model according to which each CS covers a circular area with radius $r$.

The positions of the TPs are chosen according to the following rules:

- Four people occupy each office on average, thus four TPs are randomly positioned in each office.
- Thirty master students occupy the Open Space on average, thus thirty other TPs are randomly positioned in the Open Space.

**Table 4.** TPNumber=300, uniform instances, values of the various objective functions calculated with the solution of the quadratic heuristic

| | Radius | PCH | QPC | SCP |
|---|---|---|---|---|
| | 50m | 24.2 | 24.005 | 29.1 |
| CS=30 | 100m | 14.249 | 12.766 | 23.6 |
| | 200m | 5.671 | 5.192 | 10.6 |
| | 50m | 29.943 | 29.517 | 38.2 |
| CS=40 | 100m | 15.603 | 14.162 | 27.3 |
| | 200m | 5.902 | 5.529 | 10.9 |
| | 50m | 34.211 | 33.58 | 45.6 |
| CS=50 | 100m | 16.859 | 15.644 | 29.1 |
| | 200m | 6.174 | 5.869 | 11 |

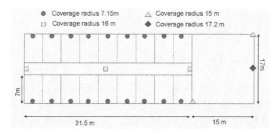

**Fig. 2.** Area to be covered through a WLAN

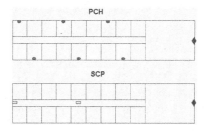

**Fig. 3.** Positions of the installed Access Points in the two cases of PCH and SCP approach

The results of the planning procedure with the full coverage constraint are presented in Figure 3 which shows the APs actually installed when solving at optimum the PCH and the classical SCP models. The quality of the solutions in terms of network capacity, and number of installed APs is reported in Table 5. The results have been obtained averaging on ten instances of TPs' positions.

**Table 5.** Planning the Telecommunications Section. Comparison between the PCH and the SCP approaches

|       | Capacity | # APs |
| ----- | -------- | ----- |
| **PCH** | 5.649  | 7     |
| **SCP** | 1.913  | 3     |

As expected our capacity oriented approach does provide a WLAN with higher capacity with respect to the classical SCP approach, which, on the other hand, tends to install a smaller number of APs.

## 5   Concluding Remarks

We have addressed the problem of coverage planning in WLANs, which is starting to attract the attention of both industry and research community. In particular, we have proposed and analyzed effective heuristics to tackle hyperbolic and quadratic formulations of this problem which aim at maximizing the overall network capacity. Our combined greedy and local search algorithms turn out to provide near-optimum solutions in a reasonable amount of computing time. In contrast, the classical approach based on the minimum cardinality set covering problem tends to yield networks with poor overall capacity. This stresses the need for appropriate planning models and procedures that are specific to WLANs.

## References

1. E. Amaldi, A. Capone, M. Cesana, F. Malucelli, *Optimizing WLAN Radio Coverage*, in proceedings of the IEEE International Conference on Communications 2004 (ICC 2004), June 20-24 2004, Paris, France.
2. S. Ceria, P. Nobili, A. Sassano , *Set Covering Problem*, in Annotated bibliographies in Combinatorial Optimization, Dell'Amico M., F. Maffioli, S. Martello eds, John Wiley and Sons - Chichester.
3. P. Hansen, M. V. Poggi de Aragão, *Hyperbolic 0-1 programming and query optimization in information retrieval*, Mathematical Programming 52 (1991), 255-263.
4. S. Hurley, *Planning Effective Cellular Mobile Radio Networks*, IEEE Transactions on Vehicular Technology, vol. 51, no. 2, March 2002, pp. 243-253.
5. http://grouper.ieee.org/groups/802/11/

6. M. Kamenetsky, M. Unbehaun, *Coverage planning for outdoor wireless LAN systems*, 2002 International Zurich Seminar on Broadband Communications Access, Transmission, Networking, 2002, Page(s): 491-496.
7. Y. Lee, K. Kim, Y. Choi, *Optimization of AP placement and Channel Assignment in Wireless LANs*, IEEE Conference on Local Computer Networks, 2002. LCN 2002.
8. R.C. Rodrigues, G.R. Mateus, A.A.F. Loureiro, *On the design and capacity planning of a wireless local area network*, Network Operations and Management Symposium, 2000. NOMS 2000, Page(s): 335-348.

# Optimization Models for Designing Aggregation Networks to Support Fast Moving Users

Frederic Van Quickenborne, Filip De Greve,
Filip De Turck, Ingrid Moerman, Bart Dhoedt, and Piet Demeester

Department of Information Technology (INTEC)
Ghent University - IMEC
Sint-Pietersnieuwstraat 41, B-9000 Gent, Belgium
{frederic.vanquickenborne|filip.degreve}@intec.ugent.be

**Abstract.** In this paper, the focus is on the design of an aggregation network for offering high bandwidth services to fast moving users (e.g., users in trains or cars). The overall considered network architecture consists of two parts: an access network part and an aggregation network part. The users in the fast moving vehicles are connected to the access network via a wireless connection. In the aggregation part, traffic of different users is bundled together in tunnels, and as the users move from one access network to another access network, tunnels have to move with them. Two problems concerning this issue are tackled in this paper. The first one can be described as follows: how to determine the tunnel paths in the aggregation network to meet the fast moving traffic demand of requests while achieving low congestion and minimizing the network dimensioning cost. Secondly we need protocols to manage the tunnels by means of configuration and activation at their due time. GVRP (GARP (Generic Attribute Registration Protocol) VLAN Registration Protocol) and a new GARP protocol, called G2RP, were designed and implemented as protocols for the automatic tunnel configuration and activation, respectively. Finally, the performance of the different algorithms used for the network capacity planning and the tunnel path determination is compared on basic train scenarios.

**Keywords.** Capacity assignment, traffic engineering, mobility support

## 1 Introduction

Nowadays, a lot of multimedia applications are taken for granted in fixed networks. These applications, such as managed home networking, multimedia content delivery, video phoning and on-line gaming require a high level of Quality of Service and are generally characterized by high bandwidth requirements. Current telecom-operators have mainly designed their broadband networks to cope with rather static or slowly evolving traffic demands while fast moving traffic conditions have never been taken into account. The challenge is to design telecom networks in such a way that high bandwidth services can be provided to fast moving users (e.g., in the car or on the train). These networks can typically

G. Kotsis and O. Spaniol (Eds.): Mobile and Wireless Systems, LNCS 3427, pp. 66–81, 2005.

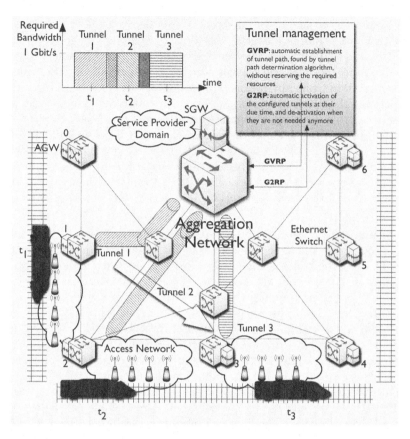

**Fig. 1.** Schematic representation of considered network architecture, which consists of an access part and an aggregation part. The designed protocols for tunnel configuration and tunnel activation are shown as well.

be deployed in metropolitan areas, along railroad tracks or along highways. For an example of such a network, the reader is referred to [3].

The considered network architecture in our paper is depicted in figure 1. As can be seen in this figure, the architecture is divided in an access network part and an aggregation network part. The main difference between these two parts is that in the access network part, traffic demands from separate users are considered, whereas in the aggregation network part, groups of users are aggregated together. We define one or more groups of users per train. The traffic of each group of moving users is multiplexed in the Access Gateways (AGWs) into a tunnel. These AGWs provide the connections between the access networks and the aggregation network. The aggregation of the groups is done by taking the users together in tunnels in the aggregation network, as depicted in figure 1. In this figure we consider three consecutive time-events: $t_1$, $t_2$ and $t_3$ on which one train is connected to one of the different access networks. The total required bandwidth for the train is 1 Gbit/s, based on a calculation made in [8]. On $t_1$, Tunnel 1 is used to meet the traffic demand of the train. On $t_2$, Tunnel 2 is used, and on $t_3$, Tunnel 3. The aggregation network is responsible for the transport of aggregated data traffic, by means of high bandwidth tunnels moving at high speed, between the access networks and service provider (SP) domain such as Internet service providers (ISPs), content providers and telephony operators. The connection between the SPs and the aggregation network is realized by Service Gateways (SGWs). The fast moving aspect of the traffic demands (leading to rapidly moving tunnels) has not been extensively studied for aggregation networks. E.g., a detailed description of the UMTS technology in [11] gives only a brief description of the used protocols for interaction with the fixed network.

The main problem, tackled in the paper, can be described as follows: how to calculate and set up dynamic tunnels between the gateways in the aggregation network to meet the traffic demand of requests while achieving low congestion and minimizing the network dimensioning cost. In order to automatically invoke the set-up of the required tunnels and activate the tunnels at their due time, protocols are required. Two different protocols are designed for handling the tunnel configuration and activation requests. But first the optimal path for each tunnel needs to be determined. Therefor a theoretical network capacity planning and dimensioning model is implemented that optimizes the use of resources under rapidly moving but quite predictable traffic conditions. Due to the complexity of the problem, rigorous optimization by means of ILP (Integer Linear Programming [9]) techniques only delivers solutions in a reasonable calculation times for limited network sizes. Therefore, we present several approaches to shorten the solution times. The model also includes a path calculation algorithm that is specifically designed for fast moving user conditions.

Mainly for economical reasons telecom operators [1] tend towards networks consisting of standard QoS-aware Ethernet switches (IEEE 802.1d [4], IEEE 802.1q [5] & p, IEEE 802.1s [6] compliant). We do not consider satellite or UMTS technology, due to their respective limitations of latency and bandwidth for fast moving users. The protocols for tunnel configuration and activation are implemented for Ethernet aggregation networks. The designed protocols allow to make optimal use of VLANs (Virtual LANs [5]) to support Multiple Spanning Trees in the Switched Ethernet networks. In this way network resources are optimally used.

The remainder of this paper is structured as follows: section 2 describes the self designed and implemented protocols for tunnel configuration and tunnel activation and section 3 details the implemented model for optimal network capacity planning and tunnel path determination. Section 5 considers the evaluation results, found for the considered scenarios, as described in section 4. In the final part of the paper in section 6, some interesting conclusions are summed up.

# 2  Tunnel Configuration and Activation

Based on the determined optimal path for each tunnel, found by the solution method described in section 3, the tunnels are configured in the network by means of GVRP (GARP (Generic Attribute Registration Protocol) VLAN Registration Protocol). At activation time the necessary resources are reserved by means of the G2RP (GARP Reservation Parameters Registration Protocol) protocol. This section gives a brief operational description of both protocols. For an extensive description, the reader is referred to [10], which also contains extensive performance measurements of both protocols.

## 2.1  GVRP

Based on the output of the network dimensioning process, the paths for each required tunnel are calculated. The path calculation aims at minimizing the total resource usage by applying optimization algorithms, which are detailed in the next section. Based on the determined path for each tunnel, these tunnels are configured in the network by means of GVRP. This protocol automatically establishes the tunnel path, without reserving the required resources. It is a GARP compatible protocol (standardized by IEEE 802.1q [5]) and sets up the tunnel path by means of automatic VLAN registration on every switch of the network. Due to the fact that GVRP was initially not designed for a VLAN tunnel, but rather for a sub-tree of the topology, the protocol suffers from a lot of overhead registrations. To deal with this problem, we developed the "Scoped Refresh" extension of GVRP. More details of this extension are also given in [10].

## 2.2  G2RP

The main purpose of this protocol is to activate the configured tunnels at their due time, and de-activate them when they are not needed anymore. Instead of extending GVRP to support (i) propagation of reservation parameters (bandwidth parameters, QoS class, burst size and the size of the time sample window) and (ii) activation and de-activation of tunnels, a new GARP protocol is designed. This protocol is called GARP Reservation Parameters Registration Protocol (G2RP). By separating the configuration of tunnels from the distribution of reservation parameters, G2RP remains independent of the applied tunnel configuration mechanism. G2RP is designed according to the GARP standard. G2RP will translate the activation and de-activation triggers into hardware operations. Basically, the switch hardware (bandwidth shapers, classifiers, queues, etc.) will be configured according to the reservation parameters for the associated configured tunnel. Before any activation takes place, G2RP will consult the admission control. Admission control is added to keep track of the existing bandwidth reservations. If at any point along the VLAN tunnel the available hardware resources are not sufficient to support a specific reservation, the activation will fail and this will lead to an error indication.

# 3   Network Capacity Planning and Tunnel Path Determination

Subsection 3.1 proves the need for a model for optimal network capacity planning, while subsections 3.2 and 3.3 details the assumptions concerning the considered network and traffic parameters. A formal definition of the aggregation network capacity planning and related tunnel path determination will be presented in subsection 3.4. Subsection 3.5 details the developed solution technique.

## 3.1   Motivation

To prove the need for a model that optimizes the network cost for aggregation networks under rapidly moving demand requests, we consider a simple problem, depicted in figure 2. The considered network is part of the network depicted in figure 1, as we do not consider AGWs 0, 1, 5 and 6. The remaining nodes (7 in total: (i) one connected to the SGW, (ii) 3 connected to AGWs 2, 3 and 4 and (iii) 3 core nodes) are connected as shown in figure 1. To each of the AGWs, an

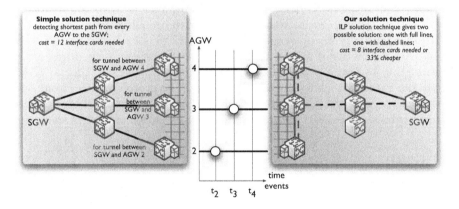

**Fig. 2.** Two different solutions for a simple problem: on the left side a simple solution technique, on the right are the solutions found by our implemented solution technique.

access network is connected, that provides a wireless connection to the passing trains. In this simple problem, one single train is considered, starting at AGW 2, passing AGW 3 and ending at AGW 4. This is visualized at the center of the figure: the train (depicted with a little circle) is connected to AGW 2 (shown on the Y-axis) on $t_2$ (time events are indicated on the X-axis). We consider three consecutive time events, similarly to the situation described in the introduction of the paper. Intuitively, the best solution seems to be the one which detects the shortest path from each AGW to the SGW and adds them all to the network topology. This solution is shown in the left part of figure 2. With respect to the routing cost, this is certainly the cheapest solution, but does this solution also has the cheapest network cost? The found solution needs 12 interface cards installed over the network, which is more than the solutions found by our developed method, as they only need 8 interface cards around the network. This means a total reduction of 33% in network cost. But still, two possible solutions are found by the developed model, the first one is depicted with full lines in the right part of figure 2, the second solution with dashed lines. The overall optimal solution depends on other model parameters, namely the availability of types of interface cards, the maximum number of interface cards and ports per node, the importance of routing cost with respect to the network cost, etc. If all types of interface cards are available and no limit is set to the number of interface cards and ports per node, the solution with the dashed lines will be the optimal one. However, if the maximum number of ports per node is limited to 2, the solution with the dashed lines is no longer possible and only the solution with the full lines will be appropriate.

## 3.2   Network Model

For now, we assume a network with one or more service gateways and we assume that successive access gateways are positioned along the railroad track. Passing trains will connect to the closest access network and will hop from one AGW to another. The SGWs are constantly updated with the current position (and future positions) of the train and updates at every turn the next hop gateway for the IP routing towards the moving user [7]. To optimize the cost of the network we assume the links to be already installed and we only take the node cost into account. We distinguish between different line card types of different speeds and with different port ranges. The model will ensure that link and node capacities are adjusted appropriately. The model allows a large flexibility: removing certain card ranges on nodes, different prices of different hardware vendors can be taken into account. We assume that for every traffic class a single path is used for routing for every AGW-SGW pair at a certain moment. This path may vary in time but it will always be the same for a traffic class. In other words, this supports that different traffic classes of one train may be routed differently. Traffic demands vary depending on wether the application is symmetric (video conference) or asymmetric (video broadcasting). Both symmetric and asymmetric demands can be taken into account in the proposed model.

We define a set of access gateways: $AGW = \{agw_i\}$, with index $i$ indicating the different access gateways and a set of service gateways: $SGW = \{sgw_k\}$, with index $k$ indicating the different service gateways. To characterize the network, we define a given set of unidirectional edges: $E = \{e\}$ and a given set of nodes: $N = \{n\}$. In addition we define a set of links: $L = \{l\}$ with every (bi-directional) link consisting of two unidirectional edges given by set $E_l = \{e_l, e_l'\}$ with same source-destination node pair as link $l$. We like to remark that $\forall l : |E_l| = 2$. Each node is characterized by the speed of every interface and the number of interfaces, possibly grouped together on one card (e.g., one card with two Gigabit interfaces):

$$C_v = \text{e.g.}, \{100|1000|10000\}, v = 1\dots|V|;\tag{1}$$

$$\forall v : O_{vw} = \text{e.g.,} \{1|2|4\}, w = 1 \ldots |O_v|. \tag{2}$$

$V$ gives the set of strings, each describing a different type of card which are present on a node; $C_v$ defines the different speed of every type of the set $V$ (where $v$ is used to distinguish the different types of cards): in this example speeds from 100 Mbit/s to 10 Gbit/s are considered; $O_v$ gives the set of possible configurations of the cards of a certain type (the type is indicated by index $v$); more specific, $O_{vw}$ gives the number of interfaces present on a card for every type of card.

### 3.3   Traffic Model

In order to describe the traffic demands, we define flows $j$ as being the basic routing unit: this allows different levels of abstraction. We can define one flow per train, one flow for every QoS class per train, etc. Traffic loads per AGW are associated with the flows as they move along the AGWs. It is important to notice that flows are associated with a moving train, so flows are not directly connected to one specific AGW nor SGW. Each train that passes the antennas connected to an AGW results in a certain demand for the specific *agw* from a specific server: $D_{ik} = \{d_{ijk}(t)\}$ with index $i$ indicating the AGW, $k$ indicating the SGW and $j$ is used to make a difference between the different flows, in order to distinguish the different trains and/or QoS classes. To indicate if the demand at a certain *agw* is above zero and thus active, we introduce

$$a_{ij} = \begin{cases} 1, \text{if} \sum_t \sum_k d_{ijk}(t) > 0 \\ 0, \text{otherwise} \end{cases}. \tag{3}$$

Due to the moving aspect of trains, the traffic demands are time dependent. However, the dimensioning problem is not continuous and can be solved for a limited set of discrete events. Therefore, we define a set of events that are critical for the dimensioning. These events are all the discrete time points when the traffic conditions change. However, this set contains a lot of events which are redundant for the dimensioning problem. In order to minimize the amount of constraints for the dimensioning problem, the set of events is reduced: e.g., for a single AGW scenario, if the network must be able to support a certain demand to this AGW, all the events with lower demands for the AGW (under same other circumstances) are already covered and are removed from the set of events. The set of reduced time events is given by $T' = \{t'\}$.

### 3.4   Problem Formulation: Network Capacity Planning and Tunnel Path Determination

1. Variables
   First of all, the variables of the ILP-problem are defined. The first one represents the number of line cards available in each node:

$$z_n^{vw} = \# \text{ of cards with } O_{vw} \text{ interfaces of speed } C_v \text{ on node } n. \tag{4}$$

Each card has a specific cost, $c_{vw}$, depending on the speed of the interfaces on the card ($C_v$) and the number of interfaces installed on the card ($O_{vw}$). The following parameter gives information about the number of fibres on every link:

$$x_l^v = \# \text{ of fibres with speed } C_v \text{ on link } l. \tag{5}$$

2. Node capacity constraint
Every node needs enough interfaces with appropriate specifications (given by indices $v$ and $w$) to provide the links that are connected to it:

$$\forall n, \forall v : \sum_{w=1}^{|O_v|} z_n^{vw} \cdot O_{vw} \geq \sum_{l \text{ incident to node } n} x_l^v. \tag{6}$$

**Link Flow Formulation**

1. Variable
Besides the previous defined variables, we also need a variable to indicate if a certain edge $e$ is used for a certain flow $j$:

$$y_{eijk} = \begin{cases} 1, & \text{if edge } e \text{ is used between } i \text{ and } k \text{ for flow } j \\ 0, & \text{otherwise} \end{cases}. \tag{7}$$

2. Link Capacity constraint
This constraint imposes that the traffic that is transported over a link does not exceed the capacity of that particular link:

$$\forall l, \forall t \in T' : \begin{cases} \sum_k \sum_i \sum_j y_{e_l ijk} \cdot d_{ijk}(t) \leq \sum_v x_l^v \cdot C_v, \\ \sum_k \sum_i \sum_j y_{e_l' ijk} \cdot d_{ijk}(t) \leq \sum_v x_l^v \cdot C_v. \end{cases} \tag{8}$$

3. Flow Conservation constraint
The last constraint imposes that a flow is not interrupted in the network:

$$\forall n, \forall k, \forall i, \forall j : \sum_{e \in \text{out}(n)} y_{eijk} - \sum_{e \in \text{in}(n)} y_{eijk} =$$
$$\begin{cases} a_{nj}, & \text{if node } n \text{ is the source for the flow} \\ -a_{in}, & \text{if node } n \text{ is the desired } agw \\ 0, & \text{otherwise} \end{cases}. \tag{9}$$

4. Objective function o

$$o = \sum_n \sum_v \sum_{w=1}^{|O_v|} z_n^{vw} \cdot c_{vw} + \sum_k \sum_i \sum_j \sum_e y_{eijk} \cdot p_e \cdot B_j. \tag{10}$$

The first part is the cost for the network devices in the network while the second part is the routing cost in the network, in which $p_e$ gives us the cost for every edge and $B_j$ represents the bandwidth of each flow. The aim of the optimization algorithm is to minimize $o$.

## Path Flow Formulation

1. Variables
   First we have to define a set of possible paths for each SGW-AGW pair:

$$P_{ik} = \{p_{ikq}\}, \tag{11}$$

   in which index $q$ is used to indicate the different considered paths between source and destination. They are calculated by taking the $M$ shortest paths between the two end nodes. This $M$ is also a parameter for the path flow formulation. We use the same $z_n^{vw}$ and $x_l^v$ variables as above in Link Flow formulation, but we define a new variable to indicate which path $p$ is used:

$$y_{pijk} = \begin{cases} 1, & \text{if path } p \text{ is used between } i \text{ and } k \text{ for flow } j \\ 0, & \text{otherwise} \end{cases}, \forall p \in \bigcup_{i,k} P_{ik}. \tag{12}$$

2. Link Capacity constraint
   With these parameters, we can build our constraints. The first one sets the capacity of each link, this constraint imposes that the traffic that is transported over a link does not exceed the capacity of that particular link:

$$\forall l, \forall t \in T' : \sum_k \sum_i \sum_j \sum_p y_{pijk \cdot \delta_{pl}^{ik} \cdot d_{ijk}(t)} \leq \sum_v x_l^v \cdot C_v; \tag{13}$$

$$\delta_{pl}^{ik} = \begin{cases} 1, & \text{if path } p \text{ uses link } l \text{ to get to destination } k \text{ from source } i \\ 0, & \text{otherwise} \end{cases}. \tag{14}$$

3. Path Activation constraint
   The second constraint takes care of the fact that we only need a path, and only one, from source to destination:

$$\forall i, \forall j : \sum_p y_{pijk} = a_{ij}, \tag{15}$$

   and thus we just foresee one path for each signal coming from one SGW and going to one AGW for a specific flow.

4. Objective function o

$$o = \sum_n \sum_v \sum_{w=1}^{|O_v|} z_n^{vw} \cdot c_{vw} + \sum_k \sum_i \sum_j \sum_p y_{pijk} \cdot p_p \cdot B_j. \tag{16}$$

   The difference between this objective function and the one in equation 10, is that $p_p$, the cost for every path, based on the hop count, is used, and variable $y_{pijk}$, instead of $p_e$ and $y_{eijk}$, respectively.

## 3.5    Solution Technique: Integer Linear Programming

*Network and traffic model* - The network topology, node- and link-related parameters were modeled by using the TRS (Telecom Research Software) library. TRS is a Java-library, developed by our research group, intended to be used in the telecom-research to speed up the development of tools and applications. For more information about TRS, the reader is referred to [2].

*ILP solution technique* - Based on (i) the input variables $D_{ik}$, $C_v$, $O_{vw}$, $c_{vw}$, $B_j$ and $p_e$ (for link flow approach) or $p_p$ (for path flow approach), on (ii) the constraints (6), (8), (9) for link flow approach and (6), (13), (15) for path flow approach, and on (iii) the objective function (10) for link flow approach, (16) for path flow approach, the requested matrices for ILP are constructed. The optimal values for the decision variables $z_n^{vw}$, $x_l^v$ and $y_{\{e|p\}ijk}$ are then calculated, using a Branch and Bound based ILP solution approach [9]. From the obtained values of the decision variables, the optimal path required capacity for the considered problem instance can be easily deduced.

*Link flow versus path flow* - The main difference between the link and the path flow approach is that the former is able to calculate all possible paths, whereas the latter only considers a pre-defined number of possible paths, found by the K shortest loopless paths algorithm, as described in [12].

# 4    Considered Scenarios

We consider a network (shown in figure 1) consisting of 11 nodes, which positions are fixed. One of the 11 nodes is connected to a Service Gateway (SGW) and 7 others (indicated with numbers 0 to 6) are connected to one of the 7 Access Gateways (AGWs). The last 3 nodes are core nodes ethernet switches installed between the node connected to the SGW and the nodes connected to the AGWs. The topology of the network is a tree with the node connected to the SGW as the top node and the 7 nodes connected to the AGWs positioned in lowest layer of the tree. These 7 nodes are located along the railroad track every 5 to 10 kilometers, based on a calculation made in [8]. Also in the figure, all possible fibres are depicted and we assume that the installation of the links does not have a cost. We only take into account the cost for installing interfaces at the different nodes. Also the routing costs for the different solutions are taken into account to achieve the solution with the best routing model. For the scenarios an important parameter will be the frequency of trains (number of trains per hour). The dimensioning is very sensitive to the number of trains that are simultaneously on the track. We consider 3 distinctly different train scenarios. The scenarios are based on major events, namely moving trains from one station to another, crossing trains and consecutive trains.

## 4.1    Train Scenarios

*Single train* - The first considered scenario is the simplest one. One train, demanding a basic traffic of 0.8 Gbit/s is going from AGW 0 to AGW 6, via all

intermediate AGWs 1, 2, etc. Besides the 0.8 Gbit/s traffic demand, we also
foresee an extra capacity of 300 Mbit/s to deal with sudden peak demand requests. Several options are possible to handle these two types of traffic demand:
one tunnel for both demands together or one tunnel for each demand, resulting
in two tunnels per train. Although this scenario seems very easy to solve, an
important deduction we make is that the optimal dimensioning is not straight-
forward, as shown in subsection 3.1.

*Crossing trains* - A logical next step is to consider two trains. Besides the train
described in the previous paragraph, another train goes in the opposite direction,
namely from AGW 5 to AGW 1, via the AGWs on the bottom. The bandwidth
requirement for this train is slightly lower than the other one: we consider a
bitrate of 0.6 Gbit/s as basic traffic, and an extra capacity of 200 Mbit/s for
sudden peak demand requests. We consider one or two tunnels per train, as explained in the previous paragraph. Again, the solution seems very predictable,
but the results are quite surprising. A few rules of thumb for tunnel path determination will be derived from the results.

*Three trains scenario* - In this scenario, two trains go from the upper left to the
upper right AGW as previously defined in the single train scenario, and one goes
in the opposite direction as described in the previous paragraph. In this case,
we have two moments of crossing trains. Again we consider two types of traffic
demands: one basic traffic demand and one extra capacity demand per train.

## 4.2   Demand Cases

The three considered different input demand cases for the problem will be detailed in this paragraph. A crossing trains scenario will be used consequently to
illustrate the different approaches (however a less complex crossing trains scenario as above for the sake of simplicity).

*Exact demand (figure 3(a))* - In this case we take the exact traffic demands
into account. For the crossing trains scenario, this implies that we optimize the
network resources with knowledge of the exact point (=the exact AGW, in this
case AGW 4) where the two trains cross each other and of the exact moment in
time when the two trains cross each other (in this case time event $t'_3$). However,
should one train experience a delay and the point where the two trains pass
each other changes to another AGW, the network could suffer from inability to
provide the requested resources to meet demand.

*Static demand (figure 3(b))* - This case translates the dynamic traffic demands
of the exact demand case into a static demand (and hence neglecting the time-
related aspects of the demands). This is done by adding all the demands that
are requested for a particular AGW, and this for every AGW separately. This
results in a time-independent demand from the SGW to each AGW. For the
shown scenario in figure 3, this implies that we assume that both trains could
cross in every AGW simultaneously. By doing this, we can guarantee that all
trains will achieve their asked bandwidth, even when delay occurs. This dimensioning case is required if the network is lacking a dynamic configuration and

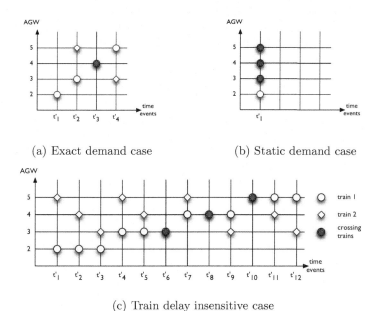

(a) Exact demand case          (b) Static demand case

(c) Train delay insensitive case

**Fig. 3.** The three traffic demand cases

activation mechanism. This results in a new definition of the traffic demand:

$$\forall i, \forall j, \forall k : d_{ijk} = \sum_{t \in T'} d_{ijk}(t); \tag{17}$$

and the link capacity constraints (8) and (13) are only evaluated for a static, time-independent demand $d_{ijk}$.

*Train delay insensitive demand (figure 3(c))* - To tackle the problem of loss of information in case of train delays, a new approach has been developed. In this case we re-interpret the traffic demands by neglecting the exact time-position relation between multiple trains. For the crossing trains scenario this implies that we assume that single trains are not connected to all the AGWs at the same time but we neglect the information of when or where the trains will cross each other exactly. In other words, the network is dimensioned to support that the trains will cross each other in any AGW along their track. Again, this results in a new definition for the demand. The demands become independent of flow $j$ in the link capacity constraints (8) and (13).

## 5 Evaluation Results of the Optimal Network Capacity Planning and Tunnel Path Determination

### 5.1 Three Traffic Demand Cases Compared

Table 1 shows the comparison between the three considered demand cases found by the ILP solution technique for the three trains scenario. For the static demand case, no difference will be found when using multiple tunnels, because all the tunnels are treated equally. From the difference between the static demand case and the other two, we can conclude that the static demand case is not advisable to use in the considered scenario, nor it is for every other scenario with rapidly moving traffic conditions. The cost for the static solution is almost twice as much as the cost for the dynamic cases. These results show that for rapidly changing traffic demands dynamic tunnel management is very useful.

Also, by splitting the traffic flows into two tunnels, one for the basic traffic demand and one for the extra demand, the routing becomes cheaper. As a comparison, in the presented scenario and for the link flow approach, the solution which uses 2 tunnels is almost 10% cheaper than the solution presented when using 1 tunnel.

The very cheap solution found for the exact demand case looks very attractive to use, but several drawbacks makes the solution less useful in real situations. The example of a train with little delay is already mentioned. Therefore a new traffic demand has been taken into account that deals with train delays: the train delay insensitive traffic demand. As shown in table 1, the cost for the network capacity planning found for this traffic demand is a little more expensive than the cheapest solution, but the benefits are huge: trains with delay will still receive their requested bandwidth.

## 5.2    Path Flow Approach Versus Link Flow Approach

As mentioned before, another solution approach is considered to deal with the reasonable calculation time of the link flow approach. Therefor the path flow approach is also evaluated. The derivations that are applied for the link flow and path flow solution approaches are both given in section 3.4. This solution technique is based on the K shortest loopless paths algorithm, as described in [12]. This method introduces an extra parameter, namely the number of considered shortest paths $M$, which also defines the maximum length of set (11). Table 2 shows the required costs for the network capacity planning calculated with the path flow approach, for different values of $M$ versus the required network cost calculated with the link flow approach. With parameter $M$ equal to 2, the cost for the path flow approach is 25% higher than the link flow approach. If we choose $M$ equal to 7, the cost is only 7.5% higher than the optimal solution.

**Table 1.** Required cost for the three demand cases, found by ILP solution technique and for three trains scenario, with one or two tunnels per train

| Traffic demand case | Required cost (%) for one tunnel per train | Required cost (%) for two tunnels per train |
|---|---|---|
| Static demand | 100 | 100 |
| Train delay insensitive demand | 49 | 45 |
| Exact demand | 48 | 44 |

If we compare the solution approaches with respect to calculation times (also shown in table 2), we observe growing calculation times with higher M-values. Though, finding the optimal solution using the link flow approach, takes the longest time.

## 5.3   Rules of Thumb for Path Determination

Besides the cost of the network capacity planning, the routing is also calculated with the solution technique. It is important to mention that only the exact demand case will determine the paths for the different flows, as for the other demand cases it is not known in advance where different trains will cross each other. We can derive two global rules of thumb concerning the routing. The routing depends on the number of tunnels per train that are used to solve the design problem. First, we consider one tunnel for all the traffic demand. Second, we consider a tunnel for each demand, resulting in two tunnels per train. For both rules of thumb, we use the crossing trains scenario.

**One Tunnel per Train** In this scenario, the shortest path between the SGW and the AGW where the crossing of the two trains occurs, is part of the design. The other links of the network design are the links that are located along the train-rail. This is the optimal path determination solution obtained through the ILP link flow solution technique. We can explain this by looking at the asked bitrate from the SGW to every AGW. At every moment two separate AGWs require about 1 Gbit/s each, except the moment the crossing takes place. That moment the sum of all flows are going from the SGW to one AGW. It is logical that the tunnel between this AGW and the SGW must be as short as possible. As a rule of thumb we can say that all the links along the train-rail are part of the design, together with the shortest path between the stressed AGW (where the crossing takes place) and the SGW.

**Two Tunnels per Train** The set of figures in figure 4 shows the tunnel activation for the crossing trains scenario. The set of figures are 4 snapshots taken at 4 different moments, starting when the dashed train comes into play and ending

**Table 2.** Required cost and calculation times for path flow approach with different value for parameter $M$ versus link flow approach for crossing trains scenario and for the exact demand case (*=measured on an AMD Athlon$^{TM}$ XP 1700+ with 256 MB RAM)

| Solution approach | Required cost (%) | Calculation time* (sec.) |
|---|---|---|
| Path flow approach, M=2 | 100 | 1 |
| Path flow approach, M=5 | 88 | 30 |
| Path flow approach, M=7 | 86 | 922 |
| Link flow approach | 80 | 2114 |

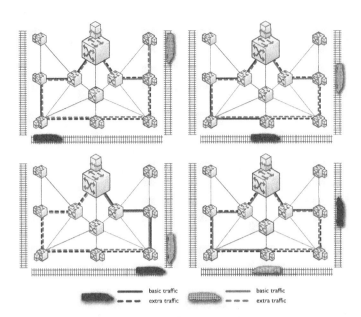

**Fig. 4.** Tunnels used for demand requests for crossing trains scenario with two tunnels per train, found by the ILP link flow approach for the exact demand case

when the dark train reaches his end station. The two trains cross each other in the lower right AGW, as shown in the lower left figure. Again, as described in 4.1, the dark train requests a bandwidth of 1.1 Gbit/s, divided into 800 Mbit/s basic traffic and 300 Mbit/s extra traffic. The dashed train also has two different tunnels, but a slightly lower overall demand: 600 Mbit/s basic traffic and 200 Mbit/s of extra traffic demand. The routes for the basic traffic are indicated with full lines (dark ones for the dark train and lighter ones for the dashed train), the routes for the extra traffic are indicated with dashed lines. Contrary to the previous case, the shortest path between the SGW and the stressed AGW is no longer part of the network design. The optimal network design is almost a ring. Indeed, only the upper left and upper right AGWs are not included in the ring. This can be explained as follows: due to the separation of the traffic into two tunnels, it becomes possible to use a shorter path to route the largest traffic demand, which leads to a cheaper network cost. In the first two figures, the left-side hand tunnel between AGW 1 and the core switch is used for the basic traffic of the dark train and for the smaller extra traffic of the dashed train. On the other side, we also have two tunnels, but now one for the basic traffic tunnel of the dashed train and for the extra demand tunnel of the dark train. This is exactly what we want: the basic traffic should be routed over a shorter path than the path for the extra traffic. After the crossing point, as shown in the lower right figure, the biggest tunnels switch from the left side to the right one for the dark train and from the right to the left side for the other train.

# 6 Conclusion

In this paper, we focused on optimization models for designing aggregation networks to support fast moving users. More specifically, we focused on the service realisation for the aggregation network, the core part of the considered network architecture. First the need for a network capacity planning model for aggregation networks under fast moving demand requests has been proven for a simple example. By the developed optimization algorithms it has been proven that using dynamical tunnel configuration and activation strongly reduces the cost of the network capacity planning. For the configuration of VLAN-based tunnels, a "Scoped Refresh" extension of the GVRP standard has been implemented and for the activation of the tunnels, a new GARP-based protocol (G2RP) has been developed. Finally, a few rules of thumb for designing aggregation network for fast moving users and the related determination of the tunnel paths, have been motivated for particular scenarios.

# Acknowledgment

Research funded by PhD grant for Frederic Van Quickenborne (IWT-Vlaanderen) and by postdoc grant for Filip De Turck (FWO-V).

# References

1. C. Bouchat and S. van den Bosch. Qos in dsl access. *IEEE Communications Magazine*, pages 108–114, September 2003.
2. K. Casier and S. Verbrugge. Trs, telecom research software. http://www.ibcn.intec.ugent.be/projects/internal/trs, 2003.
3. G. Fleishman. Destination wi-fi, by rail, bus or boat. *The New York Times*, july 2004.
4. IEEE 802.1D. Standards for local and metropolitan area networks: Media access control (mac) bridges. 1990.
5. IEEE 802.1q. Standards for local and metropolitan area networks: Virtual bridged local area networks. 1998.
6. IEEE 802.1s. Standards for local and metropolitan area networks: Multiple spanning trees. 2002.
7. D. B. Johnson, C. Perkins, and J. Arrko. Mobility support in ipv6. *IETF Internet draft*, http://www.ietf.org/internet-drafts/draft-ietf-mobileip-ipv6-24.txt, 2003.
8. B. Lannoo, D. Colle, M. Pickavet, and P. Demeester. Radio over fibre technique for multimedia train environment. *NOC*, 2003.
9. G.L. Nemhauser and A.L. Wolsey. Integer and combinatorial optimization. *John Wiley & Sons*, 1988.
10. F. Van Quickenborne, F. De Greve, P. Van Heuven, F. De Turck, B. Vermeulen, S. Van den Berghe, I. Moerman, and P. Demeester. Tunnel set-up mechanisms in ethernet networks for fast moving users. *NETWORKS*, 2004.
11. B. Walke, P. Seidenberg, and M. P. Althoff. Umts, the fundamentals. *Wiley*, page 75, 2003.
12. J. Y. Yen. Finding the k shortest loopless paths. *Management Science*, 17:712–716, 1971.

# Some Game-Theoretic Problems in Wireless Ad-Hoc Networks

E. Altman[1], Vivek S. Borkar[2], Arzad A. Kherani[1], P. Michiardi[3], and R. Molva[3]

[1] INRIA, 06902 Sophia Antipolis, France
{Eitan.Altman,alam}@sophia.inria.fr
[2] School of Technology and Computer Science, Tata Institute
of Fundamental Research, Mumbai, 400 005, India
borkar@tifr.res.in
[3] GET/EURECOM, Sophia-Antipolis, France
{Pietro.Michiardi,molva}@eurecom.fr

**Abstract.** Wireless Ad-hoc networks are expected to be made up of energy aware entities (nodes) interested in their own perceived performance. We consider a simple random access model for a wireless ad hoc network to address problems of finding an optimal channel access rate and providing incentive for cooperation to forward other nodes' traffic. By casting these problems as noncooperative games, we derive conditions for the Nash equilibrium and provide distributed algorithms to learn the Nash equilibrium.

**Keywords.** Game theory, Stochastic approximation algorithm.

## 1 Introduction

Wireless ad hoc networks (also referred to as packet radio networks and multihop radio networks) consist of mobile nodes communicating over a shared wireless channel. Contrary to cellular networks, where the nodes are restricted to communicate with a set of carefully placed base stations, in wireless ad hoc networks there are no base stations; any two nodes are allowed to communicate directly if they are close enough. A wireless ad hoc network can be considered as a system of various mobile wireless devices that is dynamically changing and self-organizing in arbitrary networks. These wireless devices are usually constantly changing their location because they are, for example, carried by people (for example, PDAs). These devices need to form a dynamic network without a pre-existing communication infrastructure. For such networks we address two problems mentioned in the subsections below.

### 1.1 Optimal Channel Access Rate

These networks are expected to use medium access protocols similar to the IEEE 802.11 protocol [12]. The 802.11 protocol is inherently a random access protocol

G. Kotsis and O. Spaniol (Eds.): Mobile and Wireless Systems, LNCS 3427, pp. 82–104, 2005.

since the protocol running in each wireless device keeps a backoff timer whose mean value essentially denotes the node's willingness to attempt a transmission, thus also risking a collision. Clearly, the nodes can not have a very large mean backoff timer value as this can add significantly to the delay in their packet transmission and also the node may miss opportunities of transmission. On the other hand, if all the nodes set their mean backoff timer value at a very small value, there will be singnificant amount of collision, thus again having an adverse effect on the nodes' performance. It is thus clear that there is some optimal attempt probability for the wireless devices at which the risk of collision could be balanced by the benefit of successfull transmission (and hence less delay) while making use of the most of the transmission opportunities available. Since, in such networks the nodes are rational, i.e., a node wants to maximize its own performance, a node needs to compute its own attempt probability such that it gets best performance for what other nodes do.

Much of the work on wireless ad hoc networks (with some exceptions) has been on the protocol design issues for medium access (the various variants of the IEEE 802.11 protocol, for example [5]) or dynamic routing in such networks [13,19]. The authors of [8] also look at the problem of tuning of the IEEE 802.11 parameters but they assume that all the nodes are cooperative and do not consider the rational behaviour of the nodes. Relatively little has been done on the resolution of 'optimal' self-organization as an optimization problem which amounts, roughly, to finding optimum parameters for the various protocols. As an example of the latter, consider [14] where the problem of adapting transmission attempt probabilities is viewed as a single optimization problem with a stated performance metric to be minimized and the optimization task is executed by a stochastic gradient method implemented in a distributed fashion. This approach, though suitable for sensor networks where each wireless device (or sensor) cooperates to acheive a common goal, is not suitable for a wireless ad hoc network with rational entities.

In Section 3 and 4, we view the problem as a noncooperative game with each node trying to optimize its own objective. By assuming a particularly simple performance metric for each node we get an explicit characterization of a Nash equilibrium. This in turn can be adaptively learnt by an iterative scheme that uses local information exchange. The required information for the algorithm should be available from a standard topology learning procedure.

## 1.2  Incentive for Forwarding

In order to maintain connectivity in an Ad-hoc network, mobile terminals should not only spend their resources (battery power) to send their own packets, but also for forwarding packets of other mobiles. Since Ad-hoc networks do not have a centralized base-station that coordinates between them, an important question that has been addressed is to know whether we may indeed expect mobiles to collaborate in such forwarding. If mobiles behave selfishly, they might not be interested in spending their precious transmission power in forwarding of other mobile's traffic. A natural framework to study this problem is noncooperative game theory. As already observed in many papers that consider noncooperative behavior in Ad-hoc networks, if we restrict to simplistic policies in which each mobile determines a fixed probability of forwarding a packet, then this gives rise to the most "aggressive" equilibrium in which no one forwards packets, see e.g. [11, Corollary 1], [18], thus preventing the system to behave as a connected network. The phenomenon of aggressive equilibrium that severely affects performance has also been reported in other noncooperative problems in networking, see e.g. [10] for a flow control context (in which the aggressive equilibrium corresponds to all users sending at their maximum rate).

To avoid very aggressive equilibria, in Section 5 we propose strategies based on threats of punishments for misbehaving aggressive mobiles, which is in the spirit of a well established design approach for promoting cooperation in Ad-hoc networks, carried on in many previous works [11,24]. In all these references, the well known "TIT-FOR-TAT" (TFT) strategy was proposed. This is a strategy in which when a misbehaving node is detected then the reaction of other mobiles is to stop completely forwarding packets during some time; it thus prescribes a threat for very "aggressive" punishment, resulting in an enforcement of a fully cooperative equilibrium in which all mobiles forward all packets they receive (see e.g. [11, Corollary 2]). The authors of [22] also propose use of a variant of TFT in a similar context.

## 2 A Model for Wireless Ad Hoc Networks

We consider a wireless adhoc network where all the terminals transmit on a common carrier frequency so that a terminal can either receive or transmit at a time. The transmission range of a terminal is denoted by $R_0$. Henceforth we use the terms terminal and node to mean the same entity.

We assume that the condition for node $j$ to successfully decode the transmission of its neighbouring node $i$ is that none of the other neighbours of node $j$ transmit when $i$ is transmitting.

A node is assumed to be in exactly one of the following modes at any time:

1. be transmitting to its neighbours, or
2. sensing the channel for the transmission from its neighbour, or
3. can be in the *sleep mode*, i.e., it is neither transmitting nor receiving and also not wasting its battery power in sensing the channel. Note that in this mode of operation a node may lose an opportunity of reception of a transmission from one of its neighbours.

Time is assumed to be slotted and channel access is random, i.e., in each slot, a node $i$ either decides to transmit with probability $\alpha_i$, or enters sleep mode with probability $\gamma_i$ or decides to receive with probability $(1 - \gamma_i - \alpha_i)$. $\alpha_i$ is called the *attempt probability* of node $i$, $\alpha_i + \gamma_i \leq 1$.

A node can be *heard* by only certain nodes called the neighbours. The neighbours of a node $i$ are the nodes within a distance $R_0$ from node $i$. A node is assumed to have some amount of data in its transmit queue at all times. For ease of presentation, we first assume that a transmission of a data packet from node $i$ is considered successful iff *all* the neighbours of node $i$ can decode the transmission successfully. Later we remove this restriction and show how to accommodate the possibility that a node $i$ transmits to a specific neighbouring node $j$ with probability $\alpha_{i,j}$. In the latter case a transmission is declared successful if the node that the transmission was destined for can decode the transmission successfully.

We assume that the topology of the network is fixed but the nodes need not be aware of the complete topology. The network consists of $N$ nodes. Denote the set of nodes by $\mathcal{N}$. For $i, j \in \mathcal{N}$ say $i \to j$ if node $i$ can receive node $j$'s transmission, i.e., node $j$ is within a distance of $R_0$ from node $i$. For ease of presentation we assume in this section that $i \to j$ iff $j \to i$, i.e., $R_0$ is same for all the nodes; we use the notation $i \leftrightarrow j$ to mean either of these two. Associate with each node $i \in \mathcal{N}$, a neighbourhood set $\mathcal{N}(i) := \{j \in \mathcal{N} : i \leftrightarrow j\}$. Denote the node incidence matrix thus obtained by $\Phi$, i.e.,

$$\Phi(i,j) = \Phi(j,i) = \begin{cases} 1 \text{ if } & i \leftrightarrow j \text{ or } j \in \mathcal{N}(i) \\ 0 \text{ otherwise.} \end{cases} \tag{1}$$

We assume that $\Phi$ is an irreducible matrix, i.e., every node $i \in \mathcal{N}$ has a *path* to any other node $j \in \mathcal{N}$; this amounts to assuming that the network is connected.

## 3   Finding Optimal Channel Access Rates

Assume for now that $\gamma_i = 0$ for all nodes $i$ in the network, i.e., in any slot a node is either transmitting a packet (which contains an update information) or is listening to the channel. It is clear from the model described above that if $\alpha_i$ is very small for all the nodes, there will be significant delay in information processing though the battery power consumption will be less. On the other hand increasing $\alpha_i$s to large values will result in increased collisions in the network and will also waste the battery power in unsuccessful transmissions. Thus there is a need to find the optimum value of these attempt probabilities.

This phenomenon is very similar to that of finding the arrival rates in a slotted Aloha system for multiple access (see [4]). It is well known (see [4]) that for such a system there exists an optimal attempt rate at which the system throughput is maximized.

Our problem here is to find, for a given network, the values of $\alpha_i$ (or, $\alpha_{i,j}$, as the case may be) which maximize a performance measure to be defined in Section 3.1. The objective then is to come up with an algorithm using which a node $i$ computes the optimal attempt probability ($\alpha_i$ or $\alpha_{i,j}$) for itself *in a distributed manner*.

### 3.1   Optimization Problem

For simplicity of presentation, in this section we assume that a transmission from a node is successful if all of its neighbours receive it correctly. In later sections we show how to modify the problem formulation and solution of this section for the case where in any slot a node $i$ transmits to a particular neighbouring node $j$ with probability $\alpha_{i,j}$.

Let $\alpha_i$, $i \in \mathcal{N}$, be the probability that node $i$ transmits in any slot. A transmission from node $i$ will be successful iff

1. None of the nodes belonging to the neighbourhood set of $i$ transmit, and
2. For each $k \in \mathcal{N}(i)$ none of the nodes belonging to the neighbourhood set of $k$ (except node $i$) transmit.

The second condition above means that none of the second hop neighbours of $i$ transmit. By second hop neighbours we mean $\cup_{j \in \mathcal{N}(i)} \mathcal{N}(j) \backslash (i \cup \mathcal{N}(i)) =: \mathcal{S}(i)$, i.e., the set of neighbours of neighbours of $i$ excluding $i$ and $\mathcal{N}(i)$. Let $\zeta$ be the second hop node incidence matrix, i.e., $\zeta(i, j) = 1 = \zeta(j, i)$ iff $j \in \mathcal{S}(i)$ and $\zeta(i, j) = 0$ otherwise.

Denote by $P_s(i)$ the probability that a transmission from node $i$ is successful. It follows from the conditions mentioned above that

$$P_s(i) = \Pi_{j \in \mathcal{N}(i)}(1 - \alpha_j)\Pi_{k \in \mathcal{S}(i)}(1 - \alpha_k) \qquad (2)$$

Thus the probability that a node $i$ made a successful transmission in any slot is $\alpha_i P_s(i)$. We want to maximise this probability for all the nodes $i$ while simultaneously reducing the probability of collision among the transmissions from node $i$ (to minimize the battery power wasted in collisions) and also the probability of missing out on a transmission opportunity. Thus the problem for node $i$ can be written as follows:

$$\text{Minimize} \qquad -A\alpha_i P_s(i) + B\alpha_i(1 - P_s(i)) + C(1 - \alpha_i)P_s(i) \qquad (3)$$

$$\text{such that } \alpha_i \geq \alpha_{min} > 0 \qquad (4)$$

$$\text{and } \alpha_i \leq \alpha_{max} < 1. \qquad (5)$$

Here:

- the first term in the cost (3) is the negative of the 'reward' for successful transmission, the latter being $A > 0$ times the probability of a successful transmission,
- the second is the penalty for an unsuccessful attempt, being $B > 0$ times the probability of a collision,
- and the third is the penalty for lost opportunities, being $C > 0$ times the probability of no transmission when one was possible.

The bounds on $\alpha_i$ imposed by the equations (4) and (5) are to ensure the connectivity of the network. This is because a node with attempt probability 0 or 1 will be effectively cutoff from the rest of the network and will also lead to disconnectivity between other node pairs.

Since the nodes are each trying to optimize their own objectives without any cooperation, this is a noncooperative game. The 'action space' for each node is the interval $[\alpha_{min}, \alpha_{max}]$ from which it chooses the transmission probability. This is compact convex. Also, each node's objective function (3) is separately convex continuous in each argument. Thus a standard argument based on the Kakutani fixed point theorem ensures the existence of a Nash equilibrium, i.e., a choice $\underline{\alpha}^* = [\alpha_1^*, \cdots, \alpha_N^*]$ such that if all but the $i$-th node transmit with probabilities $\alpha_j^*$'s, $j \neq i$, then it is optimal for $i$-th node also to use $\alpha_i^*$ [23]. Our aim will be to attain this Nash equilibrium. With this objective, we first seek the necessary conditions for the Nash equilibrium.

Since for fixed values of $\alpha_j$, $j \neq i$, this is a single agent optimization problem faced by the $i$-th node, we consider the corresponding Kuhn-Tucker conditions. Let $\theta = \frac{B}{A+B+C}$ and $\eta = \ln \frac{B}{A+B+C}$. For any vector $\underline{\alpha}$ of attempt probabilities, let $A^*(\underline{\alpha}) = \{i : \alpha_{min} < \alpha_i < \alpha_{max}\}$. The (equivalent of) Kuhn-Tucker necessary conditions [23] for a vector $\underline{\alpha}$ to be a Nash equilibrium, i.e., a componentwise local minimum of corresponding cost functions when the other components are unperturbed, are

$$\theta - P_s(i) = 0, \qquad \forall\ i \in A^*(\underline{\alpha}) \tag{6}$$

$$\theta - P_s(i) \geq 0, \qquad \forall\ i : \alpha_i = \alpha_{min} \tag{7}$$

$$\theta - P_s(i) \leq 0, \qquad \forall\ i : \alpha_i = \alpha_{max} \tag{8}$$

where $\theta - P_s(i)$ is in the direction of the gradient at point $\underline{\alpha}$ for the cost function of node $i$.

Let $\alpha^*$ be the Nash equilibrium for the game problem and assume, for simplicity, that $A^*(\alpha^*) = \mathcal{N}$. The case where $A^*(\alpha^*) \neq \mathcal{N}$ will be studied in a later section. Let $\beta_j = \ln(1 - \alpha_j)$. After taking logarithms, Kuhn-Tucker necessary conditions of (6) can be rewritten as,

$$\sum_{j \in \mathcal{N}(i) \cup \mathcal{S}(i)} \beta_j = \eta, \qquad \forall i \tag{9}$$

This set of equations can be written in matrix form as

$$\underline{\eta} - (\Phi + \zeta)\beta = 0, \tag{10}$$

where $\beta$ and $\underline{\eta}$ are column vectors of same size with the $j^{th}$ entry being $\beta_j$ and $\eta$ respectively.

This suggests the iteration

$$\underline{\beta}(n+1) = \underline{\beta}(n) + a(n)(\underline{\eta} - (\Phi + \zeta)\underline{\beta}(n)),$$

where $\{a(n)\}$ are the usual stochastic approximation stepsize schedules, i.e., positive scalars satisfying

$$\sum_n a(n) = \infty, \quad \sum_n a(n)^2 < \infty.$$

By the standard 'o.d.e. approach' to stochastic approximation, this tracks the asymptotic behaviour of the o.d.e. [16]

$$\dot{x}(t) = \underline{\eta} - (\Phi + \zeta)x(t).$$

This is a linear o.d.e. which would indeed converge to the solution of (10) if it were stable. Unfortunately, the stability cannot be a priori assumed. Thus we consider the iteration

$$\underline{\beta}(n+1) = \underline{\beta}(n) + a(n)(\Phi + \zeta)(\underline{\eta} - (\Phi + \zeta)\underline{\beta}(n)), \tag{11}$$

corresponding to the o.d.e.

$$\dot{x}(t) = (\Phi + \zeta)(\underline{\eta} - (\Phi + \zeta)x(t)). \tag{12}$$

This will be stable if $(\Phi + \zeta)$ is nonsingular, whence $(\Phi + \zeta)^2$ will be positive definite. The solution will correspond to the linear system

$$(\Phi + \zeta)\underline{\eta} - (\Phi + \zeta)^2\beta = 0, \tag{13}$$

which then has the same solution as (10). Thus node $i$ will be solving the $i^{th}$ row of (13). This will need further modification when either the nonsingularity of $(\Phi + \zeta)$ does not hold or when one of the constraints on some $\alpha_i$ is active so that either (7) or (8) is operative. The basic iteration described above then needs to be modified.

**Remark**: There is one further complication that needs to be underscored, viz., that our distributed implementation cannot ensure that all components are updated equally often. Thus the theory of [6] suggests that the limiting o.d.e. will be not (12), but

$$\dot{x}(t) = \Lambda(t)(\Phi + \zeta)(\underline{\eta} - (\Phi + \zeta)x(t)), \tag{14}$$

where $\Lambda(t)$ is a diagonal matrix for each $t$ with nonnegative entries $\{\lambda_i(t)\}$ on the diagonal. These reflect the differing comparative frequencies of updating for different components. (See [6] for details.) We shall assume that the latter are strictly positive, which means that the components get updated comparably often, though not necessarily equally often. In our case, this change of o.d.e. does not alter the conclusions. To see this, first note that (12) is of the form

$$\dot{x}(t) = -\nabla F(x(t)),$$

for $F(x) \overset{defn}{=} ||\underline{\eta} - (\Phi + \zeta)x||^2$. Thus $F(\cdot)$ itself serves as a 'Liapunov function' for it, with

$$\frac{d}{dt}F(x(t)) = -||\nabla F(x(t))||^2 \leq 0,$$

the equality holding only on the solution set of (13). When we replace (12) by (14), one has instead

$$\frac{d}{dt}F(x(t)) = -||\sqrt{\Lambda(t)}\nabla F(x(t))||^2 \leq 0,$$

leading to identical conclusions, whence the original convergence claims continue to hold.

## 3.2   The Algorithm

The following algorithm implements the iterations suggested in Section 3.1.

**Algorithm 1**

1. *Set the slot number $n = 0$.*
2. *Initialize $\alpha_i^{(0)}$, $1 \le i \le N$, to some small positive values. Also let $N(i) = 0$, the last slot number when node i updated its attempt probability.*
3. *For $1 \le i \le N$, node i does the following sequence of operations:*

   (a) *It either decides to transmit with probability $\alpha_i^{(n)}$, or decides to go into sleep mode with probability $\gamma_i$, or, if not any of the above, senses the channel for any transmission.*

   (b) *If decided to transmit, a node does the following:*

      i. *Sends the data packet (measurements) destined for all the neighbouring nodes.*

      ii. *It also transmits the information relevant for its nodes for updating their attempt probabilities based on (11). In particular, node i transmits $\alpha_i^{(n)}$, $N(i)$, $\mathcal{N}(i)$ and all the information (attempt probabilities and the last time the node updated its attempt probability) it has about the nodes it can reach in three hops.*

   (c) *If decided to sense the channel, a node does the following:*

      i. *If node i receives a signal that can be decoded correctly, then it checks if the received signal contains the update information. If yes, update node i's local information about its four hop neighbours based on the information it extracted from the transmission received from its first hop neighbour. Here node i updates its estimate of $\alpha_j$ only if the value of $N(j)$ that it has now received is more than node i's copy of $N(j)$.*

      ii. *Update $\alpha_i^{(n)}$ based on the updated information.*

      iii. *Set $N(i) = n$.*

4. *$n = n + 1$.*
5. *Go to step 3.*

**Remarks:**

1. This algorithm is similar to the DSDV protocol [19] for route discovery in the ad hoc 802.11 networks as each node keeps its own copy of the local information of the connectivity between the neighbouring 4 hop nodes and transmits a part of this information to the neighbouring nodes. This implies that mobility or failure of the nodes can also be taken into account in this algorithm as a node $i$ can consider another node $j$ (which is reachable in at most 4 hops from node $i$) as failed or nonexistent if node $i$'s information about node $j$ says that $N(j)$ has not been updated for a long time, say $M\lceil \frac{1}{\hat{\alpha}_j} \rceil$, where $M$ is a large integer and $\hat{\alpha}_j$ is node $i$'s most recent information about $\alpha_j$.

2. The property of the nodes being dense is not required here and the exact physical distance between two nodes is no longer relevant now as the required information, i.e., $(\Phi + \zeta)^2$ is already obtained.
3. A node keeps information only about its four hop neighbours. The amount of storage required for this information grows with the density of the network (which should be true for any such algorithm). Note that the storage required for the required information does *not* change by increasing the span of the network for a fixed node density (i.e., increasing the area of the network by adding more nodes so as to keep the node density fixed). Compare this with DSDV or the algorithm of [14] where a node keeps information about the *complete* network.

### 3.3   Problem Formulation to Incorporate Sleep Mode

Algorithm 1 was for the case where, in any slot, a node either decides to transmit or else decides to receive. To accommodate for the possibility that a node $i$ can decide to be in sleep mode with a fixed probability $\gamma_i$ (known to node $i$), for this case equation (2) for $P_s(i)$ can be modified to

$$P_s(i) = \Pi_{j \in \mathcal{N}(i)}(1 - \gamma_j - \alpha_j)\Pi_{k \in \mathcal{S}(i)}(1 - \gamma_k - \alpha_k) \qquad (15)$$

Similarly, in the penalty term for missed opportunities in equation (3), $(1-\alpha_i)$ should be replaced by $(1 - \gamma_i - \alpha_i)$. Algorithm 1 needs to be modified to take care of this possibility. Now, a node $i$ transmits $\gamma_i$ along with its other update information meant for its neighbours. The rest of the algorithm works similarly.

One can also consider $\{\gamma_i\}$ as additional decision variables that can be tuned to find the optimal trade-off between sleep and alert modes. To do this, one may add to node $i$'s 'cost' (3) the additional terms $D(1 - \gamma_i) + G\gamma_i P_s(i)$, $D, G > 0$. The first is the cost on battery power utilization (this could be fine tuned further to allow for different costs for different kinds of usage), the second is the cost of missed opportunities due to sleep mode. The algorithm can be easily modified to incorporate optimization over $\{\gamma_i\}$.

### 3.4   Problem Formulation for Transmissions Destined for Fixed Nodes

Algorithm 1 was for the case where a node's transmission is meant for all of its neighbouring nodes and a node $i$ has only one attempt probability $\alpha_i$. Now we show how to modify Algorithm 1 for the case where a node's transmission is destined for a particular node $j \in \mathcal{N}(i)$. In this case a node $i$, in any slot and *for each of its neighbour* $j \in \mathcal{N}(i)$, decides to send a packet destined for node $j$ with probability $\alpha_{i,j}$ *independent of anything else*. Note that it is possible that node $i$ decides to send data to two or more of its neighbours simultaneously in which case the transmission is unsuccessful. We again assume here that $\gamma_i = 0$. For this case (2) can be written as

$$P_s(i,j) = \Pi_{l \in \mathcal{N}(i) \setminus j}(1 - \alpha_{i,l})\Pi_{l \in \mathcal{N}(j)}(1 - \alpha_{j,l})\Pi_{l \in \cup_{k \in \mathcal{N}(j) \setminus i}\mathcal{N}(k) \setminus i} \qquad (16)$$
$$\Pi_{m \in \mathcal{N}(j) \setminus i}(1 - \alpha_{l,m}).$$

Thus a node computes $\alpha_{i,j}$ using Algorithm 1 based on the information that it receives from its neighbouring nodes. Note that now a node sends the $\alpha_{i,j}$'s of its 3 hop neighbours instead of just the $\alpha_i$'s.

Numerical results based on an implementation of the algorithm are presented in [7].

## 4   Optimal Channel Access Rate with Reward on Reception

In the previous section we assumed that a node is interested in its performance as a traffic source. Typically a node in an ad hoc network is both sender as well as receiver of packets and hence will be interested in a *combined* performance measure that reflects its performance as a sender and as a receiver. These are two conflicting requirements: a node, if it tries to be too aggressive in sending packets, may lose opportunity to receive packets meant for itself and vice versa.

We now assume that nodes never go into sleep mode, i.e., they are either transmitting or ready to receive. The channel access is again random, i.e., in each slot, a node $i$ decides to transmit (broadcast) with probability $\alpha_i$ and decides to receive with probability $(1 - \alpha_i)$. The quantity $\alpha_i$ is called the *attempt probability* of node $i$. What follows can be easily modified to account for a node $i$ keeping a attempt probability $\alpha_{i,j}$ for its neighboring node $j$, or to some subset of its neighbors (multicast).

Our problem now is to find, for a given network, the values of $\alpha_i$ (or $\alpha_{i,j}$, as the case may be) which maximizes node $i$'s performance.

Let $P_s(i)$ be the conditional probability that a transmission attempt from node $i$ is *successful* (conditioned on the event that node $i$ transmits), and $P_r(j, i)$ denote the probability that a transmission from node $j$ is successfully received by node $i$.

Here one can have various notions of node $i$'s transmission being *successful*. We use the simple (though not restrictive) criteria: node $i$'s transmission is successful if *all* of it's neighboring nodes correctly receive the transmission.

Each node wants to maximise its own utility function which reflects the performance obtained by the node under the sending probabilities selected by the nodes in the network. A common ingredient of the utility function of node $i$ is a combination of the rates at which node $i$ successfully transmits and receives packets. Thus the problem for node $i$ is to maximise

$$U_i(\underline{\alpha}) = A_i \alpha_i P_s(i) + \sum_{j \in \mathcal{N}(i)} A_{i,j} \alpha_j P_r(j, i) - C_i \bar{\alpha}_i P_s(i) \qquad (17)$$

such that $\alpha_i \geq 0$ and $\bar{\alpha}_i = 1 - \alpha_i \geq 0$. Here $A_i$, $C_i$ and $A_{i,j}$ are some non-negative constants. The first and second terms here are "rewards" for *success* owing to, respectively, transmission and reception. $A_{i,j}$ will be zero for node $j$ whose transmission can not be directly received by node $i$. The third term is included to act as a punishment for missed opportunities, thus aiming at maximising node $i$'s use of network. Note that the last term also is the probability of the event where none of the neighboring nodes of node $i$ are sending to node $i$ when node $i$ is ready to receive, thus this term also represents the time wasted by node $i$ in trying to receive when there is nothing to receive.

Our definition of $P_s(i)$ means that none of the first or second hop neighbors of $i$ transmit when node $i$ does. Thus

$$P_s(i) = \Pi_{j \in \mathcal{N}(i)}(1 - \alpha_j)\Pi_{k \in \mathcal{S}(i)}(1 - \alpha_k). \tag{18}$$

Similarly, it is seen that, for $j \in \mathcal{N}(i)$, $P_r(j,i)$ is,

$$P_r(j,i) = \Pi_{k \in \mathcal{N}(i) \cup \{i\} \setminus \{j\}}(1 - \alpha_k). \tag{19}$$

This is again viewed as a concave $N$-person game thus a Nash equilibrium exists, i.e., a choice $\underline{\alpha}^* = [\alpha_1^*, \cdots, \alpha_N^*]$ such that if all but the $i$-th node transmit with probabilities $\alpha_j^*$'s, $j \neq i$, then it is optimal for $i$-th node also to use $\alpha_i^*$ [20].

Again, since for fixed $\alpha_j$, $j \neq i$, this is a single agent optimization problem faced by the $i$-th node, we consider the corresponding Kuhn-Tucker condition. For any vector $\underline{\alpha}$ of attempt probabilities, let $A^*(\underline{\alpha}) = \{i : 0 < \alpha_i < 1\}$. The (equivalent of) Kuhn-Tucker conditions for a vector $\underline{\alpha}$ to be a Nash equilibrium, i.e., a componentwise local maximum of corresponding utility functions when the other components are unperturbed, are (with $A_{i,i} := A_i + C_i$)

$$A_{i,i}P_s(i) - \sum_{j \in \mathcal{N}(i)} A_{i,j}\alpha_j \frac{P_r(j,i)}{1 - \alpha_i} = 0, \qquad \forall\, i \in A^*(\underline{\alpha}) \tag{20}$$

$$A_{i,i}P_s(i) - \sum_{j \in \mathcal{N}(i)} A_{i,j}\alpha_j \frac{P_r(j,i)}{1 - \alpha_i} \geq 0, \qquad \forall\, i : \alpha_i = 1 \tag{21}$$

$$A_{i,i}P_s(i) - \sum_{j \in \mathcal{N}(i)} A_{i,j}\alpha_j \frac{P_r(j,i)}{1 - \alpha_i} \leq 0, \qquad \forall\, i : \alpha_i = 0. \tag{22}$$

Let $\alpha^*$ be a Nash equilibrium for the game problem and assume, for simplicity, that $A^*(\alpha^*) = \mathcal{N}$. Let $\underline{\alpha}$ be a column vector whose $i^{th}$ entry is $\alpha_i$. Also introduce $\mathbf{G}(\underline{\alpha}) := \frac{\partial}{\partial \alpha_i}U_i(\underline{\alpha}) = A_{i,i}P_s(i) - \sum_{j \in \mathcal{N}(i)} A_{i,j}\alpha_j \frac{P_r(j,i)}{1-\alpha_i}$.

## 4.1 Effect of Imposing Power Constraints

Till now we have not imposed any restriction on the possible values that $\alpha_i$'s are allowed to take (except that $\alpha_i \in [0,1]$). Since the nodes are battery power constrained, one would like to see the effect of imposing a constraint on $\alpha_i$ so as to use the battery power efficiently. A natural candidate for such a constraint for node $i$ is $T_i\alpha_i + R_i(1 - \alpha_i)P_r(i) \leq P_i$, where $T_i$ and $R_i$ are the average power required for transmission and reception of packets, $P_i$ is the average battery power of node $i$ and $P_r(i)$ is the probability that node $i$ is trying to receive while it is not transmitting. $P_r(i) = 1 - \Pi_{j \in \mathcal{N}(i)}(1 - \alpha_j)$, i.e., that a node spends $R_i$

amount of power whenever there is a transmission attempt from at least one neighboring node. In practice, the case of interest would be $T_i \geq P_i \geq R_i$. (If $P_i \geq \max(T_i, R_i)$ then, effectively, the $\alpha_i$'s are not battery power constrained.) Note now that the action space of the nodes are dependent on the actions of other nodes. The existence of a Nash equilibrium would follow if the constraint set so obtained is convex [20]. For a general network topology, it can be shown that the constraint defining functions $P_i - T_i\alpha_i - R_i(1 - \alpha_i)P_r(i)$ are quasi-concave [17] so that the constraint set is convex. Further, the constraint set is easily seen to be nonempty because the point $\alpha_i = 0$, $\forall i$ is always feasible. Details of proof showing quasi-concavity of the power constraint functions is omitted.

## 4.2   A Distributed Algorithm

To compute $\alpha_i$, the Kuhn-Tucker condition of Equation 20 suggests the following (gradient ascent type) iteration

$$\underline{\alpha}(n + 1) = \underline{\alpha}(n) + a(n)\mathbf{G}(\underline{\alpha}), \tag{23}$$

where $\{a(n)\}$ are the usual stochastic approximation stepsize schedules. By the standard 'o.d.e. approach' to stochastic approximation [16], this tracks the asymptotic behavior of the ordinary differential equation (o.d.e.)

$$\dot{x}(t) = \mathbf{G}(x).$$

For a general network and coefficients $A_i, A_{i,j}, C_i$, the stability of the equilibrium points of the o.d.e. cannot be a priori assumed (see also [20] for this issue). However, for a special case where all the nodes are neighbors of each other, it can be shown that the (slightly modified) o.d.e. is globally asymptotically stable and hence the suggested iteration above is guaranteed to converge irrespective of the coefficients.

## 4.3   The Case of All Nodes Neighbor of Each Other

Consider the special case where for any node $i$, $\mathcal{N}(i) = \mathcal{N}$, i.e., all the nodes are neighbors of each other. This is a common scenario in wireless LANs spanning a small area (office etc.). The standard Slotted ALOHA system is yet another example of such scenario.

Recently, [1] has also considered a game theoretic approach to delay minimization in Slotted Aloha systems with the *retransmission probabilities* as decision variables. However, it does not consider the problem of nodes computing the optimal retransmission probabilities. The problem there also assumes symmetry, i.e., (unlike our case) all nodes have equal weightage thus resulting in equal optimal retransmission probabilities for each node.

For the present case where $S(i)$ is empty, it is seen that $P_s(i) = \Pi_{j \neq i}(1 - \alpha_j)$, and $P_r(j, i) = \Pi_{k \neq j}(1 - \alpha_k) = P_s(j)$. Note that $P_r(j, i) = P_r(j, k)$ for any $k, i \neq j$. The Kuhn-Tucker condition (Equation 20) can be written as

$$\sum_{j \neq i} A_{i,j} \frac{\alpha_j}{1 - \alpha_j} = A_{i,i}, \quad \forall i.$$

Let $\beta_j := \frac{\alpha_j}{1-\alpha_j}$, $\zeta_{i,j} = A_{i,j}$, $i \neq j$ and $\eta_i = A_{i,i}$. The above condition in matrix form is then,

$$\zeta \underline{\beta} = \underline{\eta}. \tag{24}$$

**Remark:** Equation 24 gives a complete characterization of the solution of optimization problem under consideration as a solution to a set of linear equations. This is a considerable simplification given the complex set of equations representing the optimization problem. Now we proceed to give a method to compute this optimum in a distributed manner.

## 4.4   The Algorithm

To solve Equation 24, the iteration to be considered is

$$\underline{\beta}(n+1) = \underline{\beta}(n) + a(n)(\underline{\eta} - \zeta\underline{\beta}(n)),$$

corresponding to the o.d.e. $\dot{x}(t) = (\underline{\eta} - \zeta x(t))$, whose stability, again, can not be apriori assumed. We thus consider the modified o.d.e. having same critical points

$$\dot{x}(t) = \zeta(\underline{\eta} - \zeta x(t)). \tag{25}$$

This will be stable if the matrix $\zeta$ is invertible, whence $\zeta^2$ will be positive definite. The solution will correspond to the linear system

$$\zeta\underline{\eta} - \zeta^2\underline{\beta} = 0, \tag{26}$$

which then has the same solution as (24). Thus node $i$ will be solving the $i^{th}$ row of (26). The iteration at node $i$ is thus

$$\underline{\beta}(n+1) = \underline{\beta}(n) + a(n)\zeta(\underline{\eta} - \zeta\underline{\beta}(n)). \tag{27}$$

The algorithm run by the nodes based on the above iteration is detailed as follows.

1. Set the slot number $n = 0$. Initialize $\alpha_i^{(0)}$, $1 \leq i \leq N$, to some small positive values. Also let $N(i) = 0$, the last slot number when node $i$ updated its attempt probability.
2. For $1 \leq i \leq N$, node $i$ does the following operations:

   – It either decides to transmit with probability $\alpha_i^{(n)}$, or decides to receive with probability $1 - \alpha_i^{(n)}$.
   – If decided to transmit, a node sends the data packet destined for all the neighboring nodes. It also transmits the information relevant for other nodes for updating their attempt probabilities based on (27). In particular, node $i$ transmits $\alpha_i^{(n)}$, $N(i)$, $\mathcal{N}(i)$.
   – If decided to sense the channel, do the following:

- If node $i$ receives a signal that can be decoded correctly, then it checks if the received signal contains the update information. If yes, update node $i$'s local information about its neighbors based on information extracted from the transmission received from its first hop neighbor. Here node $i$ updates its estimate of $\alpha_j$, $j \neq i$, only if the value of $N(j)$ that it has now received is more than node $i$'s copy of $N(j)$.
- Update $\alpha_i^{(n)}$ based on the updated information.
- Set $N(i) = n$.

3. $n = n + 1$, Go to step 2.

For numerical results based on an implementation of the algorithm, see [2].

## 5    Non-cooperative Forwarding in Ad Hoc Networks

As mentioned in the Introducion, in this work we consider a less aggressive punishment policy as an incentive for cooperation in ad hoc networks. We simply assume that if the fraction $q'$ of packets forwarded by a mobile is less than the fraction $q$ forwarded by other mobiles, then this will result in a decrease of the forwarding probability of the other mobiles to the value $q'$. We shall show that this will indeed lead to non-aggressive equilibria, yet not necessarily to complete cooperation. The reasons for adopting this milder punishment strategy are the following:

1. There has been criticism in the game-theoretical community on the use of aggressive punishments. For example, threats for aggressive punishments have been argued not to be credible threats when the punishing agent may itself loose at the punishing phase. This motivated equilibria based on more credible punishments known as subgame perfect equilibria [21].
2. An individual that adopts an "partially-cooperative" behavior (i.e. forwards packets with probability $0 < q < 1$) need not be considered as an "aggressive" individual, and thus the punishment needs not be "aggressive" either; it is *fair* to respond to such a partially-cooperative behavior with a partially-cooperative reaction, which gives rise to our mild punishment scheme.
3. The TFT policy would lead to complete cooperation at equilibrium. However, our milder punishment seems to us more descriptive of actual behavior in the society in which we do not obtain full cooperation at equilibrium (for example in the behavior of drivers on the road, in the rate of criminality etc.) It may indeed be expected that some degree of non-cooperative behavior by a small number of persons could result in larger and larger portions of the society to react by adopting such a behavior.

As already mentioned, incentive for cooperation in Ad-hoc networks have been studied in several papers, see [11,18,22,24]. Almost all previous papers however only considered utilities related to successful transmission of a mobile's packet to its neighbor. In practice, however, multihop routes may be required for a packet to reach its destination, so the utility corresponding to successful transmission depends on the forwarding behavior of all mobiles along the path. The goal of our paper is therefore to study the forwarding taking into account the multihop topological characteristics of the path.

Most close to our work is the paper [11] which considers a model similar to ours (introduced in Section 5.1 below). [11] provides sufficient condition on the network topology under which each node employing the "aggressive" TFT punishment strategy results in a Nash equilibrium. In the present section, we show that a less aggressive punishment mechanism can also lead to a Nash equilibrium which has a desirable feature that it is less resource consuming in the sense that a node need not accept all the forwarding request.

## 5.1   The Model

Consider an Ad-hoc network described by a directed graph $G = (N, V)$. Along with that network, we consider a set of source-destination pairs $O$ and a given routing between each source $s$ and its corresponding destination $d$, of the form $\pi(s, d) = (s, n_1, n_2, \ldots, n_k, d)$, where $k = k(s, d)$ is the number of intermediate hops and $n_j = n_j(s, d)$ is the $j$th intermediate node on path $\pi(s, d)$. We assume that mobile $j$ forwards packets (independently from the source of the packet) with a fixed probabilty $\gamma_j$. Let $\underline{\gamma}$ be the vector of forwarding probabilities of all mobiles. We assume however that each source $s$ forwards its own packets with probability one. For a given path $\pi(s, d)$, the probability that a transmitted packet reaches its destination is thus:

$$p(s, d; \underline{\gamma}) = \prod_{j=1}^{k(s,d)} \gamma(n_j(s, d)).$$

If $i$ belongs to a path $\pi(s, d)$ we write $i \in \pi(s, d)$. For a given path $\pi(s, d)$ of the form $(s, n_1, n_2, \ldots, n_k, d)$ and a given mobile $n_j \in \pi(s, d)$, define the set of intermediate nodes before $n_j$ to be the set $S(s, d; n_j) = (n_1, \ldots, n_{j-1})$. The probability that some node $i \in \pi(s, d)$ receives a packet originating from $s$ with $d$ as its destination is then given by

$$p(s, d; i, \underline{\gamma}) = \prod_{j \in S(s,d;i)} \gamma(j).$$

Note that $p(s, d; d, \gamma) = p(s, d; \underline{\gamma})$, the probability that node $d$ receives a packet originating from source $s$ and having $d$ as its destination.

Define $O(i)$ to be all the paths in which a mobile $i$ is an intermediate node. Let the rate at which source $s$ creates packets for destination $d$ be given by some constant $\lambda_{sd}$. Then the rate at which packets arrive at node $i$ in order to be forwarded there is given by

$$\xi_i(\underline{\gamma}) = \sum_{\pi(s,d) \in O(i)} \lambda_{sd} p(s, d; i, \underline{\gamma}).$$

Let $E_f$ be the total energy needed for forwarding a packet (which includes the energy for its reception and its transmission). Then the utility of mobile $i$ that we consider is

$$U_i(\underline{\gamma}) = \sum_{n:(i,n)\in O} \lambda_{in} f_i(p(i,n;\underline{\gamma}))$$

$$+ \sum_{n:(n,i)\in O} \lambda_{ni} g_i(p(n,i;\underline{\gamma})) - aE_f \xi_i(\underline{\gamma}), \qquad (28)$$

where $f_i$ and $g_i$ are utility functions that depend on the success probabilities associated with node $i$ as a source and as a destination respectively and $a$ is some multiplicative constant. We assume that $f_i(\cdot)$ and $g_i(\cdot)$ are nondecreasing concave in their arguments. The objective of mobile $i$ is to choose $\gamma_i$ that maximizes $U_i(\underline{\gamma})$. We remark here that similar utility function is also considered in [11] with the difference that node's utility does not include its reward as a destination, i.e., they assume that $g_i(\cdot) \equiv 0$.

**Definition:** *For any choices of strategy $\underline{\gamma}$ for all mobiles, define $(\gamma_i', \underline{\gamma}^{-i})$ to be the strategy obtained when only player $i$ deviates from $\gamma_i$ to $\gamma_i'$ and other mobiles maintain their strategies fixed.*

In a noncooperative framework, the solution concept of the optimization problem faced by all players is the following:

**Definition:** *A Nash equilibrium, is some strategy set $\underline{\gamma}^*$ for all mobiles such that for each mobile $i$,*

$$U_i(\underline{\gamma}^*) = \max_{\gamma_i'} U_i(\gamma_i', (\underline{\gamma}^*)^{-i}).$$

*We call $\mathrm{argmax}_{\gamma_i'} U_i(\gamma_i', \underline{\gamma}^{-i})$ the set of optimal responses of player $i$ against other mobiles policy $\underline{\gamma}^{-i}$ (it may be an empty set or have several elements).*

In our setting, it is easy to see that for each mobile $i$ and each fixed strategy $\underline{\gamma}^{-i}$ for other players, the best response of mobile $i$ is $\gamma_i = 0$ (unless $O(i) = \emptyset$ in which case, the best response is the whole interval $[0, 1]$). Thus the only possible equilibrium is that of $\gamma_i = 0$ for all $i$. To overcome this problem, we consider the following "punishing mechanism". in order to incite mobiles to cooperate.

**Definition:** *Consider a given set of policies $\underline{\gamma} = (\gamma, \gamma, \gamma, ...)$. If some mobile deviates and uses some $\gamma' < \gamma$, we define the punishing policy $\kappa(\gamma', \gamma)$ as the policy in which all mobiles decrease their forwarding probability to $\gamma'$.*

When this punishing mechanism is enforced, then the best strategy of a mobile $i$ when all other mobiles use strategy $\gamma$ is $\gamma'$ that achieves

$$J(\gamma) := \max_{\gamma' \leq \gamma} U_i(\underline{\gamma}') \qquad (29)$$

where $\underline{\gamma}' = (\gamma', \gamma', \gamma', ....)$.

**Definition:** *If some $\gamma^*$ achieves the minimum in (29) we call the vector $\underline{\gamma}^* = (\gamma^*, \gamma^*, \gamma^*, ...)$ the equilibrium strategy (for the forwarding problem) under threats. $J(\gamma)$ is called the corresponding value.*

**Remark:** Note that $\gamma^* = 0$ is still a Nash equilibrium.

## 5.2   Utilities for Symmetrical Topologies

By symmetrical topology we mean the case where $f_i$, $g_i$ and $\xi_i$ are independent of $i$. This implies that for any source-destination pair $(s, d)$, there are two nodes $s'$ and $d'$ such that the source-destination pairs $(s', s)$ and $(d, d')$ are identical to $(s, d)$ in the sense that there view of the network is similar to that of $(s, d)$. This implies that, under the punishment mechanism where all nodes have same forwarding probability, we have $p(s, d; \underline{\gamma}) = p(s', s; \underline{\gamma})$. Thus we can replace the rewards $f_i + g_i$ by another function that we denote $f(\cdot)$.

Consider $\underline{\gamma}$ where all entries are the same and equal to $\gamma$, except for that of mobile $i$. For a path $\pi(s, d)$ containing $n$ intermediate nodes, we have $p(s, d; \underline{\gamma}) = \gamma^n$. Also, if a mobile $i$ is $n + 1$ hops away from a source, $n = 1, 2, 3, ...$, and is on the path from this source to a destination (but is not itself the destination), then $p(s, d; i, \underline{\gamma}) = \gamma^n$. We call the source an "effective source" for forwarding to mobile $i$ since it potentially has packets to be forwarded by mobile $i$. Let $h(n)$ be the rate at which all effective sources located $n + 1$ hops away from mobile $i$ transmit packets that should use mobile $i$ for forwarding (we assume that $h$ is the same for all nodes). Let $\lambda^{(n)}$ denote the rate at which a source $s$ creates packets to all destinations that are $n + 1$ hops away from it. Then we have

$$U_i(\underline{\gamma}) = \sum_{n=1}^{\infty} \lambda^{(n)} f(\gamma^n) - aE_f \sum_{n=1}^{\infty} h(n)\gamma^n. \qquad (30)$$

The equilibrium strategy under threat is then the value of $\gamma$ that maximizes the r.h.s.

**Remark:** If we denote by $\Lambda(z) = \sum_{n=1}^{\infty} z^n \lambda^{(n)}$ the generating function of $\lambda^{(n)}$ and $H(z) := \sum_{n=1}^{\infty} z^n h(n)$ the generating function of $h$. Then

$$\max_{\gamma} \left( \Lambda(\gamma) - aE_f H(\gamma) \right)$$

is the value of the problem with threats in the case that $f$ is the identity function.

## 5.3   Examples

In this section we present, by means of two examples, the effect of imposing the proposed punishment mechanism.

## 5.4   An Asymmetric Network

Consider the network shown in Figure 1. For this case nodes 1 and 4 have no traffic to forward. Note also that if we assume that $g_3(\cdot) \equiv 0$ in Equation 28 then node 3 has no incentive even to invoke the punishment mechanism for node 2. This will result in no cooperation in the network. Assume for the time being that $f_2(x) = g_3(x) = x$, i.e., $f_2$ and $g_3$ are identity functions. In this case it is seen that the utility functions for nodes 2 and 3 are, assuming $\lambda_{13} = \lambda_{24} = 1$, $U_2(\gamma_2, \gamma_3) = \gamma_3 - aE_f\gamma_2$ and $U_3(\gamma_2, \gamma_3) = \gamma_2 - aE_f\gamma_3$. When we impose the punishment mechanism, it turns out that the equilibrium strategy for the two nodes is to always cooperate, i.e., $\gamma_2 = \gamma_3$. This is to be compared with the TFT strategy of [11] which would imply $\gamma_2 = \gamma_3 = 0$.

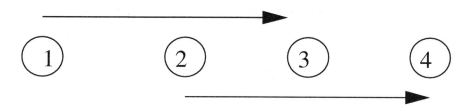

**Fig. 1.** An asymmetric network

## 5.5 A Symmetric Network: Circular Network with Fixed Length of Paths

We consider here equally spaced mobile nodes on a circle and assume that each node $i$ is a source of traffic to a node located $L$ hops to the right, i.e. to the node $i + L$.

Let the rate of traffic generated from a source be $\lambda$. For this case, $h(n) = \lambda I_{\{n \leq L-1\}}$. Also, $\lambda^{(n)} = \lambda I_{\{n=L\}}$, for some $\lambda$. It follows from Equation 30 that the utility function for mobile $i$ is

$$U_i(\underline{\gamma}) = \lambda f(\gamma^{L-1}) - aE_f \lambda \sum_{n=0}^{L-2} \gamma^n.$$

For $f(\cdot)$ an identity function, we see that $U_i(\underline{\gamma}) = \lambda \left[ \gamma^{L-1} - aE_f(\gamma^{L-2} + \gamma^{L-3} + \ldots + \gamma + 1) \right]$. Note that if $L = 2$ and $a = \frac{1}{E_f}$, the utility function is independent of $\gamma$ hence in this case the equilibrium strategy is any value of forwarding probability. Also, if $aE_f \geq 1$, the equilibrium strategy is $\gamma = 0$. We will have more to say on this in th next section where we study the structure of equilibrium strategy for symmetric network.

## 5.6 Algorithm for Computing the Equilibrium Strategy in a Distributed Manner

It is interesting to design distributed algorithms which can be used by the mobiles to compute the equilibrium strategy and simultaneously enforce the proposed punishment mechanism. The obvious desirable features of such an algorithm are that it should be decentralised, distributed scalability and should be able to adapt to changes in network.

We propose such an algorithm in this section. We present it, for ease of notation, for the case of symmetric network. Assume for the moment that $f(\cdot)$ is the identity function. In this case each node has to solve the equation (recall the notation of Section 5.2)

$$U'(\gamma) = \Lambda'(\gamma) - KH'(\gamma) = 0, \tag{31}$$

where the primes denote the derivatives with respect to $\gamma$. In general this equation will be nontrivial to solve directly. For the case of more general network, one needs to compute the derivative of the utility function of Equation 28, the rest of procedure that follows is similar.

Note that in the above expression we first assume that the forwarding probabilities of all the nodes in the network are same (say $\gamma$) and then compute the derivative with respect to this common $\gamma$. This is because in the node must take the effect of punishment mechanism into account while computing its own optimal forwarding probability, i.e., a node should assume that all the other nodes will use the same forwarding probability that it computes.

Thus, solving Equation 31 is reduced to a single variable optimization problem. Since the actual problem from which we get Equation 31 is a maximization problem, a node does a gradient *ascent* to compute its optimal forwarding probability. Thus, in its $n^{th}$ computation, a node $i$ uses the iteration

$$\gamma_i^{(n+1)} = \gamma_i^{(n)} + a(n)(\Lambda'(\gamma_i^{(n)}) - KH'(\gamma_i^{(n)})), \tag{32}$$

where $a(n)$ is a sequence of learning parameters in stochastic approximation algorithms.

The relation to stochastic approximation algorithm here is seen as follows: the network topology can be randomly changing with time owing to node failures/mobility et cetera. Thus a node needs to appropriately modify the functions $\Lambda(\cdot)$ and $H(\cdot)$ based on its most recent view of the network (this dependence of $\Lambda(\cdot)$ and $H(\cdot)$ on $n$ is suppressed in the above expression).

It is a matter of choice when a node should update its estimate of its forwarding probability, i.e., does the computations mentioned above. One possibility, that we use, is to invoke the above iteration whenever the node receives a packet that is meant for it.

Though the above is a simple stochastic approximation algorithm, it requires a node to know the topology of the part of network around itself. This information is actually trivially available to a node since it can extract the required information from the packets requesting forwarding or using a neighbour discovery mechanism. However, in case of any change in the network, there will typically be some delay till a node completely recognizes the change. This transient error in a node's knowledge about the network whenever the network changes is ensured to die out ultimately owing to the assumption of finite second moment for the learning parameters.

It is known by the o.d.e. approach to stochastic approximation algorithm that the above algorithm will asymptotically track the o.d.e. [15]:

$$\dot{\gamma}_i(t) = \Lambda'(\gamma_i(t)) - KH'(\gamma_i(t)), \tag{33}$$

and will converge to one of the *stable* critical points of o.d.e. of Equation 33. It is easily seen that a local maximum of the utility function forms a stable critical point of Equation 33 while any local minimum forms an unstable critical point. Thus the above algorithm inherently makes the system converge to a local maximum and avoids a local minimum.

However, it is possible that different nodes settle to different local maxima (we have already seen that there can be multiple maxima). The imposed punishment mechanism then ensures that all the nodes settle to the one which corresponds to the lowest values of $\gamma$. This is a desirable feature of the algorithm that it inherently avoids multiple simultaneous operating points. An implementation of the punishment mechanism is described next.

## 5.7    Distributed Implementation of the Punishment Mechanism

An implementation of punishment mechanism proposed in Section 5.1 requires, in general, a node to know about the misbehaving node in the network, if any. Here we propose a simple implementation of the punishment mechanism which requires only local information for its implementation.

Let $\mathcal{N}(i)$ be the set of neighbours of node $i$. Every node computes its forwarding policy in a distrubuted manner using the above mentioned stochastic approximation algorithm. However, as soon as a neighboring node is detected to misbehave by a node, the node computes its forwarding policy as follows:

$$\gamma_i^* = \min\{\gamma_i, \min_{j \in \mathcal{N}(i)} \hat{\gamma}_j\} \tag{34}$$

where $\gamma_i$ and $\hat{\gamma}_j$ represents, respectively, the forwarding policy adopted by node $i$ and the estimate of node $j$'s forwarding probability available to node $i$. $\gamma_i^*$ represents the new policy selected by node $i$. Note here that $\gamma_i$ is still computed using iteration of Equation 32. We are also assuming here that a node can differentiate between a misbehaving neighbouring node and the failure/mobility of a neighbouring node.

This punishment propagates in the network until all the nodes in the network settle to the common forwarding probability (corresponding to that of the misbehaving node). In particular, the effect of this punishment will be seen by the misbehaving ndoe as a degradation in its own utility. Suppose now that the misbehaving node, say $n_i$, decides to change to a cooperative behavior: at that point, it will detect and punish its neighbors because of the propagation of the punishment that induced its neighbouring nodes to decrease their forwarding policy. Thus, the intial punishment introduces a negative loop and the forwarding policy of every node of the network collapses to the forwarding policy selected by the misbehaving node. Since now every node in the network has same value of forwarding probability, none of the nodes will be able to increase its forwarding probability even if none of the node is misbehaving now.

An example of this phenomenon can be seen from the network of Figure 1. Assume that $\gamma_2 = \gamma_3 = \gamma$ and now node 2 reduces $\gamma_2$ to a smaller value $\gamma'$. Owing to the punishment mechanism, node 3 will respond with $\gamma_3 = \gamma'$. This will result in a reduced utility for node 2 which would then like to increase $\gamma_2$. But, since $\gamma_3 = \gamma'$, the punishing mechanism would imply that $\gamma_2 = \gamma'$ as well. This *lock-in* problem is avoided by the solution proposed below.

We modify our algorithm to account for the above mentioned effect. Our solution is based on timers of a fixed duration. When a node enters in the punishing phase (starts punishing some of its neighbour) the local timer for that node is set and the forwarding policy is selected as in equation 34. When the timer expires, the punishing node evaluates its forwarding policy as if there were no misbehaving nodes, then uses some of standard mechanism to detect any persistent misbehavior (this also helps distinguishing between a misbehaving node and a failed/moved node). In the case no misbehaviors are detected, depending on the choice of the learning parameter of the stochastic apporximation algotithm, the forwarding policy of the network eventually returns to the optimal value for the network. If the neighboring node continues to misbehave, the timer is set again and the punishment mechanism is re-iterated. We assume that the sequence of learning parameters by a node is restarted each time the timer is set.

**Remark**: It is interesting to see that the proposed implementation of the punishing mechanism is actually having a storage complexity for a node that grows only with the number of its neighbouring nodes (Equation 34). Computational complexity is also not large as it depends only on the distance (hops) from a node to its farthest destination (Equation 32).

See [3] for numerical results and discussions on the implementation of the algorithm.

# 6    Conclusion

We have proposed and analysed a distributed scheme for adapting the random access probabilities in a wireless ad hoc network and tested it on some simple scenarios. The advantage of the scheme is its simplicity, made possible by a simplified model and a judicious choice of the performance measures. This makes it attractive from an implementation point of view.

We use the framework of non-cooperative game theory to provide incentives for cooperation in the case of wireless Ad-hoc networks. The incentive proposed in the paper is based on a simple punishment mechanism that can be implemented in a completely distributed manner with very small computational complexity. The advantage of the proposed strategy is that it results in a less "aggressive" equilibrium in the sense that it does not result in a degenerate scenario where a node either forwards all the requested traffic or does not forward any of the request.

**Acknowledgements** The work of the E. Altman, V.S. Borkar and A.A. Kherani was supported in part by project no. 2900-IT-1 from the *Centre Franco-Indien pour la Promotion de la Recherche Avancee* (CEFIPRA). The work of E. Altman was partially supported by the European Network of Excellence EURO NGI.

# References

1. E. Altman, R. El Azouzi and T. Jimenez: Slotted Aloha as a Stochastic Game with Partial Information, WiOpt'03, Sophia Antipolis, France, (2003).
2. E. Altman, V. S. Borkar and A. A. Kherani: Optimal Random Access in Networks with Two-Way Traffic, in PIMRC 2004, Spain.
3. E. Altman, A. A. Kherani, P. Michiardi and R. Molva: Non-cooperative Forwarding in Ad-hoc Networks, INRIA Report No. RR-5116, Sophia-Antipolis, France, February 2004.
4. Bertsekas, D., Gallager, R.: Data Networks. Prentice Hall, (1992).
5. Bharghavan, V., Demers, A., Shenker, S., Zhang, L.: MACAW: A Media Access Protocol for Wireless LANs. ACM SIGCOMM, (1994).
6. Borkar, V. S.: Asynchronous Stochastic Approximation. SIAM Journ. of Control and Optimization, **36** (1998).
7. V. S. Borkar and A. A. Kherani: Random Access in Wireless Ad Hoc Networks as a Distributed Game, in proceedings of WiOpt 2004, Cambridge.
8. Cali, F., Conti, M., Gregori, E.: Dynamic tuning of the IEEE 802.11 protocol to achieve a theoretical throughput limit. IEEE/ACM Transactions on Networking, (2000).
9. J. Crowcroft, R. Gibbens, F. Kelly, and S. Ostring. Modelling incentives for collaboration in mobile Ad-hoc networks. In *Proceedings of WiOpt'03*, Sophia-Antipolis, France, 3-5, March 2003.
10. D. Dutta, A. Goel and J. Heidemann, "Oblivious AQM and Nash Equilibria", IEEE Infocom, 2003.
11. M. Félegyházi, L. Buttyán and J. P. Hubaux, "Equilibrium analysis of packet forwarding strategies in wireless Ad-hoc entworks – the static case", PWC 2003 Personal Wireless Communications, Sept. 2003, Venice, Italy.
12. IEEE Computer Society LAN MAN Standards Committee.: Wireless LAN Medium Access Control (MAC) and Physical Layer (PHY) Specifications. IEEE Standard 802.11-1997, (1997).
13. Johnson, D., Maltz, D., Broch, J.: DSR: The Dynamic Source Routing Protocol for Multi Hop Wireless Ad Hoc Networks. Ad Hoc Networking, Addision-Wesley, (2001).
14. Karnik, A., Kumar, A.: Optimal Self-Organization of Wireless Sensor Networks. Infocom 2004.
15. H. J. Kushner and G. Yin, "Stochastic Approximation Algorithms and Applications," Springer-Verlag, 1997.
16. Kushner, H. J., Yin, G.: Stochastic Approximation Algorithms and Applications. Springer-Verlag, (1997).
17. A. Mas-Colell, M. D. Whinston and J. R. Green: Microeconomic Theory, Oxford Univ. Press, (1995).
18. P. Michiardi and R. Molva. A game theoretical approach to evaluate cooperation enforcement mechanisms in mobile Ad-hoc networks. In *Proceedings of WiOpt'03*, Sophia-Antipolis, France, 3-5, March 2003.
19. Perkins, C. E., Bhagwat, P.: Highly Dynamic Destination-Sequenced Distance-Vector Routing (DSDV) for Mobile Computers. Computer Communications Review, (1994).
20. J. B. Rosen: Existence and Uniqueness of Equlibrium Points for Concave N-Person Games, Econometrica, (1965).

21. L. Samuelson, "Subgame Perfection: An Introduction," in John Creedy, Jeff Borland and Jürgen Eichberger, eds., Recent Developments in Game Theory, Edgar Elgar Publishing, 1992, 1-42.
22. V. Srinivasan, P. Nuggehalli, C. F. Chiasserini and R. R. Rao, "Cooperation in wireless Ad-hoc networks", *Proceedings of IEEE Infocom*, 2003.
23. Sundaram, R. K.: A First Course in Optimization Theory. Cambridge University Press, (1999).
24. A. Urpi, M. Bonuccelli, and S. Giordano. Modelinig cooperation in mobile Ad-hoc networks: a formal description of selfishness. In *Proceedings of WiOpt'03*, Sophia-Antipolis, France, 3-5, March 2003.

# Admission Region of Multimedia Services for EDCA in IEEE 802.11e Access Networks

Rosario G. Garroppo, Stefano Giordano, Stefano Lucetti, and Luca Tavanti

Dept. of Information Engineering, University of Pisa,
Via Caruso, I-56122, Pisa, Italy
{r.garroppo, s.giordano, s.lucetti, luca.tavanti}@iet.unipi.it,
http://netgroup.iet.unipi.it

**Abstract.** This paper presents a simulation analysis for the evaluation of the admission region of a IEEE 802.11e network adopting the EDCA (Enhanced Distributed Channel Access) mechanism. In particular, this study gives an estimate of the number of QoS-aware applications, namely videoconference and Voice over IP (VoIP), that can be admitted to the transport service offered by the EDCA while satisfying their QoS requirements. The traffic sources adopted for the simulation are obtained from measurement campaigns led on the emulation of VoIP and videoconference services based respectively on the G.723.1 and the H.263 codecs. The results emphasize the bottleneck role played by the Access Point when services producing symmetrical traffic are conveyed over an 802.11e access network. Furthermore, the QoS parameters experienced in a mix of VoIP, videoconference and TCP traffic under EDCA are compared with those obtained when the DCF mechanism is adopted. This comparison clearly highlights the efficiency in traffic differentiation of the EDCA algorithm.

## 1   Introduction

While the IEEE 802.11 technology [11] is gaining wide popularity, particularly in its 11 Mbps extension known as 802.11b [12], it is also becoming clear that it can hardly be adopted to face the growth of multimedia services over wireless LANs. It does not provide any means to differentiate the transport service offered to various applications and cannot provide any guarantee on the timely delivery of frames[1].

The IEEE 802.11 working group has therefore created a new Task Group (TG11e) whose target is the definition of mechanisms for differentiating the radio channel access depending on the requirements of the supported traffic types. One of the most recent 802.11e draft standards [13] introduces two new modes of operation: an enhanced version of the legacy DCF, called EDCA, and an hybrid access method, called HCCA. EDCA, which we have focused our work on, defines four different transport modes, indicated as Access Categories (AC),

---

[1] The PCF mode partly accomplishes these tasks, but it is seldom implemented.

G. Kotsis and O. Spaniol (Eds.): Mobile and Wireless Systems, LNCS 3427, pp. 105–120, 2005.
© Springer-Verlag Berlin Heidelberg 2005

each having its own queue and MAC parameters (a detailed description is given in Section 2). The basic philosophy of this scheme is to give quicker access to medium to high priority traffic, i.e. traffic which is more sensitive to delay.

The activity carried out in the standardization body has been complemented by frenetic activity from research centers and universities that has produced a number of papers describing the behavior of the 802.11e service differentiation mechanism in the most diverse contexts[2]. While there is broad consensus about its fair capability to support real-time applications with a reasonable quality of service, it has also been shown that this does not come without pains. This relatively simple protocol provides less predictable performance than a reservation-based method and also suffers from network congestion. Scarce reliability of QoS guarantees, starvation of low priority traffic and unbalanced uplink/downlink bandwidths are the most serious drawbacks hampering the use of a distributed access mechanism such as EDCF or EDCA for multimedia services.

Just to cite a few examples, the authors of [4] remark that the EDCF could be optimized by adapting the access parameters at run-time, depending on network load and applications, and, for acceptable QoS provisioning, there should be an admission control process in place. The same conclusions are confirmed by [9], which, after performing several simulations under heavy load conditions, is able to show that low priority traffic rapidly experiences bandwidth shortage.

For these reasons, it can be argued that the support for service differentiation in wireless LAN cannot be easily achieved if disjoined from the relevant issue of admission control. In detail, it assumes a paramount relevance the determination of the number of users for each class that can be admitted to the service while satisfying the respective QoS requirements.

Works on the topic of the identification of the admission region have been recently proposed considering the plain 802.11 access method, which, however, does not provide service differentiation. In [6] the authors estimate an upper bound to the number of VoIP users that can be admitted in a 802.11(a/b) coverage area while maintaining the service level of already active voice traffic. The bound, calculated as a function of VoIP codec and length of the audio payload, proves the inadequacy of base-stations to handle a large number of VoIP calls and the inherent channel inefficiency of 802.11b at small frames sizes, as pointed out in several papers, such as [3][1][7]. The maximum number of VoIP calls is very low, and is further reduced by spatial distribution of the clients. A similar analysis, supported by extensive simulations, has been recently presented in [10], where the authors evaluate the capacity of an 802.11b system for a variety of scenarios. The capacity is found to be very sensitive to delay constraints and packet sizes, while almost independent of channel conditions. Furthermore, the impact on network capacity of different MAC-layer parameters has been discussed.

---

[2] Most of the works actually refers to previous versions of the 802.11e draft, thus taking into consideration the precursor of EDCA, called EDCF (Enhanced Distributed Coordination Function).

At present, to the best of our knowledge, the only work on admission control specifically designed for 802.11e networks is exposed in [8]. The authors propose and evaluate, through simulations, the behavior of a new admission control mechanism, but do not care of estimating the capacity of the system. The 802.11e draft itself suggests a distributed admission control algorithm in which the Access Point can control the traffic load from each AC as well as each station by periodically announcing the available bandwidth for each AC. This algorithm, however, is rather complex and of difficult implementation and has therefore received scarce attention from both the research and the industrial communities.

The main contribution of our activity is the determination of an admission region for videoconference and VoIP sources multiplexed with TCP traffic in a WLAN system supporting the EDCA mechanism, thus conforming to one of the most recent available versions of the draft. The number of videoconference and VoIP sources that can be accepted in the 802.11e coverage area has been evaluated by means of simulation, considering the actual QoS requirements that can be assumed for these services. In the study, a mapping between these services and the Access Categories defined in the draft standard is assumed.

## 2    Description of IEEE 802.11e EDCA

In this section we present an overview of the enhancements introduced by the EDCA access mechanism to guarantee service differentiation in IEEE 802.11 wireless LANs. Note that a Basic Service Set (BSS) supporting the new priority schemes of the 802.11e is now called QoS-capable BSS (QBSS). Stations operating under the 802.11e are called QoS-capable STAtions (QSTAs) and a QoS station which works as the centralized coordinator is called QoS-capable Access Point (QAP) [13].

EDCA maintains the distributed approach of the CSMA/CA protocol as in legacy DCF, but introduces four Access Categories (ACs), each one defining a priority level for channel access and having a corresponding transmission queue at the MAC layer. Payload from higher levels is assigned to a specific AC following its QoS requirements; according to the IEEE 802.1D standard [2], eight User Priority (UP) classes are defined. The mapping from UPs to ACs is defined by the 802.11e draft standard [13].

The medium contention rules for EDCA are the same as of legacy DCF, i.e. wait until the channel is idle for a given amount of time, then access/retry following exponential backoff rules in case of collision or transmission failures. In legacy DCF, each station (or STA) must sense the channel idle for Distributed Inter Frame Spacing (DIFS) time, which is equal for all the STAs. EDCA differentiates this value, as well as the other involved in the backoff procedure, in order to perform prioritization of the medium access for the different ACs.

Each one of the four ACs in a QSTA behaves like a virtual STA, independently contending with the others to gain access to the medium. Each AC having a frame to transmit listens on the medium and, when it senses the channel idle for a period of time equal to its Arbitration IFS (i.e. AIFS[AC]), starts decrementing its backoff timer, suspending it as soon as it detects that some other STA has started transmitting. A simplified time diagram of the mechanism is reported in Fig. 1. The AIFS for a given class is equal to a DIFS plus a certain number ($AIFSN$) of time-slots (whose duration is $20\mu s$ for DSSS PHY layer), depending on the considered AC; the higher the priority class, the lower the value of $AIFSN$. The exact values are reported in Table 1, along with the other relevant parameters used in 802.11e EDCA to differentiate the channel access procedure, which will be described further on. The corresponding values for legacy DCF stations are also reported (last row of the table).

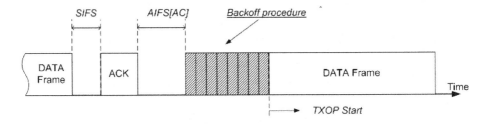

**Fig. 1.** The channel access procedure

**Table 1.** EDCA parameters

| AC | $AIFSN$ | $CW_{min}$ | $CW_{max}$ | $TXOPLimit$ |
|----|---------|------------|------------|-------------|
| 0 | 2 | 7 | 15 | 3.008 ms |
| 1 | 2 | 15 | 31 | 6.016 ms |
| 2 | 3 | 31 | 1023 | - |
| 3 | 7 | 31 | 1023 | - |
| DCF | 2 | 31 | 1023 | - |

The backoff time depends on a random integer number drawn from a uniform distribution between 1 and CW[AC]+1, where CW indicates the current value of the Contention Window. The values assumed by CW are in the interval $[CW_{min}[AC], CW_{max}[AC]]$, where $CW_{min}[AC]$ and $CW_{max}[AC]$ are further parameters used to differentiate the traffic treatment. Clearly, lower values of $CW_{min}[AC]$ and $CW_{max}[AC]$ will be assigned to high priority classes, as results from Table 1.

CW is updated after every transmission, being it successful or not. If the previous transmission was successful, CW assumes the value $CW_{min}$ for the related AC; otherwise, CW assumes the next value in the series $2^n - 1$, up to $CW_{max}$ value. After a predefined number of retransmission attempts, as defined in the standard, the frame is dropped.

Should two or more ACs in the same QSTA (or QAP) terminate their backoff period simultaneously, the contention is solved by an internal scheduler which assigns the grant to transmit (or Transmission Opportunity, TXOP) to the highest priority AC. Other virtual stations behave as if an external collision occurred. As in legacy DCF, when the medium is determined busy before the backoff counter is zero, the QSTA freezes its countdown until the medium is sensed idle for an AIFS again.

One of the most noticeable differences between DCF and EDCA is the adoption of packet bursting, introduced in IEEE 802.11e to achieve better medium utilization. Once a station (to be precise, an AC) has gained access to the medium, i.e. it has acquired a TXOP, it may transmit more than one frame without contending for the medium again: the station (AC) is allowed to send as many frames as it wishes, provided that the total medium access time does not exceed the $TXOPLimit[AC]$ bound, another parameter used to differentiate the service offered to the various ACs (higher priority ACs have higher $TXOPLimit$ values). To ensure that no other station interrupts the packet bursting, a Short IFS (SIFS) is used between the burst frames[3]. Should a collision occur during this period, packet bursting terminates. Note that IEEE 802.11e draft standard establishes that the QAP may dynamically adjust the contention window parameters as well as the $TXOPLimit$ for each AC by advertising the access parameters associated to each AC; this is done by setting the QoS Parameter Set Element in the beacon frame.

Summarizing, the transport service differentiation with EDCA is obtained giving different values to the $CW_{min}$, $CW_{max}$, the $AIFSN$ and the $TXOPLimit$ for each AC. Furthermore, these parameters may be dynamically adjusted by the QAP, and the adopted values communicated to every QSTA by means of the beacon frame. In our simulation study, the QoS Parameter Set Element is not set, thus all the QSTAs adopt the standard values of the EDCA parameters.

## 3   Simulation Model

The simulation study has been carried out using Network Simulator 2 (NS2) version v2.26 [16]. In particular, we used a patch developed by the Technical University of Berlin that models the EDCA mechanism [17]. The MAC layer of the patch has been updated in order to consider the four different AC parameters defined in the EDCA. This means that for each queue we can configure the values of the channel access parameters characterizing the AC, i.e. $AIFSN$, $CW_{min}$, $CW_{max}$ and $TXOPLimit$. In our simulation we have considered the AC and the channel access function parameters as defined in the Draft Standard 5.0 of 802.11e [13]. The model permits to establish a mapping among traffic flows and

---

[3] The SIFS is the shortest allowed IFS, therefore no other STA can sense the medium idle long enough to decrement its backoff counter or to start a transmission.

the AC by means of an appropriate field in the IP header of NS2. A relevant feature of the patch is the implementation of the Contention Free Burst (CFB), which permits a station to transmit frames for a time equal to *TXOPLimit* after winning the contention.

## 3.1    Validation of the Simulation Model

We performed a few tests in order to validate the simulation model. The tests consisted in comparing simulation and theoretical results in a simple scenario. In particular, we focused on the ACs having the *TXOPLimit* equal to zero. This implied considering the channel access function parameters defined for AC 2 and AC 3. In these conditions, when using a simple point-to-point connection, we could evaluate the maximum goodput[4] by analyzing the time budget necessary for the transmission of a frame, as presented in [7]. The obtained results are reported in Table 2, which details the simulation and theoretical maximum goodput for two different packet sizes (the worst case, 64 bytes, and the best case, 1472 bytes). It is relevant to emphasize that the maximum goodput has been evaluated at the 11 Mbps data rate considering a single point-to-point connection, hence, without collisions. The table shows a good accordance among theoretical and simulation results, with differences within the 1% in the worst cases.

**Table 2.** Comparison of theoretical and simulation results for the maximum goodput

|      | Packet Size | Theoretical goodput | Simulation goodput | Difference (%) |
|------|-------------|---------------------|--------------------|----------------|
| AC 3 | 64          | 0.511               | 0.506              | 0.98           |
| AC 3 | 1472        | 5.81                | 5.79               | 0.34           |
| AC 2 | 64          | 0.555               | 0.549              | 1.08           |
| AC 2 | 1472        | 6.05                | 6.03               | 0.33           |

# 4    Simulation Study

The simulation study is mainly aimed at evaluating the admission region for two relevant QoS-aware services such as VoIP and videoconference. The region is defined in a cartesian plane, where abscissa and ordinate components represent, respectively, the number of VoIP and videoconference sources that can be admitted in the system while guaranteeing their QoS requirements. The definition

---

[4] The maximum goodput is defined as the maximum rate at which user data, without considering the protocol overhead, is transferred.

of the QoS parameters is outlined in subsection 4.2, while the adopted traffic sources are presented in the next subsection. Then, the following subsections describe the simulation scenario and the obtained results.

## 4.1  Traffic Sources

The traffic data acquisition has been carried out in an experimental testbed, by means of the software protocol analyzer Ethereal [5]. From the acquired data, through the use of an ad hoc post processing routine, we have obtained the trace file, which holds the inter-arrival times and the sizes of the IP packets belonging to a particular traffic flow.

The voice call employed the G.723.1 codec with VAD (Voice Activity Detection), which produces information at 6.3 Kbps when the voice activity is detected. The codec fills every packet with 24 bytes (obviously, to obtain the packet size at IP or lower levels we must consider the protocol overhead). For the videoconference service, that employed the H.263 codec of Microsoft Net-Meeting, we have taken two different traffic data sets, each referring to audio and video packets transmitted by one of the two involved users. The statistics on the acquired traffic are summarized in Table 3.

**Table 3.** Voice and Videoconference traffic characteristics

|                             | Voice | Videoconference |
|-----------------------------|-------|-----------------|
| Mean packet rate (pps)      | 21.58 | 58.82           |
| Mean IP packet size (bit)   | 512   | 5664            |
| Mean throughput (Kbps)      | 11.05 | 333.16          |

The length of the traffic data acquisition has been set long enough to permit an accurate estimation of the QoS parameters. Considering a packet loss rate of $10^{-3}$, we have assumed that each source should transmit at least $10^4$ packets. This means that, being the VoIP source the most critical (it has the lower mean packet rate, 21.58 pps), our acquisition period is about 1000 seconds (actually, 1000 seconds enable the transmission of about $2 \cdot 10^4$ packets).

## 4.2  QoS Parameters

For the definition of the QoS parameters associated to the considered services, we refer to the ITU-T recommendations Y.1540 [14] and Y.1541 [15]: the first defines the QoS parameters and how to measure them, the second introduces the Class of Service (CoS) concept and defines six different classes. For each CoS, the Y.1541 recommendation indicates the maximum values that the QoS parameters should not exceed. Table 4 summarizes these values (NS indicates that the value for the parameter is Not Specified). The significance of the parameters considered in the table is described in the following:

- IPTD (IP Packet Transfer Delay) is the time necessary to transfer a packet from the network interface of a measurement point (e.g a transmitter) to that of the companion measurement point (e.g. the receiver).
- The Mean IP Packet Transfer Delay is the arithmetic average of IPTD for a population of interest.
- IPDV (IP Packet Delay Variation) is the difference between the IPTD and a fixed reference IPTD value, which can be assumed equal to the Mean IPTD.
- IPLR (IP Packet Loss Ratio) represents the ratio of the total lost IP packets to the total transmitted IP packets.
- IPER (IP Packet Error Ratio) can be estimated as the ratio of the total errored IP packets to the total of successful and errored IP packets.

The performance parameters are estimated considering the single packet flow, which can be identified by all or some of the following fields: the destination IP address, the source IP address, the transport protocol port and the CoS. As can be observed from the table, in Class 0 and Class 1 the upper bounds of the four considered QoS parameters are well defined. This feature let us deduce that Classes 0 and 1 have been thought for real time services. Classes 2 and 3 differ from Classes 0 and 1 only in terms of IPDV, which is not specified. Hence, Classes 2 and 3 can be adopted for data transfer requiring only IPTD constraints. Finally, Class 4 is defined for services with no strict delay constraints, such as videostreaming, while Class 5 permits to support best effort services. Features and examples of the services that can be supported are the following:

- Class 0 is for real-time, sensitive to delay jitter, high interactivity services such as Voice over IP and videoconference;
- Class 1 is like Class 0, but for a medium-low interactivity service such as some kind of Voice over IP or videoconference services;
- Class 2 is for data transfer with high interactivity, such as signaling services;
- Class 3 is like Class 2 but for low interactivity services, such as some kind of signaling;
- Class 4 is for only data loss sensitive services, such as data transfer and video streaming;
- Class 5 is for best effort services.

It is worth mentioning that user traffic can be dropped by the network when it exceeds the figures specified in the traffic contract between the user and the network operator. The packets dropped by this preventive action of congestion control performed by the network are not considered in the estimation of the IPLR.

## 4.3   Simulation Scenario

The simulation scenario is depicted in Fig. 2. In order to have ideal channel conditions, we set a very low distance between QAP and QSTAs. Furthermore,

**Table 4.** Objective values (upper bounds) for different QoS parameters for each CoS

| Class | 0 | 1 | 2 | 3 | 4 | 5 |
|---|---|---|---|---|---|---|
| Mean IPTD $[ms]$ | 100 | 400 | 100 | 400 | 1000 | NS |
| IPDV $[ms]$ | 50 | 50 | NS | NS | NS | NS |
| IPLR | $10^{-3}$ | $10^{-3}$ | $10^{-3}$ | $10^{-3}$ | $10^{-3}$ | NS |
| IPER | $10^{-4}$ | $10^{-4}$ | $10^{-4}$ | $10^{-4}$ | $10^{-4}$ | NS |

we considered high transmission rate and low latency for the wired link in order to have in the EDCA mechanism the only bottleneck of the system. The scenario is then composed by a variable number of VoIP and Videoconference users, whose traffic is generated from the data acquired in our experimental session as previously described. Each QSTA supports the EDCA mechanism and has a VoIP or videoconference session active with a companion station on the wired network. During each active session, traffic is produced in both directions. Among the sources, a single couple of stations simulates a data transfer, based on the TCP protocol, by setting up a greedy file transfer. The use of a single client-server connection for data transfer can be backed by two reasons: first, TCP sources can modify their data rate according to the congestion state of the network and, second, the issues associated to guarantee a minimum bandwidth to TCP sources are outside of the scope of this study.

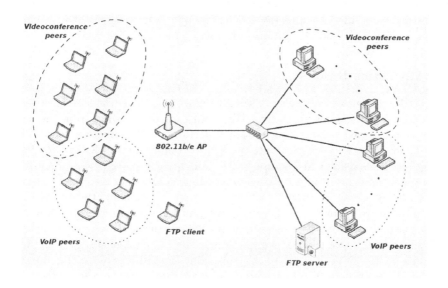

**Fig. 2.** Simulation scenario

For the estimation of the admission region, we assume that packets exceeding the Mean IPTD and the IPDV are dropped by the application. Then, we compute a Virtual IPLR (vIPLR) as the ratio between the total number of discarded packets and the transmitted packets of the considered traffic flow. The total number of discarded packets is obtained as the sum of the number of lost packets (due, for example, to buffer overflow or to reaching the maximum number of retransmissions at MAC layer) and of the packets exceeding the Mean IPDT and IPDV limits. Finally, we suppose that a new user service cannot be accepted by the system if its activation implies that the estimated vIPLR of at least one of the active CoS exceeds the IPLR upper bound.

The constraints for the determination of the admission region are obtained from Table 4 after associating a Class of Service to VoIP and videoconference services. In particular, we reckoned VoIP services to require the QoS parameter constraints defined for Class 0, while the videoconference those for Class 1. Then, in the mapping of EDCA's AC to the CoS, we have assumed that VoIP traffic can be transported with AC 0, while AC 1 is used by the videoconference traffic; the traffic of the TCP connection has been transmitted using AC 2.

Several sets of simulation have been carried out using different number of VoIP and Videoconference sessions simultaneously active. For each set we carried out at least 10 different simulations having diverse seeds for the random number generators in order to estimate mean values and 95% Confidence Interval for the vIPLR parameter.

The admission region has been obtained as the set of scenarios, each one characterized by a different number of VoIP and videoconference users, where the constraints on the upper value of IPLR are satisfied (i.e. a value lower than $10^{-3}$, found for the 95%-CI of vIPLR). The analysis of the QoS parameters has been carried out in both directions of the traffic flows exchanged in a single session, i.e. from the mobile station to the wired one and vice versa.

### 4.4   Simulation Results

We start the discussion of the simulation results considering the simple scenario where only VoIP sources are active. We recall that in our simulation the TCP connection is always present. The obtained performance parameters, reported in Table 5, refer to two scenarios with zero videoconference and 21 and 22 VoIP sources (columns named "0-21" and "0-22") and are the arithmetic averages over simulations carried out with different seeds. Each parameter has been observed for both the upstream (from mobile towards wired stations) and the downstream flows, in order to point out if there is a different behavior in the two directions of traffic. For both flows we observed about 20000 packets.

From the table, we can deduce that the system is unable to satisfy the QoS requirements for 22 VoIP sources: the constraint on vIPLR is not satisfied in the downlink stream[5] (see Table 4, where the constraints are reported). Hence, a first point delimiting the admission region is represented by the scenario where

---

[5] The value exceeding the constraint is reported in bold.

**Table 5.** Simulation results for the 0-21 and 0-22 scenarios

|  | 0-21 | | 0-22 | |
|  | Uplink | Downlink | Uplink | Downlink |
| --- | --- | --- | --- | --- |
| Mean IPTD (ms) | 1.72 | 2.87 | 1.82 | 3.06 |
| Lost packets | 1.55 | 5.95 | 2.66 | 9.09 |
| Discarded packets for IPTD | 0.08 | 2.23 | 0.21 | 5.46 |
| Discarded packets for IPDV | 0.6 | 4.31 | 0.86 | 8.72 |
| vIPLR $(10^{-4})$ | 1.11 | 6.29 | 1.85 | **11.7** |
| 95%-CI $(10^{-4})$ | 0.789 | 2.06 | 1.14 | 4.03 |

**Table 6.** Simulation results for the 5-0 scenario

|  | Uplink | Downlink |
| --- | --- | --- |
| Mean IPTD (ms) | 3.59 | 9.05 |
| Lost packets | 0.12 | 3.78 |
| Discarded packets for IPTD | 0 | 0 |
| Discarded packets for IPDV | 0.06 | **206.38** |
| vIPLR $(10^{-4})$ | 0.03 | **35.5** |
| 95%-CI $(10^{-4})$ | 0.18 | 27.2 |

zero videoconference and 21 audio sources are active. It should be noted, however, that in the uplink the vIPLR is always under the $10^{-3}$ upper bound, even in the 0-22 scenario. This remark highlights the bottleneck role played by the QAP: considering all the four ACs, the QAP has the same probability to acquire the right to transmit a frame as whatever QSTA, while it is expected to transmit a traffic that is about N times the traffic generated by a single mobile station (with N being the number of mobile stations having an active symmetrical and bidirectional session in the coverage area of the AP). For completeness, we report Fig. 3 and Fig. 4 showing the complementary probability of IPTD and IPDV parameters observed for upstream and downstream traffic in the 0-21 and 0-22 scenarios. From these figures, we can note the different behavior of the downstream link with respect to the uplink.

A second set of simulations shows that the considered system is unable to satisfy the QoS requirements of 5 videoconference users (scenario 5-0). The details on the observed performance parameters are summarized in Table 6. In this case the number of transmitted packets for each direction is about 59000. In this case too, the maximum number of active sources satisfying their QoS requirements is imposed by the IPDV parameter in the downlink. In addition, the large packet sizes produced by videoconference sources lead to higher performance differences between uplink and downlink: the vIPLR experimented by the downlink flow is three order of magnitude higher than that observed in the

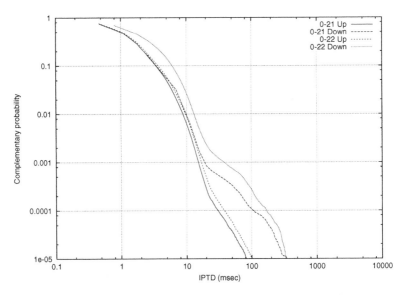

**Fig. 3.** Complementary probability of audio IPTD for the 0-21 and 0-22 scenarios

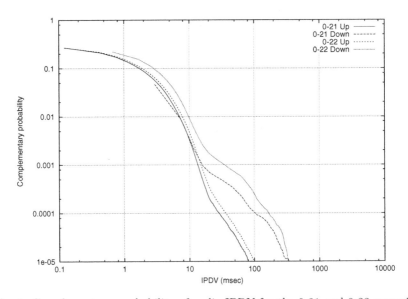

**Fig. 4.** Complementary probability of audio IPDV for the 0-21 and 0-22 scenarios

uplink flow ($3.55 \cdot 10^{-3}$ vs. $3 \cdot 10^{-6}$). This is a further proof of the congesting behavior of the AP. It is also worth noting that the main contribution to the vIPLR is given by the packets discarded for overcoming the IPDV upper bound.

This time, for the sake of simplicity, we report just the complementary probability of the IPTD parameter observed for upstream and downstream traffic, see Fig. 5. Similar behavior has been observed for the complementary probability of IPDV parameter.

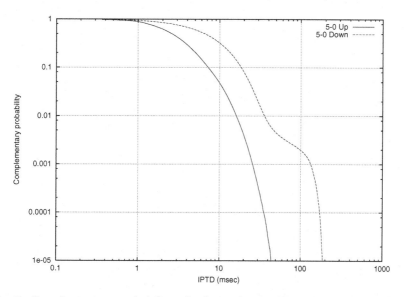

**Fig. 5.** Complementary probability of videoconference IPTD for the 5-0 scenario

After the evaluation of the boundaries of the admission region in case of homogeneous QoS aware sources (i.e. only VoIP or videoconference sources), we have taken into account all the other points of the admission region mixing active VoIP and videoconference sources. The results of this work are depicted in Fig. 6 where the x-axis represents the number of VoIP sources and the y-axis represents the number of videoconference sources. The grayed area indicates the admission region, in terms of joint number of voice and videoconference applications which can be activated concurrently in the QBSS satisfying the QoS requirements. The results show the low number of simultaneous videoconferences that can be admitted. A similar statement holds for the VoIP services: in spite of the low traffic produced by a single source (a VoIP service requires about 11 Kbps for each direction), only 21 VoIP sessions can be simultaneous active if we want to satisfy their QoS requirements. The number of QoS-aware services that can be simultaneously supported by the 802.11e technology is therefore surprisingly low. This is due to the constraints of QoS imposed to the transport service,

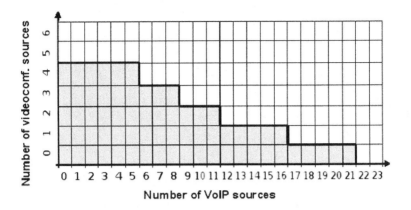

**Fig. 6.** The admission region

to the distributed EDCA mechanism and to the presence of just a single TCP traffic session.

## 4.5   Comparison Between 802.11b and 802.11e

To verify the actual performance improvement of the EDCA, we carried out the same tests on the admission region with the 802.11b version [12], keeping the same QoS limits and the same traffic parameters to provide for a fair comparison. The "b" version of IEEE 802.11 does not allow to split the different streams into separate queues, but they are handled together by the same queue with no priority levels. Therefore we should expect highly variable delivery times for all the streams.

The results, reported in Table 7, have been obtained for the scenario with 0 videoconference and 1 VoIP sessions. We can easily deduce that the DCF does not allow any VoIP communication when a TCP connection is active. Moreover, we can observe that this is once again due to the bottleneck represented by the AP in the downlink: for the uplink traffic the vIPLR limit is satisfied.

The reason for the non-admission of the real-time streams is the presence of the TCP traffic, which is kept active. To confirm this statement, we ran a simulation where the data traffic has been turned off and where 10 VoIP calls have been inserted. Under this configuration the obtained values were well below the imposed limits. The figures for the considered QoS parameters in the downlink are shown in Table 8.

The difficulties in maintaining the real-time communications come from the excessive delay that the packets experience, resulting in a high drop rate. We can put this fact in relation with the presence of the TCP traffic if we consider that the TCP protocol expects a confirmation for the correct reception of each packet. This confirmation translates into another packet, the ACK packet, that is

**Table 7.** Statistics for the audio streams in the 0-1 bidirectional configuration

|  | Uplink | Downlink |
|---|---|---|
| Mean IPTD (ms) | 3.02 | 3.29 |
| Lost packets | 0 | 0.2 |
| Discarded packets for IPTD | 0.6 | 17.6 |
| Discarded packets for IPDV | 4 | 9 |
| vIPLR $(10^{-4})$ | 2.27 | **13.1** |
| 95%-CI $(10^{-4})$ | 1.39 | 34.4 |

**Table 8.** Downlink statistics for the 10 audio streams without TCP traffic

|  | Downlink |
|---|---|
| Mean IPTD (ms) | 0.58 |
| Lost packets | 0.06 |
| Discarded packets for IPTD | 0 |
| Discarded packets for IPDV | 0 |
| vIPLR $(10^{-4})$ | 0.03 |
| 95%-CI $(10^{-4})$ | 0.06 |

a further burden on the AP's queue. Hence all the packets, including multimedia ones, are subject to increased delivery times.

# 5    Conclusions

The aim of this work was determining, via simulation, the admission region for multimedia streams for the 802.11e EDCA protocol. In particular, we focused on VoIP and videoconference services, adopting G.723.1 and H.263 codecs respectively. The simulator has been fed with values drawn from measurements of real VoIP and videoconference sessions.

The results highlights on one hand the efficiency of transport differentiation offered by the EDCA's ACs, while, on the other hand, it has emerged the presence of a bottleneck at the AP's transmission queue (towards the mobile nodes). Hence the admission region turned out to be dependent on the overcoming of the limits imposed by the ITU-T Y1541 recommendation by the streams originated at the fixed stations.

Simulations have also been run to quantify the improvements with respect to the legacy 802.11 DCF mode, whose inability to guarantee the QoS requirements has been proven in the presence of TCP traffic.

# References

1. G. Anastasi, E. Borgia, M. Conti, E. Gregori, IEEE 802.11 ad hoc networks: performance measurements, in *Proc. of the 23rd International Conference on Distributed Computing Systems Workshops*, 2003, Pages 758-763.
2. ANSI/IEEE Std 802.1D, Information technology - telecommunications and information exchange between systems - local and metropolitan area networks - common specifications. Part 3: Media Access Control (MAC) bridges, 1998 Edition.
3. M.G. Arranz, R. Aguero, L. Munoz, P. Mahonen, Behavior of UDP-based applications over IEEE 802.11 wireless networks, in *Proc. of the 12th IEEE International Symposium on Personal, Indoor and Mobile Radio Communications*, 30 Sept.-3 Oct. 2001, Volume 2, Pages F72-F77.
4. S. Choi, J. del Prado, S. Shankar, S. Mangold, IEEE 802.11e Contention-Based Channel Access (EDCF) Performance Evaluation, in *Proc. of IEEE International Conference on Communications*, 11-15 May 2003, Volume 2, Pages 1151-1156.
5. Ethereal network protocol analyzer, http://www.ethereal.com.
6. S. Garg, M. Kappes, Can I add a VoIP call?, in *Proc. of the IEEE International Conference on Communications*, 11-15 May 2003, Volume 2, Pages 779-783.
7. R. G. Garroppo, S. Giordano, S. Lucetti, IEEE 802.11b performance evaluation: convergence of theoretical, simulation and experimental results, in *Proc. of Networks 2004*, Volume 1, Pages 405-410.
8. D. Gu, J. Zhang, A new measurement-based admission control method for IEEE802.11 wireless local area networks, in *Proc. of the 14th IEEE Personal, Indoor and Mobile Radio Communications*, 7-10 September 2003, Volume 3, Pages 2009-2013.
9. D. He, C. Q. Shen, Simulation study of IEEE 802.11e EDCF, in *Proc. of the 57th IEEE Semiannual Vehicular Technology Conference*, 22-25 April 2003, Volume 1, Pages 685-689.
10. D. P. Hole, F. A. Tobagi, Capacity of an IEEE 802.11b Wireless LAN supporting VoIP, *Proc. of the IEEE International Conference on Communications*, 20-24 June 2004, Volume 1, Pages 196-201.
11. IEEE Std 802.11-1999, Part 11: Wireless LAN Medium Access Control (MAC) and Physical Layer (PHY) Specifications, 1999 Ed.
12. IEEE Std 802.11b-1999, Part11: Wireless LAN Medium Access Control (MAC) and Physical Layer (PHY) specifications: Higher-Speed Physical Layer Extension in the 2.4 GHz Band, September 1999.
13. IEEE Std 802.11e/D5.0, Draft Supplement to Part 11: Wireless Medium Access Control (MAC) and Physical Layer (PHY) specifications: Medium Access Control (MAC) Enhancements for Quality of Service (QoS), July 2003.
14. ITU-T Rec. Y.1540, IP Packet Transfer and Availability Performance Parameters, December 2002.
15. ITU-T Rec. Y.1541, Network Performance Objectives for IP-Based services, May 2002.
16. The Network Simulator - ns-2, http://www.isi.edu/nsnam/ns.
17. Sven Wiethölter, Christian Hoene, An IEEE 802.11e EDCF and CFB Simulation Model for ns-2, http://www.tkn.tu-berlin.de/research/802.11e_ns2.

# Admission Control Policies in Multiservice Cellular Networks: Optimum Configuration and Sensitivity

David García, Jorge Martínez, and Vicent Pla

Universidad Politécnica de Valencia (UPV)
ETSIT, Camino de Vera s/n, 46022 Valencia, Spain
dagarro@doctor.upv.es, (jmartinez, vpla)@dcom.upv.es

**Abstract.** We evaluate different call admission control policies in various multiservice cellular scenarios. For each of the studied policies we obtain the maximum calling rate that can be offered to the system to achieve a given QoS objective defined in terms of blocking probabilities. We propose an optimization methodology based on a hill climbing algorithm to find the optimum configuration for most policies. The results show that policies of the trunk reservation class outperform policies that produce a product-form solution and the improvement ranges approximately between 5 and 15% in the scenarios studied.

## 1   Introduction

Call Admission Control (CAC) is a key aspect in the design and operation of multiservice cellular networks that provide QoS guarantees. Different CAC strategies have been proposed in the literature which differ in the amount of information that the decision process has available. Obviously, as more information is fed into the process that decides if a new call is accepted or rejected both the system performance and the implementation complexity increase. We study a class of CAC policies for which the decision to accept a new call, say for example of service $r$, depends only on either the number of resource units occupied by the calls in progress of service $r$ (which produce a product-form solution) or the number of free resource units in the system (trunk reservation). The physical meaning of a unit of resources will depend on the specific technological implementation of the radio interface.

Two sets of parameters are required to obtain the optimum configuration for these policies: those that describe the services as Markovian processes and those that specify the QoS objective. The QoS objective is defined in terms of the blocking probabilities for both new setup requests and handover requests. In a wireless scenario this distinction is required because a call being forced to terminate due to a handover failure is considered more harmful than the rejection of a new call setup request.

The configuration of a CAC policy specifies the action (accept/reject a new/handover request from each service) that must be taken at each system state in order to maximize the offered calling rate while meeting the QoS objective.

For the class of CAC policies under study, an important question that arises is how the performance of simple policies that produce a product-form solution compare to the performance of the trunk reservation policies and how sensitive these policies are to the tolerance of system parameters and to overloads. Surprisingly, and to the best

G. Kotsis and O. Spaniol (Eds.): Mobile and Wireless Systems, LNCS 3427, pp. 121–135, 2005.
© Springer-Verlag Berlin Heidelberg 2005

of our knowledge, no studies have been published so far comparing the performance and sensitiveness of these policies when deployed in cellular access networks.

For a monoservice scenario, it has been shown in [1] that two trunk reservations polices named the *Guard Channel* and the *Fractional Guard Channel*[1] are optimum for common QoS objective functions. More recently, the multiservice scenario has been studied in [2], where using an approximate fluid model the optimum admission policy is also found to be of the trunk reservation class.

We study a representative selection of policies that produce a product-form solution, which include: i) *Complete Sharing*; ii) *Integer Limit* [3]; iii) *Fractional Limit* [4]; iv) *Upper Limit and Guaranteed Minimum* (ULGM) [5]; v) *Fractional Limit and Integer Limit*; vi) *ULGM and Integer Limit*; vii) *ULGM and Fractional Limit*; and, viii) *ULGM with Fractional and Integer Limits*. We also study a representative selection of trunk reservation policies, which include: ix) *Multiple Guard Channel* [6]; and, x) *Multiple Fractional Guard Channel* [7,8]. Details for all these policies are given in the next section.

For each policy and for each possible configuration of them we determine the maximum calling rate that can be offered to the system in order to satisfy the QoS objective. The result of this study is called the solution space and its peak value is called the system capacity for the CAC policy. We obtain the solution space for each policy in five different scenarios.

The main contributions of our work are: i) the determination of the optimum configuration for different multiservice CAC policies in various common scenarios using a novel hill-climbing algorithm; ii) the determination of the system capacity for each scenario (which is attained at the optimum configuration); and iii) the sensitivity analysis of the performance of the different policies to both the tolerance of the values of the configuration parameters and to overloads. The deployment of a hill-climbing algorithm drastically reduces the computational complexity of the process that determines the optimum configuration of a policy and, for example, compares quite favorably to the one proposed in [8] for the Multiple Fractional Guard Channel policy.

We use the theory of Markov Decision Processes (MDP) [10] along with linear programming techniques to obtain the optimum CAC policy and its configuration and we find that the policy is of the Randomized Stationary (RS) type [9]. This policy outperforms previous policies and is considered as a performance upper bound in the comparative study. Clearly the performance of the Complete Sharing policy defines the lower bound.

The remaining of the paper is structured as follows: in Section 2 we describe the model of the system as well as the CAC policies under study. In Section 3 we describe the RS policy in detail, formulating a method for the design of the CAC policy as the solution to a linear program. Section 4 justifies the applicability of the hill climbing algorithm for the determination of the optimum configuration of a policy. In Section 5 we compute the system capacity for each of the CAC policies under study. Section 6 discuses how the CAC policies behave under overload conditions. Finally, Section 7 concludes the paper.

---

[1] In [1] FGC is referred to as *Limited FGC*.

# 2    System Model and Admission Control Policies

We consider a single cell, where a set of $R$ services contend for $C$ resource units. For any service $r$ ($1 \leq r \leq R$), new setup requests arrive according to a Poisson process with mean rate $\lambda_r^n$ and request $c_r$ resource units per call. The duration of a service $r$ call is exponentially distributed with rate $\mu_r^c$, the cell residence time or dwell time of a service $r$ call is exponentially distributed with rate $\mu_r^d$. Hence, the holding time of the resources occupied by a service $r$ call is exponentially distributed with rate $\mu_r = \mu_r^c + \mu_r^d$. We will also consider that handover requests arrive according to a Poisson process with mean rate $\lambda_r^h$. Although the value of $\lambda_r^h$ can be determined by a fixed point iteration method that balances the incoming and outgoing handover flows of a cell as described [11], we will suppose it is a known fraction of the value of $\lambda_r^n$. The QoS objective is expressed as blocking probabilities for both new setup requests ($B_r^n$) and handover requests ($B_r^h$). The handover blocking probabilities are related to the forced termination probabilities of accepted calls through the expression [11]

$$B_r^{ft} = \frac{B_r^h}{\left(\mu_r^c / \mu_r^d\right) + B_r^h}$$

Let the system state vector be $n \equiv (n_1^n, n_1^h, ..., n_R^n, n_R^h)$, where $n_r^{n,h}$ is the number of service $r$ calls in progress in the cell that where initiated as a successful setup request or a handover request respectively. We will denote by $c(n) = \sum_{r=1}^{R} \left(n_r^n + n_r^h\right) \cdot c_r$ the number of busy resource units in state $n$. Let $S_p$ be the state space under policy $P$. For example, for the Complete Sharing policy $S_{CS} = \left\{ n \in N^{2R} \middle| \sum_{r=1}^{R} \left(n_r^n + n_r^h\right) \cdot c_r \leq C \right\}$. The stochastic process $n(t)$, which gives the system state at time $t$, is an irreducible finite-state continuous-time Markov chain with a unique steady-state probability vector $\pi$.

The definition of each CAC policy under study is as follows:
1. Complete Sharing (CS). A request is admitted provided there are enough free resource units available in the system.
2. Integer Limit (IL). Two parameters are associated with service $r$: $l_r^n$ for new setup requests and $l_r^h$ for handover requests, $l_r^n, l_r^h \in N$. A service $r$ request that arrives in state $n$ is accepted if $(n_r^{n,h} + 1) \leq l_r^{n,h}$ and blocked otherwise.
3. Fractional Limit (FL). Four parameters are assigned to service $r$: $t_r^n, t_r^h \in N$ and $q_r^n, q_r^h \in [0,1]$. A service $r$ request is accepted with probability one if $(n_r^{n,h} + 1) \leq t_r^{n,h}$, otherwise new setup requests are accepted with probability $q_r^n$ and handover requests with probability $q_r^h$.
4. Upper Limit and Guaranteed Minimum (ULGM). Service $r$ requests have access to two sets of resources: a private set and a shared set. The number of resource units in the private set available for new setup requests is denoted as $(s_r^n \cdot c_r)$ and for handover requests as $(s_r^h \cdot c_r)$, $s_r^n, s_r^h \in N$. Therefore the size of the shared set is $C - \sum_{r=1}^{R} (s_r^n + s_r^h) \cdot c_r$. A service $r$ request is accepted if $(n_r^{n,h}+1) \leq s_r^{n,h}$ or if there are enough free resource units in the shared set, otherwise it is blocked.
5. Fractional Limit and Integer Limit (FL+IL). Six parameters are associated with service $r$: $t_r^n, t_r^h, l_r^n, l_r^h \in N$, $q_r^n, q_r^h \in [0,1]$. A service $r$ request is accepted with probability one if $(n_r^{n,h} + 1) \leq t_r^{n,h}$, it is accepted with probability $q_r^{n,h}$ if $t_r^{n,h} < (n_r^{n,h}+1) \leq l_r^{n,h}$, and blocked otherwise.

6. ULGM and Integer Limit (ULGM+IL). Four parameters are associated with service $r$: $s_r^n, s_r^h, l_r^n, l_r^h \in N$. A service $r$ request is accepted if $(n_r^{n,h}+1) \leq s_r^{n,h}$ or if there are enough free resource units in the shared set and $(n_r^{n,h}+1) \leq l_r^{n,h}$, and blocked otherwise.

7. ULGM and Fractional Limit (ULGM+FL). Six parameters are associated with service $r$: $s_r^n, s_r^h, t_r^n, t_r^h \in N$ and $q_r^n, q_r^h \in [0,1]$. A service $r$ request is accepted with probability one if $(n_r^{n,h}+1) \leq s_r^{n,h}$ or if there are enough free resource units in the shared set and $(n_r^{n,h}+1) \leq t_r^{n,h}$, it is accepted with probability $q_r^{n,h}$ if there are enough free resource units in the shared set and $(n_r^{n,h}+1) > t_r^{n,h}$, and blocked otherwise.

8. ULGM with Fractional and Integer Limits (ULGM+FL+IL). Eight parameters are associated with service $r$: $s_r^n, s_r^h, t_r^n, t_r^h, l_r^n, l_r^h \in N$ and $q_r^n, q_r^h \in [0,1]$. A service $r$ request is accepted with probability one if $(n_r^{n,h}+1) \leq s_r^{n,h}$ or if there are enough free resource units in the shared set and $(n_r^{n,h}+1) \leq t_r^{n,h}$, it is accepted with probability $q_r^{n,h}$ if there are enough free resource units in the shared set and $t_r^{n,h} < (n_r^{n,h}+1) \leq l_r^{n,h}$, and blocked otherwise.

9. Multiple Guard Channel (MGC). Two parameters are associated with service $r$: $l_r^n, l_r^h \in N$. A service $r$ request that arrives in state $n$ is accepted if $c(n) + c_r \leq l_r^{n,h}$ and blocked otherwise.

10. Multiple Fractional Guard Channel (MFGC). Four parameters are associated with service $r$: $t_r^n, t_r^h \in N$ and $q_r^n, q_r^h \in [0,1]$. A service $r$ request that arrives in state $n$ is accepted with probability one if $c(n) + c_r < t_r^{n,h}$, accepted with probability $q_r^{n,h}$ if $c(n) + c_r = t_r^{n,h}$, and blocked otherwise.

11. Randomized Stationary (RS). Each system state is assigned with a set of probabilities $q(n) = \{ q_1^n(n), q_1^h(n), \dots, q_R^n(n), q_R^h(n) \}$, $q(n) \in [0,1]^{2R}$. A service $r$ request that arrives in state $n$ is accepted with probability $q_r^{n,h}(n)$.

## 3    Randomized Stationary (RS) Policies

In this section we redefine the notation of the system state vector as $x \equiv (x_1, \dots, x_R)$, where $x_r = n_r^n + n_r^h$. In memoryless systems this redefinition does not suppose a loose of generality because once a request of service $r$ has been accepted in a cell, the time the resources will be held is a random variable which distribution is independent of the fact that the call had been initiated as new or as handover. Therefore the state space is $S_{RS} = \{ x \in N^R | \sum_{r=1}^R x_r \cdot c_r \leq C \}$. Each state has an associated set of actions $A(x) \in A$, where $A$ is the set of all actions, $A \equiv \{ a = (a_1, \dots, a_R) | a_r = 0,1,2 \}$. Element $a_r$ of an action $a$ encodes how service $r$ requests are handled, and its meaning is as follows: $a_r = 0$ reject both new and handover requests; $a_r = 1$ accept handover requests and reject new requests; and $a_r = 2$ accept both new and handover requests. When an RS policy is applied, one of the possible actions $A(x)$ is chosen at random according to the probability distribution $p_x(a)$, $a \in A(x)$, each time the process visits state $x$. The transition rate between states depends on the action chosen. Let $r_{xy}(a)$ denote the transition rate between states $x$ and $y$ when action $a$ is chosen. Transitions rates can be expressed as:

associated to arrivals ( $y = x + e_r$ )           associated to departures ( $y = x - e_r$ )

$$r_{xy}(a) = \begin{cases} 0 & \text{if } a_r = 0 \\ \lambda_r^h & \text{if } a_r = 1 \\ \lambda_r^n + \lambda_r^h & \text{if } a_r = 2 \end{cases} \qquad\qquad r_{xy}(a) = x_r \mu_r$$

where $r$ denotes the service type and $e_r$ is a vector whose entries are all 0 except for the r-th one which is 1.

The continuous time process is converted to a discrete time one by applying the uniformization approach. This is possible since a uniform upper bound $\Gamma$ can be found for the total outgoing rate from each state, where $\Gamma = \sum_{r=1}^{R} (\lambda_r^n + \lambda_r^h + C\mu_r)$. The transition probabilities for the uniformized discrete time Markov chain can be written as:

$$p_{xy}(a) = \begin{cases} r_{xy}(a)/\Gamma & y \neq x \\ 1 - \sum_{\substack{z \in S_{RS} \\ z \neq x}} p_{xz}(a) & y = x \end{cases}$$

Let us define the following cost functions:

$$c_r^n(a) = \begin{cases} 1 & \text{if } a_r = 0,\, 1 \\ 0 & \text{if } a_r = 2 \end{cases} \qquad\qquad c_r^h(a) = \begin{cases} 1 & \text{if } a_r = 0 \\ 0 & \text{if } a_r = 1,\, 2 \end{cases}$$

Note that the cost associated to any action is independent of the state, i.e. $c_r^{n,h}(x,a) = c_r^{n,h}(a) \forall x$. Cost functions are defined in such a way that their time average equals the corresponding blocking probability, i.e.

$$p_r^{n,h} = \lim_{k \to \infty} \frac{\left( E\left[ \sum_{t=0}^{k} c_r^{n,h}(x(t),a(t)) \right] \right)}{(k+1)}$$

where $x(t)$ and $a(t)$ represent the state and action at time t.

Let $p(x)$ denote the stationary probability of state $x$. If we introduce $p(x,a) = p(x)p_x(a)$, which denotes the probability of being in state x and choosing action x, then the following equation holds: $p(x) = \sum_{a \in A(x)} p(x,a)$.

## 3.1   Constrains

We now define several constraint sets that are subsequently used to formulate the design criterion:

**S0**
$$\sum_{a \in A(x)} p(x,a) = \sum_{\substack{y \in S_{RS} \\ a \in A(y)}} p_{yx}(a) p(y,a), \quad x \in S_{RS}$$

$$\sum_{\substack{x \in S_{RS} \\ a \in A(x)}} p(x,a) = 1 , \quad p(x,a) \geq 0$$

Constraints in S0 stem from the associated Markov chain equations.

**S1**
$$\sum_{\substack{x \in S_{RS} \\ a \in A(x)}} p(x,a) \cdot c_r^J(x,a) \leq B_r^J, \quad J = n,h, \quad r = 1,...,R$$

Parameters $B_r^{n,h}$ represent the maximum allowed values for the blocking probabilities.

## 3.2    Design Criterion

The design criterion considered here is made up of an objective function, which is to be minimized, plus the constraint sets defined above. As both objective functions and constraints are linear, the design problem can be formulated as a linear program. Thus the simplex method or other well-known algorithms can be used to solve the linear program. Different design criterion can be used [9] but in this work we only use the following:

**Minimize**    $\sum_{\substack{r= \\ x \in S_{RS} \\ a \in A(x)}}^{R} p(x,a)\left(c_r^n(x,a) + c_r^h(x,a)\right)$    subject to: S0 and S1

The solution of the linear program yields the values of $p(x,a)$ from which the steady-state probabilities $p(x)$ and the CAC policy configuration $p_x(a)$ are obtained; note that the values of $p_x(a)$ can be readily mapped to the RS policy description given in Section 2. In this way, the blocking probability for each service is minimized and upper bounded by the QoS objective. From a practical perspective it is worth noting that there may not exist a feasible solution if the value of $C$ is not high enough. Finding the minimum value of $C$ so that a feasible solution exists or, equivalently, finding the maximum offered traffic so that a feasible solution exists for a given value of $C$, are typical problems at the planning phase that can be solved by applying this design criterion.

# 4    Determination of the Optimum Policy Configuration

The common approach to carry out the CAC synthesis process in multiservice systems is by iteratively executing an analysis process. We refer to a synthesis process as the process that having as inputs the values of the system parameters ($\lambda_r^{n,h}, \mu_r, c_r$ and $C$) and the QoS objective ($B_r^{n,h}$), produces as output the optimum configuration (the thresholds $l_r^{n,h}, t_r^{n,h}, s_r^{n,h}$) for a given CAC policy. In contrast the analysis process is a process that having as inputs the value of the system parameter and the configuration for a given CAC policy produces as output the blocking probabilities for the different services.

Given that in general, the blocking probabilities are non-monotonic functions both of the offered load and the thresholds that specify most policy configurations; the common approach is to carry out a multidimensional search using for example meta-heuristics like genetic algorithms which are able to find a *good* configuration in a reasonable amount of time. It should also be pointed out that each execution of the analysis process requires solving the associated continuous-time Markov chain, for which we use the Gauss-Seidel algorithm when the solution has not a product-form. As shown before, the first eight policies are created by defining multiple thresholds with multiple weights for each traffic stream. It has been shown in [4] that these policies result in product-form solutions.

In this respect, formulating the problem of finding the optimum CAC policy by the theory of MDPs has as advantage that both the value of the system parameters and the

QoS objective become part of the inputs and as output we obtain the optimum configuration. Therefore no additional search is required.

The study of the optimum configuration for each policy is done for five different scenarios (A, B, C, D and E) that are defined in Table 1, where the $B_r^{n,h}$ are specified as percentages. The parameter $f_r$ represents the percentage of service $r$ new call requests, i.e., we suppose that the aggregated new call request rate is $\lambda = \sum_{r=1}^{R} \lambda_r^n$, $\lambda_r^n = f_r \lambda$. This simplification reduces the complexity of the multidimensional search and seems to be a common approach among operators. The parameters in Table 1 have been selected to explore possible trends in the numerical results, i.e., taking scenario A as a reference, scenario B represents the case where the ratio $c_1 / c_2$ is smaller, scenario C where $f_1 / f_2$ is smaller, scenario D where $B_1 / B_2$ is smaller and scenario E where $B_1$ and $B_2$ are equal.

**Table 1.** Definition of the scenarios under study

| | A | B | C | D | E |
|---|---|---|---|---|---|
| $c_1$ | 1 | 1 | 1 | 1 | 1 |
| $c_2$ | 2 | 4 | 2 | 2 | 2 |
| $f_1$ | 0.8 | 0.8 | 0.2 | 0.8 | 0.8 |
| $f_2$ | 0.2 | 0.2 | 0.8 | 0.2 | 0.2 |
| $B_1^n \%$ | 5 | 5 | 5 | 1 | 1 |
| $B_2^n \%$ | 1 | 1 | 1 | 2 | 1 |

| | A, B, C, D, E |
|---|---|
| $B_r^h \%$ | $0.1 B_r^n$ |
| $\lambda_r^n$ | $f_r \lambda$ |
| $\lambda_r^h$ | $0.5 \lambda_r^n$ |
| $\mu_1$ | 1 |
| $\mu_2$ | 3 |

In order to illustrate the algorithm we have chosen a simple example with only two service classes but without their associated handover streams. This allows us to represent the solution space in only three dimensions. Fig. 1 and Fig. 2 show the solution spaces when policies IL and MGC are deployed in scenario A with $C = 10$ resource units (recall that $c_1 = 1$, $c_2 = 2$, $B_1 = 5\%$ and $B_2 = 1\%$).

The configuration of both policies is defined by two parameters $l_1$ and $l_2$. Remember that when deploying the IL policy a call setup request from service $r$ is accepted only if $(n_r + 1) \le l_r$. On the other hand, when deploying the MGC policy a call setup request from service $r$ is accepted only if $c(n) + c_r \le l_r$. These two policies were selected because they have solution spaces with shapes that can be considered as representing two different families (with and without product form solution respectively). The MGC has been chosen instead of the MFGC policy, because it has the same number of configuration parameter as the IL policy.

The form of the solution spaces shown in Fig.1 and Fig.2 suggests that a hill-climbing algorithm could be an efficient approach to obtain the optimum configuration for most CAC policies. The hill-climbing algorithm works as follows. Given an

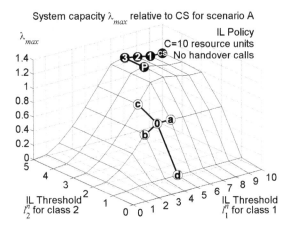

**Fig. 1.** Example of the use of a hill-climbing algorithm to determine the optimum configuration for the IL policy

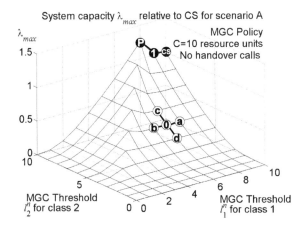

**Fig. 2.** Example of the use of a hill-climbing algorithm to determine the optimum configuration for the MGC policy

starting point in a $k$-dimensional discrete search space (for example, point 0 in both figures), the hill-climbing algorithm begins by computing the value of the function (the system capacity $\lambda_{max}$) for the two adjacent neighbors in each of the $k$ dimensions (points a, b, c and d in both figures). Then the algorithm selects as the new starting point the adjacent point with the largest function value (point c in both figures) and the process repeats iteratively until a local maximum is found. In this way the algorithm makes a number of successive unitary steps along each dimension of the search space and stops when it reaches the peak.

As defined in Section 1, each point of the solution space defines the maximum aggregated call request rate ( $\lambda = \lambda_1 + \lambda_2$ , $\lambda_r = f_r \lambda$ ) that can be offered to the system in order to satisfy the QoS objective. The plotted surfaces are obtained as follows. At each point, $\lambda_{max}$ is computed by a binary search process which has as input the value of the system parameters $\mu_r, c_r, C$ and the thresholds $l_r$, and produces as output the blocking probabilities $p_r$. The binary search process stops when it finds the $\lambda_{max}$ that meets the QoS objective $B_r$, $r=1,\dots, R$.

It should be noted that the system capacity is expressed as a relative value to the capacity obtained for the CS policy. When the solution space is continuous, for example for the MFGC policy, a gradual refinement process is used to reduce the size of the step once a promising region has been found, which is possibly close to the optimum.

A further reduction of the computation complexity can be obtained by observing that the optimum configuration (point P) for any policy is near the CS configuration (point CS), and therefore it is a good idea to select it as the starting point. In Fig. 1 points 1 to 3 and in Fig.2 point 1 illustrate a typical progression of the algorithm starting from the CS configuration and ending at the peak.

To gain additional insight into the problem we show the solution spaces for the IL and MGC policies in the scenario A, now considering their associated handover streams. Given that each policy has now a four-dimensional solution space in the scenario under study, an appropriate representation is required. We have chosen to represent slices of the solution space: variation of system capacity $\lambda_{max}$ (expressed as a relative value to the capacity obtained for the CS policy) as a function of each configuration parameter ($l_1^n, l_1^h, l_2^n$ and $l_2^h$) while keeping the others constant at their optimum values.

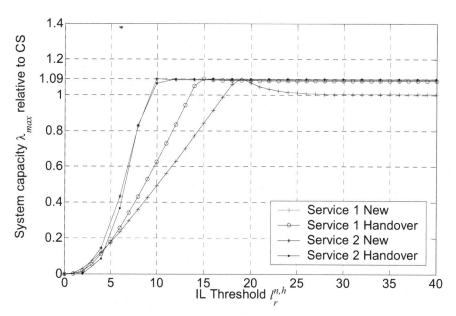

**Fig. 3.** Two-dimensional representation of the solution space for the IL policy in the scenario A with C=40

For the IL policy, Fig. 3 plots the slices of the solution space in scenario A with C=40. As it could be expected, the values of the configuration parameters at which the peak for $\lambda_{max}$ (1.09) is achieved are different. An interesting observation is that the peak value seems insensitive to the values of some configuration parameters in a quite large region. Unfortunately, the peak value seems sensitive to the value of $l_1^n$, that is, to the threshold defined for new calls of service 1.

This can be intuitively explained noting that if the system is loaded with $\lambda_{max}$ and we deploy the CS policy then the blocking probability achieved for the new calls of service 1 ( $p_1^n$ ) is far below its objective, while the blocking probabilities achieved by the other traffic streams are much closer to their objectives. In this scenario we can increase the capacity of the system by restricting the access to the new calls of service 1 (by decreasing its threshold if deploying the IL policy) and offering the new available capacity to the other traffic streams. Therefore, if a value larger than the optimum one is chosen for $l_1^n$ then the performance of the IL policy approximates the performance of the CS policy, but if a value smaller than the optimum one is chosen for $l_1^n$ then the performance of the IL policy can be even worse than the performance of the CS policy.

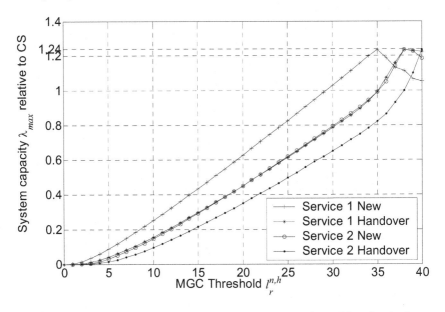

**Fig. 4.** Two-dimensional representation of the solution space for the MGC policy in the scenario A with C=40

Figure 4 plots the slices of the solution space for the MGC policy. As it could be expected, the values of the configuration parameters at which the peak for $\lambda_{max}$ (1.24) is achieved are different. For this policy, there is no plateau but a clear half-pyramidal or near-half-pyramidal shape with the maximum located at the apex. In this case, the position of the apex is of capital significance since not far away from this point the system capacity is poor compared to the one obtained for the CS policy. This solution space suggests that the definition of the configuration parameters requires more precision, unless we are willing to accept a degradation of the system capacity. Nevertheless, the slopes of the curves are now less steep. It should also be noted that, as mentioned before, the optimum configuration is close to the CS configuration (all thresholds set to $C$).

## 5  System Capacity

In this section we obtain the system capacity that can be expect when deploying one of the CAC policies under study. As defined before, the system capacity is the maximum arrival rate of new calls ($\lambda = \sum_{r=1}^{R} \lambda_r^n$) that can be offered to the system while meeting the QoS requirements, i.e. that produces blocking probabilities lower or equal than $B_r^{n,h}$.

**Table 2.** System capacity for the CAC policies under study

|  | C | CS | IL | ULGM | FL | FL +IL | ULGM +FL | ULGM +IL | ULGM +FL+IL | MGC | FMGC | RS |
|---|---|---|---|---|---|---|---|---|---|---|---|---|
|   | 10 | 1.54 | 1.13 | 1.07 | 1.13 | 1.14 | 1.18 | 1.17 | 1.18 | 1.23 | 1.33 | 1.34 |
| A | 20 | 5.61 | 1.11 | 1.06 | 1.12 | 1.13 | 1.15 | 1.14 | 1.16 | 1.26 | 1.31 | 1.31 |
|   | 40 | 15.76 | 1.09 | 1.07 | 1.10 | 1.10 | 1.14 | 1.13 | 1.14 | 1.24 | 1.25 | 1.26 |
|   | 10 | 0.37 | 1.05 | 1.00 | 1.18 | 1.18 | 1.18 | 1.05 | 1.19 | 1.10 | 1.15 | 1.20 |
| B | 20 | 2.78 | 1.03 | 1.08 | 1.11 | 1.11 | 1.12 | 1.09 | 1.13 | 1.21 | 1.25 | 1.25 |
|   | 40 | 10.39 | 1.06 | 1.04 | 1.07 | 1.10 | 1.09 | 1.06 | 1.10 | 1.21 | 1.22 | 1.23 |
|   | 10 | 1.37 | 1.07 | 1.05 | 1.07 | 1.09 | 1.10 | 1.08 | 1.10 | 1.11 | 1.21 | 1.22 |
| C | 20 | 5.77 | 1.05 | 1.05 | 1.08 | 1.08 | 1.07 | 1.06 | 1.09 | 1.20 | 1.21 | 1.21 |
|   | 40 | 17.62 | 1.05 | 1.04 | 1.07 | 1.07 | 1.07 | 1.06 | 1.07 | 1.15 | 1.16 | 1.16 |
|   | 10 | 1.74 | 1.03 | 1.00 | 1.06 | 1.06 | 1.04 | 1.03 | 1.06 | 1.13 | 1.16 | 1.17 |
| D | 20 | 6.05 | 1.04 | 1.00 | 1.05 | 1.05 | 1.05 | 1.04 | 1.05 | 1.13 | 1.15 | 1.15 |
|   | 40 | 16.54 | 1.03 | 1.00 | 1.04 | 1.04 | 1.00 | 1.03 | 1.04 | 1.10 | 1.11 | 1.11 |
|   | 10 | 1.54 | 1.05 | 1.00 | 1.06 | 1.06 | 1.05 | 1.05 | 1.06 | 1.13 | 1.17 | 1.17 |
| E | 20 | 5.62 | 1.04 | 1.02 | 1.05 | 1.05 | 1.06 | 1.05 | 1.06 | 1.13 | 1.15 | 1.16 |
|   | 40 | 15.7 | 1.03 | 1.02 | 1.04 | 1.04 | 1.05 | 1.04 | 1.05 | 1.10 | 1.10 | 1.10 |

The study is done for the five scenarios described in Table 1. Results for the capacity are displayed in Table 2. They are expressed as relative values to the capacity obtained for the CS policy, while for this policy we display absolute values. The maximum traffic that can be offered by each service can be easily determined from the parameters in Table 1, once the system capacity has been obtained.

As observed, trunk reservation policies perform better than those that produce a product-form solution and, in the scenarios studied, the improvement ranges between 5 and 15% approximately, although in some configurations can be a bit lower and in others a bit higher. However, the relative gain diminishes when the number of resource units $C$ increases.

In general, the implementation complexity is not an issue in these types of policies because at the most they only require storing a reduced set of parameters per service. For the RS algorithm, it can be shown that the maximum number of variables that need to be stored are the number of states plus $4R$ [9].

## 6  Sensitivity to Overloads

We study how the achieved handover blocking probabilities $p_r^h$ of all services increase with different degrees of overload (1% to 500%), which is defined as the ratio of the offered aggregated calling rate of new calls to the $\lambda_{max}$ that allows the system to meet the QoS requirements. It should the noted that the components of the offered aggregated calling rate are determined by $\lambda_r^n = f_r\lambda$ as shown in Table 1, and therefore, as we increase the offered aggregated calling rate $\lambda$ their relative ratios are maintained.

Given a policy and a configuration, the limiting service (LS) is the one for which its achieved $p_r^h$ or $p_r^n$ prohibits to increase $\lambda_{max}$. When deploying any of the policies that produce a product-form solution and the system is loaded with $\lambda_{max}$, typically, the achieved $p_r^h$ of the LS is the one closest to its objective, while for some very few particular cases it is the $p_r^n$ of the LS which is the one closest to its objective. When overload occurs, typically, the $p_r^h$ of the LS goes above its objective, while for the very few particular cases mentioned before it is the $p_r^n$ of the LS which goes above its objective, while all the $p_r^h$ remain below their objectives for a certain range of overload.

When deploying any of the last three policies and the system is loaded with $\lambda_{max}$, all the achieved blocking probabilities $p_r^{n,h}$ are quite close to their objectives, and this

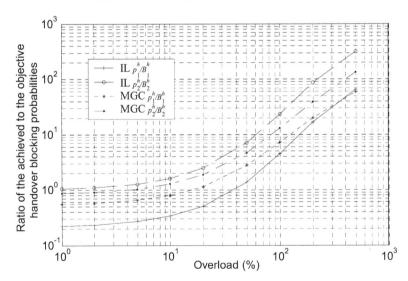

**Fig. 5.** Ratio of the achieved to the objective handover blocking probabilities in the scenario B with $C=20$

is specially true for the last two. Under a certain degree of overload, the $p_r^h$ achieved by the LS is typically smaller than the $p_r^h$ achieved by the LS of any of the policies that produce a product-form solution, except for the very few particular cases just described.

The increase ratio for the $p_r^h$ with a given increase of the overload ratio tends to be similar for all policies. All the comments of this section are especially applicable in scenarios with C=20 or 40 bandwidth units.

Fig. 5 shows the ratio of the achieved to the objective handover blocking probabilities for each service class and degree of overload. For example, for the IL policy and a 10% of overload the achieved handover blocking probability of service class 1, $p_1^h$, is 33.75% of its objective ( $B_1^h = 5\%$ ).

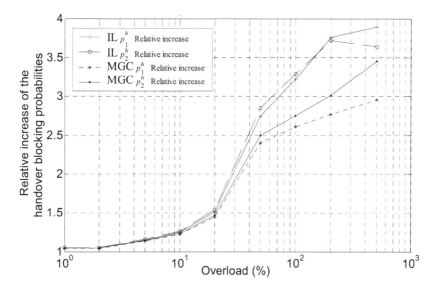

**Fig. 6.** Relative increase of the handover blocking probabilities in the scenario B with C=20

Fig. 6 shows the relative increase of the $p_r^h$ in relation to the previous degree of overload. For example, for the IL policy the achieved handover blocking probability of service class 1 for an overload of 10% is 25.23% higher (1.2523) than the achieved handover blocking probability of service class 1 for an overload of 5%.

Finally, two main conclusions can be drawn from the sensitivity analysis to overloads. First, in general, deploying an admission control policy is convenient because it introduces a certain degree of fairness since it shares among the different services the penalty due to the increase of the blocking probabilities during overloads. Second, in general, the last three policies tend to handle the overload similarly to (in the low to medium overload region) or better than (in the high overload region) those which produce a product-form solution, in the sense that the relative increase of the achieved handover blocking probabilities for the last three is lower than the relative increase for the policies that produce a product-form solution.

# 7  Conclusions

We have determined the maximum system capacity that can be expected when using different CAC policies. Due to the multidimensionality and non-monotonic behavior of the system under study the determination of the optimum configuration becomes difficult and computationally costly. The form of the solution spaces suggested us the use of a hill-climbing algorithm to reduce the computational complexity of the procedure that obtains the optimum configuration for each admission policy.

For the system capacity, numerical results show that policies of the trunk reservation class outperform policies that produce a product-form solution and the improvement ranges approximately between 5 and 15% in the scenarios studied. However, the relative gain diminishes when the number of resource units C increases. In addition, the shape of the solutions space of the trunk reservation policies shows that higher precision is required when determining the optimum configuration with respect to the product-form policies. Given that in practice the system parameters must be estimated and are non-stationary, trunk reservation policies could become less attractive.

We have also studied the sensitivity of the policies to overloads and found that, in general, trunk reservation policies handle the overload better.

It is clear that the results of our study have been obtained in quite idealistic conditions that might be difficult to achieve in a real operating system, nevertheless the study provides novel insights to a difficult problem.

Future work should address the study of the solution space for the RS policy, although intuition suggests that it could have a shape similar to the one found for the MFGC policy but probably with a more pronounced apex. We also plan to study adaptive policies which performance is insensitive to system parameters.

## Acknowledgements

The authors are grateful to the anonymous reviewers for their helpful reviews and suggestions. This work has been supported by the Spanish *Ministerio de Ciencia y Tecnología* under projects TIC2003-08272 and TIC2001-0956-C04-04, and by the *Generalitat of Valencia* under grant CTB/PRB/2002/267.

## References

1. Ramachandran Ramjee, Ramesh Nagarajan, Don Towsley, "On Optimal Call Admission Control in Cellular Networks," ACM/Baltzer Wireless Networks Journal, vol. 3, no. 1, pp 29-41, 1997.
2. E. Altman, T. Jimenez, G. Koole, "On optimal call admission control in resource-sharing system," IEEE Transactions on Communications, vol. 49, no. 9, pp.1659-1668, Sep. 2001.
3. V.B. Iversen, "The Exact Evaluation of Multi-Service Loss Systems with Access Control", in Proceedings of the Seventh Nordic Teletraffic Seminar (NTS-7), Aug. 1987, Lund, Sweden.
4. Chin-Tau Lea and Anwar Alyatama, "Bandwidth Quantization and States Reduction in the Broadband ISDN," IEEE/ACM Trans. on Networking, vol.3, no.3, pp.352-360, Jun. 1995.

5. G.L. Choudhury, K.K. Leung, and W. Whitt, "Efficiently Providing Multiple Grades of Service with Protection Against Overloads in Shared Resources", AT&T Technical Journal, vol. 74, no. 4, pp. 50-63, 1995.
6. B. Li, C. Lin, and S. T. Chanson, "Analysis of a hybrid cutoff priority scheme for multiple classes of traffic in multimedia wireless networks," ACM/Baltzer Wireless Networks Journal, vol. 4, no. 4, pp. 279-290, 1998.
7. H. Heredia-Ureta, F. A. Cruz-Pérez, and L. Ortigoza-Guerrero, "Multiple fractional channel reservation for optimum system capacity in multi-service cellular networks," Electronic Letters, vol. 39, pp. 133-134, Jan. 2003.
8. ——, "Capacity optimization in multiservice mobile wireless networks with multiple fractional channel reservation," IEEE Transactions on Vehicular Technology, vol. 52, no. 6, pp. 1519 – 1539, Nov. 2003.
9. Vicent Pla and Vicente Casares-Giner, "Optimal Admission Control Policies in Multiservice Cellular Networks," in Proceedings of the International Network Optimization Conference (INOC2003), Paris, France, Oct. 2003.
10. S. M. Ross, Applied Probability Models with Optimization Applications. Holden-Day, 1970.
11. Y.-B. Lin, S. Mohan, and A. Noerpel, "Queueing priority channel assignment strategies for PCS hand-off and initial access," IEEE Transactions on Vehicular Technology, vol. 43, no. 3, pp. 704–712, Aug. 1994.

# Admission Control in the Downlink of WCDMA/UMTS

S.-E. Elayoubi and T. Chahed

GET/Institut National des Telecommunications
{salah_eddine.elayoubi, tijani.chahed}@int-evry.fr

**Abstract.** In this paper, we develop a novel CAC algorithm that takes into account the mobility of users inside the cell with a focus on the downlink of third generation mobile systems. We first study the system capacity in a multiple cell setting and obtain effective bandwidth expressions for different calls as a function of both their positions in the cell as well as their classes of traffic (voice versus data). We then use this formulation to derive a mobility-based admission control algorithm which we analyze by Markov chains. We hence obtain several performance measures, namely the blocking probability, the dropping probability, both intra and inter-cell, as well as the overall cell throughput. We eventually investigate the performance of our CAC and show how to extend the Erlang capacity bounds, i.e., the set of arrival rates such that the corresponding blocking/dropping probabilities are kept below predetermined thresholds.

## 1 Introduction

Universal mobile Telecommunication System (UMTS) is designed to support a variety of multimedia services and its radio interface is based on Wideband Code Division Multiple Access (WCDMA). In such a context, the system is interference-limited and an efficient Connection Admission Control (CAC) is needed to guarantee Quality of Service (QoS) of the different multimedia classes.

Several CDMA-oriented CAC algorithms have been developed, considering the Signal-to-Interference Ratio (SIR) as the determinant parameter in accepting or not a new call; the idea being mainly that a new call is accepted if its contribution to the overall interference at the base station does not make the latter exceed a given value [9] , or alternatively if the new call does not make the SIR of an ongoing user fall below a target value [5][6][13]. However, these works did not compute exact values for the blocking probabilities, and hence cannot be used for an exact dimensioning of the system.

Yet, other works studied the capacity of CDMA systems using Markov chains, and obtained analytical values for the blocking probabilities, but they focused solely on the uplink [1][12]; it is well known, however, that the traffic in 3G systems is assymetric, with the major part of data traffic supported by the downlink. The only work, to our knowledge, that computed exact blocking rates

G. Kotsis and O. Spaniol (Eds.): Mobile and Wireless Systems, LNCS 3427, pp. 136–151, 2005.

in the downlink is [11], but it failed to consider the maximal transmission power of the base station as an additional CAC constraint.

Moreover, these works considered a static CDMA system, where the QoS of a user does not depend on its mobility and position in the cell. This assumption could be somehow acceptable in the uplink, where a perfect power control makes the SIR homogeneous in the cell until the maximal transmission power is reached [7]. This is not true in the downlink where the SIR is largely dependent on mobility. In fact, the level of interference at the mobile station in the downlink will depend largely on its position in the cell : the farther is the mobile terminal from the base station, the higher is the interference it experiences from adjacent cells [7]. This factor, i.e., distance $r$ between the base station and the mobile terminal, plays a discriminating role between different users in the downlink.

Our aim in this work is then to develop an admission control algorithm that handles the mobility issue in the downlink of 3G wireless systems. It shall also account for the maximal transmission power of the base station. Our algorithm also handles priorities between voice and data traffic.

To take mobility into account, we develop expressions for the SIR in a multiple cell setting, and define a larger set of classes of users that implements, in addition to the traditional voice versus data cleavage, new levels of priorities based on the distance $r$. $r$ is a random variable that changes with time accounting for the user's mobility. The idea is then to decompose the cell into a finite number of concentric circles, so-called rings, and to define an effective bandwidth expression relative to each ring.

This effective bandwidth formulation makes it possible to study the capacity of the system by Markov chains and to determine exact values of the blocking probabilities. Another important performance measure that we obtain is the dropping probability, i.e., the probability that an accepted user moving away from its base station sees its call dropped before reaching the adjacent cell, or has its handoff request blocked due to a lack of resources in the new cell.

Using these analytical tools, we associate to each ring and each class of multimedia calls a given acceptance ratio. We find out that if the aim is to reduce the dropping probability of ongoing calls at a low price in terms of blocking probability of voice calls, we need to prioritize the calls that have the lower effective bandwidth requirements. In this sense, data users near the base station may have higher priority over farther voice users.

We next study the Erlang capacity of our system and determine the set of arrival rates such that the corresponding blocking/dropping probabilities are below predetermined thresholds. We show how to extend the Erlang capacity region to include some additional arrival rates.

The remainder of this paper is organized as follows. In section II, we develop an effective bandwidth formulation for the different classes of users in the system where a class reflects both the user's type of traffic as well as its position in the cell. Based on these expressions, we define our CAC condition. In Section III, we present a Markovian analysis of our algorithm and determine the steady state probabilities. The performance measures in terms of blocking and dropping probabilities as well as cell throughput are calculated in Section IV. In Section V we investigate, through numerical applications, several CAC strategies so as to determine optimality of the algorithm. We also address the Erlang capacity issue and show the benefits of our CAC in extending it. Section VI eventually concludes the paper.

## 2   Model

### 2.1   Cell Decomposition

We consider a homogeneous DS/CDMA cellular system with hexagonal cells, of radius $R$, uniformly deployed, and numbered from 0 to $\infty$; the target cell being numbered 0 and containing $K$ users.

In a previous work [7], we developed an expression for the SIR in UMTS. In the downlink, we obtained a lower bound for the SIR :

$$\beta_j \geq \gamma_j = \frac{P_j^{(B)}}{\sigma^2 q_j + \frac{I(r_j)}{N} + \frac{1-\epsilon}{N} \sum_{i=1}^{K} P_i^{(B)}} \tag{1}$$

with $P_i^{(B)}$ the signal emitted by the base station for user $i$, $\sigma^2$ is the power of the background Gaussian noise, N is the spreading factor and $\epsilon$ is the orthogonality factor. $q_j$ is the path loss between mobile $j$ and the base station given by :

$$q_j = L \times (r_j)^\alpha 10^{(-\xi_j/10)} \tag{2}$$

where $r_j$ is the distance between mobile $j$ and the base station and $\xi_j$ is a random variable due to shadowing. $\alpha$ is usually equal to 4 and $L = 33.8$. $I(r_j)$ is the upper bound of the other-cell interference at mobile $j$ that we calculated in [7] based on a log-normal approximation of this interference. We showed that this other-cell interference varies rapidly with the distance to the base station, while its variation with the angle with an arbitrary reference axis is not significant. It can then be considered as a function of $r_j$ solely.

The downlink is limited by the maximum transmission power $W^B$ that could be emitted by the base station [6][8] and so :

$$\sum_{i=1}^{K_0} P_i^{(B)} \leq W^B \tag{3}$$

Then, the CAC equation is :

$$\sum_{i=1}^{K} \gamma_i [\frac{(1-\epsilon)W^B}{N} + \sigma^2 q_i + \frac{I(r_i)}{N}] \leq W^B \tag{4}$$

This CAC equation is more constraining than classical ones where a call is accepted if it does not degrade the SIR of ongoing users [11][13], or if it does not make the system reach its pole capacity [1], i.e., the number of users that makes the power go to infinity. In fact, the maximal transmission power is not infinite and the pole capacity can thus never be reached.

Let us introduce the following notation :

$$\mathbf{g}(r, \xi) = \frac{(1 - \epsilon)W^B}{N} + \sigma^2 r^\alpha 10^{-\xi/10} + \frac{I(r)}{N} \tag{5}$$

$\mathbf{g}(r, \xi)$ contains three interference terms. The first term, $\frac{(1-\epsilon)W^B}{N}$, due to the intra-cell interference, is a constant term that will be preponderant near the base station. The second term, $\sigma^2 r^\alpha 10^{-\xi/10}$, is due to the Gaussian noise. And the third term, $\frac{I(r)}{N}$, is generated by the other-cell interference and will have a larger effect near the cell border.

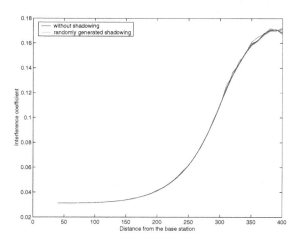

**Fig. 1.** Effect of the shadowing on the interference coefficient

However, the direct effect of the shadowing $\xi$ in the noise term $\sigma^2 r^\alpha 10^{-\xi/10}$ is not significant as this term is small compared to the other parameters, as shown in Figure 1. The latter plots the interference coefficient $\mathbf{g}(r, \xi)$ as a function of the distance $r$, with and without shadowing in the noise term, for a cell of radius $R = 400$ meters. We can see that even for a large cell where the Gaussian noise has a relatively large mean value, the effect of shadowing is not significant in the overall interference coefficient and can thus be neglected in capacity calculations. Let us note that its effect remains however important as it increases the upper bound of the othercell interference factor ($P_i^d q_i$ in $I(r_i)$). We can then neglect the shadowing in the noise term, i.e.,

$$\mathbf{g}(r, \xi) \simeq g(r) = \frac{(1 - \epsilon)W^B}{N} + \sigma^2 r^\alpha + \frac{I(r)}{N} \tag{6}$$

Without loss of generality, we limit our study to two classes of users : voice users requiring a SIR of $\gamma^v$ and data users requiring a SIR equal to $\gamma^d$. For $K^v$ and $K^d$ voice and data users in the cell respectively, Eqn. (4) becomes :

$$\sum_{i=1}^{K^v} \gamma^v g(r_i) + \sum_{i=1}^{K^d} \gamma^d g(r_i) \leq W^B \tag{7}$$

We define the effective bandwidth of class-$x$ users at distance $r$ from the base station as

$$E^x(r) = \gamma^x g(r) \tag{8}$$

Let us now divide the cell into $n$ concentric circles of radii $R_k$, $k = 1...n$, the last circle being the circumcircle of the hexagonal cell, and let us define ring $Z_k$ as the area between the two adjacent circles of radii $R_{k-1}$ and $R_k$ (see Figure 2). The system is hence quantized. Let us note that the last ring will cover parts of the adjacent cells to include calls that are in the soft handover region and are then connected to both cells in the same time.

The immediate consequence of this quantization is that each class of users is divided into $n$ subclasses depending on their position in the cell. We then have $2n$ classes : $n$ classes of voice calls, and $n$ classes of data ones, and the effective bandwidth of class-$x$ mobiles in ring $Z_k$ can be considered as constant with value

$$E_k^x = \gamma^x g(\overline{R}_k) \tag{9}$$

where $\overline{R}_k = \sqrt{\frac{R_k^2 + R_{k-1}^2}{2}}$, for instance and $R_0 = 0$.

Note that Eqn. (7) can then be rewritten as

$$\sum_{k=1}^{n} (E_k^v K_k^v + E_k^d K_k^d) \leq W^B \tag{10}$$

This effective bandwidth formulation of the load makes an abstraction of the complexity of the WCDMA radio interface by a simple combination of a finite number of traffic classes, in a circuit-switched-like system.

## 3   Analysis

### 3.1   CAC Algorithm

Our CAC algorithm is based on the idea of handling the mobility of users for taking a CAC decision. The state of the system is then defined by the instantaneous number of calls in each ring. Priorities between handoff and new calls, as well as between voice and data, are assured by means of different acceptance ratios which we now define.

Calls arrive as new or handoff : voice handoff calls are given an absolute priority over all other calls, while data handoff calls (if present) are treated as new ones. Handoff voice calls are accepted if enough resources are available

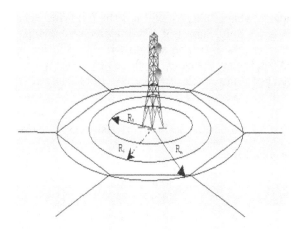

**Fig. 2.** Cell decomposition into rings

(i.e., condition (10) is verified taking into account that the handoff call is always situated in the last ring $Z_n$). For new calls of class $x$ arriving in ring $Z_k, k = 1..n$, they are accepted, if condition (10) is verified, with an acceptance ratio $a_k^x \leq 1$, $k = 1...n$. In doing so, a new call request may be blocked, even though enough resources are available, in order to leave space to higher priority users. Handoff voice calls have an acceptance ratio of 1. Note that we treat handover calls, and generally calls in last rings, in a pessimistic way, giving that they may require lower power due to the macrodiversity. An alternative way to deal with these calls is to define lower effective bandwidth for them. The whole analysis of this paper will still hold.

### 3.2 Markovian Model

In what follows, we will make use of the following assumptions :

1. The arrival process of class-$x$ new calls is Poisson with rate $\Lambda^x$ uniformally distributed over the cell surface.
2. The arrival process of class-$x$ handoff calls in $Z_n$ is Poisson with rate $\lambda_h^x$.
3. Class-$x$ calls migrate from ring $Z_i$ to ring $Z_j$, $j = i \pm 1$, with rate $\lambda_{i,j}^x$.
4. The service time of a class-$x$ call is exponential with mean $1/\mu^x$.

The arrival process of class-$x$ new calls in ring $Z_i$ is also Poisson with rate

$$\Lambda_i^x = \Lambda^x \frac{R_i^2 - R_{i-1}^2}{R^2} \tag{11}$$

For $K_i^v$ and $K_i^d$ denoting the number of voice and data calls in progress within ring $Z_i$, respectively, the system state can be defined by a row vector $\overrightarrow{s}$

$$\overrightarrow{s} := (K_1^v, ..., K_n^v, K_1^d, ..., K_n^d)$$

In the remainder of this paper, we will use the following definitions :

*Definition 1.* A is the finite subset of $\mathbf{N}^{2n}$ for which condition (10) holds. This means that a state vector $\overrightarrow{s}$ is in A if and only if $\sum_{k=1}^{n}(E_k^v K_k^v + E_k^d K_k^d) \leq W^B$.

*Definition 2.* $A_k^x$ is the subspace of A where any other new call of class $x$ in ring $Z_k$ will be blocked due to lack of resources. In other terms, $\overrightarrow{s} \in A_k^x$ if and only if $\overrightarrow{s} \in A$ and $\sum_{k=1}^{n}(E_k^v K_k^v + E_k^d K_k^d) + E_k^x > W^B$. $\overline{A}_k^x$ is the complementary subspace of $A_k^x$ in A.

Within the space of admissible states A, transitions are caused by :

1) Arrival of a new call in ring $Z_k$, $1 \leq k \leq n$.
2) Arrival of a handoff call in ring $Z_n$.
3) Termination of a class-$x$ ongoing call in ring $Z_k$.
4) Migration of an ongoing class-$x$ call from $Z_k$ to $Z_{k+1}$, $1 \leq k < n$. Note that such a migrating call may be dropped if there are not enough resources.
5) Migration of an ongoing call from ring $Z_k$ to ring $Z_{k-1}$, $2 \leq k \leq n$. Note that a call migrating from ring $Z_k$ to ring $Z_{k-1}$ is never dropped.
6) Departure of a class-$x$ call from border ring $Z_n$ to an adjacent cell.

### 3.3   Steady State Probabilities

Let $\pi(\overrightarrow{s})$ be the steady state probability of state $\overrightarrow{s}$. If we consider that the dwell time of class-$x$ mobiles in ring $Z_k$ (i.e., the time they spend in ring $Z_k$) is exponentially distributed with mean $1/\nu_k^x$, then the following theorem holds :

**Theorem 1.** *the system described above is a Markov chain and the steady state probabilities are given by*

$$\pi(\overrightarrow{s}) = \frac{1}{G} \prod_{k=1}^{n} \prod_{x=v}^{d} \frac{(\rho_k^x)^{K_k^x}}{K_k^x!}, \quad \overrightarrow{s} \in A \tag{12}$$

*where $\rho_k^x$ is the offered load of class-$x$ calls in ring $Z_k$ given by :*

$$\rho_k^x = \frac{a_k^x \Lambda_k^x + a_h^x \lambda_h^x I_{k=n} + \lambda_{k+1,k}^x I_{k\neq n} + \lambda_{k-1,k}^x I_{k\neq 1}}{\eta_k^x} \tag{13}$$

*where $\eta_k^x = (\nu_k^x + \mu_k)$ and G is the normalizing constant given by :*

$$G = \sum_{\overrightarrow{s} \in A} \prod_{k=1}^{n} \prod_{x=v}^{d} \frac{(\rho_k^x)^{K_k^x}}{K_k^x!} \tag{14}$$

*Proof.* Let $V_k^x$, $X^x$ and $Y_k^x$ be the random variables indicating the channel holding time of a class-$x$ call in ring $Z_k$, the class-$x$ call duration, and the dwell time in $Z_k$ respectively. $X^x$ and $Y_k^x$ are independent as the first depends on the amount of data to be sent and the latter on the users' mobility. We then have $V_k^x = \min(X^x, Y_k^x)$ with cumulative distribution function (CDF) :

$$F_{V_k^x}(t) = F_{X^x}(t) + F_{Y_k^x}(t) - F_{X_k^x}(t)F_{Y_k^x}(t) = 1 - \exp(-(\mu^x + \nu_k^x)t) \tag{15}$$

$V_k^x$ is then exponential and the load of calls $(c, k)$ is given by Eqn. (13).

Our system corresponds to a BCMP network with a single node (corresponding to the cell), where class-$x$ customers arrive from the outside to ring $Z_k$ with rate $\Lambda_k^x$ as new calls and $\lambda_h^x$ as handoff ones. These rates must be multiplied by their corresponding acceptance ratios. These customers are served for a time equal to $V_k^x$ and then either quit the queue (call termination or handoff), or reenter it after changing their class from $(c, k)$ to $(c, k \pm 1)$, following certain routing probabilities [2] (migration from one ring to another). The total arrival rate of class-$x$ calls in ring $Z_k$ is then $a_k^x \Lambda_k^x + a_h^x \lambda_h^x I_{k=n} + \lambda_{k+1,k}^x I_{k \neq n} + \lambda_{k-1,k}^x I_{k \neq 1}$.

According to the BCMP theorem for multiple classes of customers with possible class changes (see [3] pp. 146-150), the steady state probabilities have the product form given in Eqn. (12).

*Remark.* It can be further shown that the formulae for the steady state probabilities extend also for the case where the dwell time for class-$x$ calls in ring $Z_k$ and/or the call duration time are not exponential, but have general distributions. The system is no more a Markov chain, but Eqn. (12) holds, as the steady state distribution in a multi-service loss system is insensitive to the call duration distribution and depends only on its mean [4]. This mean is derived via the resulting CDF of the channel holding time of calls $(x, k)$ (Eqn. (15)).

## 3.4   Determination of Handoff and Migration Rates

In equilibrium, the overall system may be assumed homogeneous and a cell statistically the same as any other one. We can thus decouple a cell from the rest of the system by assuming that, for each class $x$ of calls, the mean handoff arrival rate to the given cell is equal to the mean handoff departure rate from it [10][11], i.e., $\lambda_h^x = \lambda_{n,n+1}^x$.

The migration rates from a ring $Z_k$ to its adjacent rings $Z_{k-1}$ and $Z_{k+1}$ depend on the dwell times and the number of calls in ring $Z_k$. We then have

$$\lambda_{1,2}^x = \sum_{\vec{s} \in A} \pi(\vec{s}) K_1^x \nu_1^x \tag{16}$$

$$\lambda_{i,i+1}^x + \lambda_{i,i-1}^x = \sum_{\vec{s} \in A} \pi(\vec{s}) K_i^x \nu_i^x \tag{17}$$

$$\lambda_h^x + \lambda_{n,n-1}^x = \sum_{\vec{s} \in A} \pi(\vec{s}) K_n^x \nu_i^x \tag{18}$$

On the other hand, if we assume that the trajectories followed by the different mobiles are randomly chosen, the migration rates are proportional to the perimeter of contact between two adjacent rings, which gives :

$$\lambda_{i,i+1}^x = \frac{R_i}{R_{i-1}} \lambda_{i,i-1}^x, \quad i = 2..n \tag{19}$$

One can see that these handoff/migration rates depend on the steady state probabilities, while the latter are themselves derived using the handoff/migration rates. To solve this problem, we use the following iterative algorithm that begins with an initial guess for handoff/migration rates.

*Step 1 : Set initial values for the arrival/migration rates. To do so, we suppose that the dropping probabilities are negligible and that the blocking probabilities in Eqn. (22) are essentially due to the fact that the acceptance ratios $a_k^x$ may be strictly less than 1 :*

$$p_k^x \simeq 1 - a_k^x$$

*If $p_{i,j}^x$ is the probability that a call migrates from ring $i$ to ring $j = i \pm 1$ :*

$$\lambda_{i,i+1}^x + \lambda_{i,i-1}^x \simeq (p_{i,i+1}^x + p_{i,i-1}^x)(\Lambda_i^x a_k^x + \lambda_{i+1,i} + \lambda_{i-1,i}^x) \tag{20}$$

*The migration probability is the probability that the call quits ring $Z_i$ before termination. It is given by :*

$$p_{i,i+1}^x + p_{i,i-1}^x = P(Y_k^x < X^x) = \frac{\nu_k^x}{\nu_k^x + \mu^x} \tag{21}$$

*The initial migration/handoff rates are then obtained by solving the set of equations (20), using Eqns. (19) and (21).*

*Step 2 : Obtain the steady state probabilities from Eqn. (12).*

*Step 3 : Calculate the migration rates corresponding to the obtained state probabilities using Eqns. (16)-(19).*

*Step 4 : Check the convergence of the migration rates using the relative error $e = \max |1 - \frac{\lambda_{new}}{\lambda_{old}}|$. If $e > \epsilon$, where $\epsilon > 0$ is a predetermined constant, go to Step 2, otherwise, compute the performance measures given in the next section.*

## 4   Performance Measures

### 4.1   Blocking Probabilities

The first performance measure is the blocking probability.

**Proposition 1.** *The blocking probability $p_k^x$ of a class-$x$ call in ring $Z_k$ is :*

$$p_k^x = 1 - a_k^x + a_k^x \sum_{\vec{s} \in A_k^x} \pi(\vec{s}) \tag{22}$$

*Specifically, the new call blocking probability is given by*

$$p^x = \frac{1}{\Lambda^x} \sum_{k=1}^n p_k^x \Lambda_k^x \tag{23}$$

*and the voice handoff call blocking probability is given by :*

$$p_h^v = \sum_{\vec{s} \in A_n^v} \pi(\vec{s}) \tag{24}$$

*Proof.* A new connection of class-$x$ in ring $Z_k$ is always blocked if the system is in a state $\overrightarrow{s} \in A_k^x$. Otherwise, it is blocked with probability $1 - a_k^x$. In total, the blocking probability is

$$p_k^x = (1 - a_k^x) \sum_{\overrightarrow{s} \in \overline{A_k^x}} \pi(\overrightarrow{s}) + \sum_{\overrightarrow{s} \in A_k^x} \pi(\overrightarrow{s}) = 1 - a_k^x + a_k^x \sum_{\overrightarrow{s} \in A_k^x} \pi(\overrightarrow{s}) \qquad (25)$$

The overall blocking probability in the cell is directly derived by means of the relative arrival rates $\Lambda_k^x / \Lambda^x$.

For voice handoff calls, they arrive only at the last ring $Z_n$. They are then blocked when the system is in a state of the space $A_n^v$ with probability :

$$p_h^v = \sum_{\overrightarrow{s} \in A_n^v} \pi(\overrightarrow{s})$$

Note that the blocking probability for handoff data calls is equal to that of new data ones at the cell border, i.e., $p_h^d = p_n^d$.

## 4.2  Dropping Probability

We now determine the dropping probability. In the literature [14], this term refers to the blocking of a handover call. We shall denote this particular event by inter-cell dropping. As we focus on intra-cell mobility, we should thus take into account the possibility of an intra-cell dropping event, i.e., a mobile station moving away from its base station experiences a higher interference figure and is thus dropped due to a lack of resources. The overall dropping probability is hence the result of both intra and inter-cell dropping probabilities.

**Proposition 2.** *The intra-cell dropping probability $d^x$ of a class-$x$ call due to mobility inside the cell is equal to :*

$$d^x = \frac{1}{\sum_{\overrightarrow{s} \in A} K^x (\nu_k^x + \mu^x) \pi(\overrightarrow{s})} \sum_{k=1}^{n-1} \sum_{\overrightarrow{s} \in A / \overrightarrow{s}_{k,k+1}^x \notin A} K_k^x \nu_k^x \frac{R_k}{R_k + R_{k-1}} \pi(\overrightarrow{s})$$

$$(26)$$

*where $\overrightarrow{s}_{k,k+1}^x$ is the next state when a class-$x$ call quits ring $Z_k$ to ring $Z_{k+1}$.*

*Proof.* If the system is in state $\overrightarrow{s}$, a migrating class-$x$ call from ring $Z_k$ to ring $Z_{k+1}$ is dropped if the state $\overrightarrow{s}_{k,k+1}^x \notin A$. However, not all mobiles migrate : only those whose dwell time in the ring is less then their call duration time do migrate. The rate of leaving the ring $K_k^x (\nu_k^x + \mu^x)$ must then be multiplied by the probability that an ongoing class-$x$ call quits the ring :

$$P(Y_k^x < X^x) = \frac{\nu_k^x}{\nu_k^x + \mu^x}$$

Among these calls, only a fraction of $\frac{R_k}{R_k + R_{k-1}}$ try to migrate from ring $Z_k$ to ring $Z_{k+1}$. These calls are dropped if $\overrightarrow{s}_{k,k+1}^x \notin A$.

The intra-cell dropping probability $d^x$ due to mobility within the cell is the sum of dropping rates at each ring $Z_k$, divided by the rate of leaving the system, which gives the proof.

Let us now determine the overall dropping probability.

**Corollary 1.** *The overall dropping probability $f^x$ of an ongoing class-x call due to its mobility within the cell or between adjacent ones is equal to :*

$$f^x = d^x + \frac{1}{\sum_{\overrightarrow{s} \in A} K^x(\nu_k^x + \mu^x)\pi(\overrightarrow{s})} \sum_{\overrightarrow{s} \in A} K_n^x \nu_n^x \frac{R_n}{R_n + R_{n-1}} \pi(\overrightarrow{s}) p_h^x \quad (27)$$

*Proof.* To the intra-cell dropping probability, we add the blocking rate of calls leaving the cell to adjacent ones, i.e., inter-cell dropping rate, divided by the rate of calls leaving the system. As the overall system is homogeneous in equilibrium, this blocking probability is equal to the handoff blocking probability calculated in Proposition 1. This leads to the expression (27).

*Remark.* It is envisaged that heavy loaded cells may be divided into three sectors by means of three directive transmitters, in order to limit the interference. This introduces the notion of softer handover between sectors of the same cell, which is present in all zones and not only in zone $Z_n$. The softer handoff blocking probability in zone $Z_k$ is then equal to $p_k^x$. The same analysis can be applied to calculate the overall dropping probability. In particular, if $\lambda_{sh}^x$ is the softer handover rate from zone $Z_k$ in the target sector to the adjacent sectors, we have:

$$\frac{\lambda_{sh}^x}{2(R_k - R_{k-1})} = \frac{\lambda_{k,k+1}^x}{\frac{2\pi R_k}{3}} = \frac{\lambda_{k,k-1}^x}{\frac{2\pi R_{k-1}}{3}}$$

## 4.3  Throughput

Another important performance measure is the overall cell throughput :

$$T = \sum_{\overrightarrow{s} \in A} \left\{ \sum_{k=1}^{n} (K_k^v D^v + K_k^d D^d) \right\} \pi(\overrightarrow{s}) \quad (28)$$

where $D^x$ is the throughput of a class-x single user.

## 5  Numerical Applications

The following parameters shall be used in the numerical applications:

- The cell has a radius of 400 meters, and the base station has a transmission power of 5 Watts.
- The mean call duration is equal to 120 sec.

– New calls arrive according to a Poisson process with rate $\Lambda$. A new call is randomly generated as a voice call with probability 0.75 or a data call with probability 0.25, that is, $\Lambda^v = 0.75\Lambda$ and $\Lambda^d = 0.25\Lambda$.
– Voice calls have a SIR requirement of 5 dB and a rate of 12.2 Kbps, while data calls require a SIR of 9 dB and have a rate of 64 Kbps.
– Medium mobility is studied for a mean dwell time in the cell equal to 300 sec, and the mean dwell time is proportional to the surface of each ring.

### 5.1   Acceptance Strategy

In Section IV, we analyzed the performance of our algorithm under general assumptions for the acceptance ratios. We now study it under four specific acceptance strategies which are :

1. No priorities between classes : a new call is accepted if there are enough resources, it is blocked otherwise, i.e., $a_k^x = 1$, $k = 1...n$, $x = v, d$.
2. Voice calls are given absolute priority over data ones, i.e., $a_k^v > a_l^d$, $\forall k \leq n, l \leq n$.
3. Data calls are given absolute priority over voice ones, i.e., $a_k^d > a_l^v$, $\forall k \leq n, l \leq n$.
4. The priority of a class-$x$ call is dependent on its effective bandwidth, i.e., $a_k^x > a_l^y$ if $E_k^x < E_l^y$. This will lead to a situation where data calls near the base station have higher priority than distant voice calls.

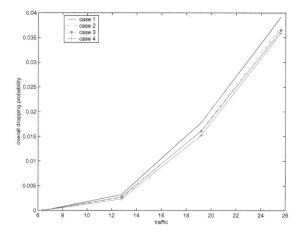

**Fig. 3.** Dropping probability for the four strategies in the Priority CAC

Our aim is to minimize the dropping probability, at low voice blocking probability. We plot in Figures 3 and 4 the dropping probability and the voice blocking probability for the four strategies, respectively.

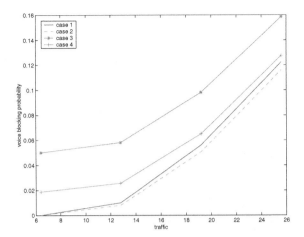

**Fig. 4.** Voice blocking probability for the four strategies in the Priority CAC

We observe that giving higher priority to data calls (strategy 3) decreases the dropping probability. However, it is very harmful to voice calls as they will experience a high blocking rate. The best lowest dropping probability is obtained when using strategy 4, where the blocking ratio is proportional to the effective bandwidth. This strategy achieves a low dropping probability at an acceptable blocking rate for voice calls. The only drawback is that this strategy results in a slightly lower throughput (see Figure 5) and may be unfair for users with large capacity demands. In the remainder of this work, we will adopt this strategy in our capacity calculations. However, the whole analysis holds for any strategy.

## 5.2   Investigating Erlang Capacity

The Erlang capacity is generally defined as the set of offered loads such that the corresponding blocking probability is smaller than a given $\epsilon > 0$ [1]. In this work, as we are also interested in the dropping probability, we will extend this definition to the following :

*Definition 3.* The Erlang capacity $EC(\epsilon_1, \epsilon_2)$ is defined as the set of offered loads such that there exists a set of acceptance ratios $(a_1^v...a_n^v, a_1^d...a_n^d)$ for which the dropping probability is less than a given $\epsilon_1 > 0$, and the blocking probability is less than $\epsilon_2 \geq \epsilon_1 > 0$.

In other words, we determine, if they exist, the acceptance ratios for each arrival rate that satisfy the constraints on blocking / dropping probabilities.

For illustration, we study the case where $\epsilon_1 = 3\%$ and $\epsilon_2 = 12\%$, and $a_{min}^v = (1 + a_{min}^d)/2$, i.e., the preventive blocking of data calls at the cell border occurs with a probability equal to $1 - a_{min}^d$, while voice calls in the same conditions are blocked in a preventive way only at a probability of $1 - a_{min}^v = (1 - a_{min}^d)/2$. We plot in Figures 6, 7 and 8 the voice blocking probabilities, the dropping proba-

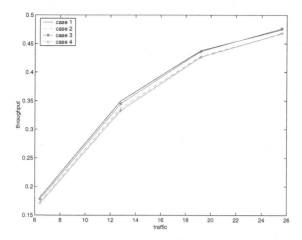

**Fig. 5.** Throughput achieved for the four strategies in the Priority CAC

bilities and the achieved throughput corresponding to those values, respectively, for six different arrival rates.

One can see that for an arrival rate $\Lambda > 0.17$ calls per sec, we cannot satisfy the performance measures with any set of acceptance ratios. In fact, we cannot satisfy jointly the conditions on the blocking and dropping probabilities for any acceptance ratio (Fig. 6 and 7). The Erlang capacity region is than limited by $\Lambda_{max} = 0.17$ calls per sec.

On the other hand, when $\Lambda = 0.17$ calls per sec, the constraint on the dropping probability is satisfied for $a^v_{min} \leq 0.88$ (Figure 7), while the constraint for the blocking probability imposes that $a^v_{min} \geq 0.84$ (Figure 6). The best choice that maximizes the throughput is then $a^v_{min} = 0.88$ (Figure 8).

Note that if no priorities were implemented, an arrival rate of $\Lambda = 0.17$ calls per sec would have generate a dropping rate larger than 3% that is not acceptable. The priority-based CAC extends then the Erlang capacity region to include even larger arrival rates.

# 6   Conclusion

In this paper, we developed a mobility-based admission control for the downlink of third generation mobile networks. We first studied the system capacity and obtained effective bandwidth expressions based on both the class of traffic and the position of the user in the cell, hence accounting for its mobility pattern.

Based on this formulation, we attributed to each class of users an acceptance ratio to handle priorities between flows, and proved that the underlying system can be modeled as a Markov chain. We then obtained the steady state probabilities and gave an iterative algorithm to determine them explicitly.

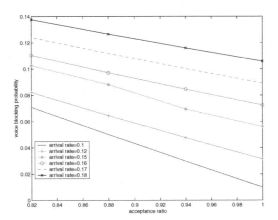

**Fig. 6.** Voice blocking probability for different arrival rates in the Priority CAC

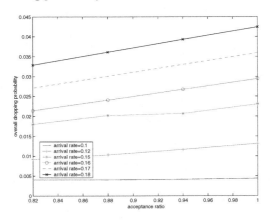

**Fig. 7.** Dropping probability for different arrival rates in the Priority CAC

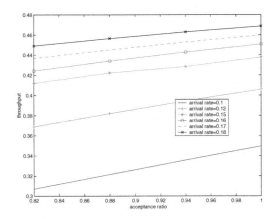

**Fig. 8.** Throughput for different arrival rates in the Priority CAC

As of the performance measures, we obtained the blocking probabilities and the dropping probabilities of ongoing calls, be they intra-cell due to their mobility or inter-cell due to handoff. We also determined the overall cell throughput. We next studied numerically our CAC algorithm and determined the Erlang capacity bounds, i.e. the set of arrival rates that satisfy predetermined constraints on blocking/dropping probabilities.

In a fucture work, we should introduce the effect of interaction between cells and show how downgrading elastic data calls affects the CAC algorithm.

**Acknowledgment.** The authors wish to thank Mr. James Roberts from France Telecom R&D for useful discussions and corrections.

# References

1. E. Altman, *Capacity of Multi-service Cellular Networks with Transmission Rate Control : A Queueing Analysis*, in proceedings of ACM MOBICOM, 2002.
2. B. Baynat, *Théorie des files d'attente*, Hermes Science Publications, 2000.
3. X. Chao, M. Miyazawa and M. Pinedo, *Queueing Networks : Customers, Signals and Product Form Solutions*, J. Wiley and Sons, England, 1999.
4. S-P. Chung and K.W. Ross, *Reduced Load Approximations for Multirate Loss Networks*, IEEE Transactions on Communications, Vol. 41. No. 8, August 1993.
5. N. Dimitriou, G. Sfikas and R. Tafazolli, *Call Admission Policies for UMTS*, in proceedings of IEEE VTC 2000-Spring, Tokyo, 2000.
6. S-E. Elayoubi, T. Chahed and G. Hébuterne, *Admission control in UMTS in the presence of shared channels*, computer communications, Vol. 27, issue 11, 2004.
7. S-E. Elayoubi, T. Chahed and G. Hébuterne, *On the Capacity of multi-cell UMTS*, in proceedings of IEEE GLOBECOM 2003, San Fransisco, december 2003.
8. C. Huang and R. Yates, *Call Admission in Power Controlled CDMA systems*, in proceedings of IEEE VTC 1996.
9. Y. Ishikawa and N. Umeda, *Capacity Design and Performance of Call Admission Control in Cellular CDMA Systems*, IEEE Journal on Selected Areas in Communications, Vol. 15, No. 8, October 1997.
10. W. Jeon and D. Jeong, *Call Admission Control for Mobile Multimedia Communications with Traffic Asymmetry between Uplink and Downlink*, IEEE Transactions on Vehicular Technology, Volume : 50 Issue: 1 , Jan. 2001.
11. W. Jeon and D. Jeong, *Call Admission Control for CDMA Mobile Communications Systems Supporting Multimedia Services*, IEEE Transactions on Wireless Communications, Volume : 1, No. 4 , Oct. 2002.
12. I. Koo, J. Ahn, J-A. Lee and K. Kim, *Analysis of Erlang Capacity for the Multimedia DS-CDMA Systems*, IEICE Transactions on Fundamentals, Vol. E82-A, No. 5, May 1999.
13. Z. Liu and M. Elzarki, *SIR-Based Call Admission Control for DS-CDMA Cellular Systems*, IEEE Journal on Selected Areas in Telecommunications, May 1994.
14. H. Wu, L. Li, B. Li, L. Yin, I. Chlamtak and B. Li, *On handoff performance for an integrated voice/data cellular system*, in proceedings of IEEE PIMRC'2002.

# Effects of WLAN QoS Degradation on Streamed MPEG4 Video Quality

Helmut Hlavacs, Karin A. Hummel, Alexander Albl, Stefan Frandl,
Jürgen Kirchler, and Boris Ilic

Institute for Computer Science and Business Informatics, University of Vienna,
Lenaug. 2/8, 1080 Vienna, Austria
`helmut.hlavacs@univie.ac.at`

**Abstract.** In this paper we evaluate different models for packet losses
in wireless networks. The used model framework is given by extended
Gilbert models, which are generalizations of the well known Gilbert
model, a two state discrete Markov chain. It is further shown that the
correlation of the packet loss indication process has a severe effect on the
quality of streamed MPEG-4 video.

## 1 Introduction

In the past, WLAN has become very popular for connecting mobile clients with
each other and the Internet. This way, mobile clients can maintain connectivity
even when being carried around, for instance, when going to a meeting in the
office, or when moving into the garden at home. Both scenarios do not require
the installation of wires to the mobile clients.

WLAN may be disturbed by multiple effects, like multipath fading, attenua-
tion, or noise sources like microwave ovens, other networks sending in the same
band, or even WLAN clients which are not aware of other senders (hidden terminal problem) [7]. If the relation from the received signal energy to added noise
energy is too small (signal-to-noise ratio, SNR), the receiver is no more able to
correctly decode the signal, and the received data contains bit errors. In this
case the network at Layer 2 may decide to try to resend the packet, or after a
few attempts, may drop the packet.

Lost packets may have different effects on the performance of the communicating application and the user perceived application quality of service (QoS). If
all of the data *must* be received, which is mostly the case for raw data transfer,
for example, then packet loss must be signalled to the sender, who has to send the
lost data anew. This is the case for TCP and all services using it. On the other
hand, audio/video (AV) streaming applications often use UDP, and lost UDP
packets simply cause a degradation of the perceived audio/video presentation.
Here, depending on the AV coding and the observed packet loss, the perceived
AV quality degradation may be acceptable to the users or not.

In order to assess the effect of packet losses to the quality of streamed video,
it is desirable to represent packet losses by a loss model. Usually, packet loss is

G. Kotsis and O. Spaniol (Eds.): Mobile and Wireless Systems, LNCS 3427, pp. 152–165, 2005.

modelled by taking into account the packet loss rate, and sometimes also the mean burst size. Furthermore, the used video encoding often is set to one fixed scheme. In this paper, more sophisticated models are used for explaining the packet loss of a WLAN following IEEE 802.11b. We apply different loss models to videos encoded with different encoding parameters and observe the objective video quality.

## 2  Loss Models

Losses are usually modelled by using a loss rate. Assume that $N$ packets have been sent, of which $L \leq N$ packets have been lost. The observed loss rate then is $r = L/N$, which for $N \to \infty$ becomes the packet loss probability $p = 1 - q$. A loss burst of size $B$ denotes the loss of $B$ consecutive packets, preceeded and followed by received packets. Furthermore it is often assumed that packet losses are *independent* from the past. In this case, the loss process follows independent Bernoulli trials, the burst size distribution is geometric, and

$$P(B = k) = p^k q, k \geq 0. \tag{1}$$

The mean burst size then is simply $\mu = p/q$, and the variance is $\sigma^2 = p/q^2$. A binary stochastic process $I_n$ for loss indication is defined by $I_n = 0$ if the $n$th packet was received (with probability $q$), and $I_n = 1$, if the $n$th packet was lost (with probability $p$). Then

$$EI_n = 0q + 1p = p \tag{2}$$
$$\text{Var}(I_n) = E(I_n - EI_n)^2 = (0 - p)^2 q + (1 - p)^2 p = pq, \tag{3}$$

and

$$\text{Cov}(I_n, I_k) = E(I_n - EI_n)(I_k - EI_k) =$$
$$(0 - p)(0 - p)q^2 + (0 - p)(1 - p)qp +$$
$$(1 - p)(0 - p)pq + (1 - p)(1 - p)p^2 = 0, n \neq k \tag{4}$$

and thus the *autocorrelation function* $\text{ACF}(k - n) = \text{Cov}(I_n, I_k)/\text{Var}(I_n)$ is always 0 for $k > n$, indicating that there is no inter-dependence between $I_n$ and $I_k$ if $n \neq k$.

However, typically, the independence assumption of packet losses is incorrect. Consider for example a simple finite queue. Packet losses occur only if the queue is full. Thus, if the $n$th packet is lost, the probability that the $(n + 1)$st packet is lost is much higher than the respective probability for the case, when the $n$th packet has been received. Another argumentation concerns WLAN. In case of interference or fading, the network is broken for a short period of time, and packets are likely to be lost in bursts rather than as single losses.

It is thus reasonable to use more sophisticated models which catch dependencies on past losses as well. A model taking into account the status of the last packet is the well-known Gilbert loss model [1]. The Gilbert loss model is

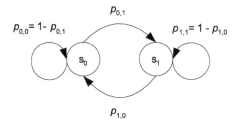

**Fig. 1.** Gilbert loss model

a two-state discrete-time Markov chain, where the state $s_0$ denotes the event that a packet has been successfully received, and $s_1$ denotes a lost packet. The model is described by its state transition probabilities $p_{i,j}, i, j \in \{0, 1\}$. Simple calculation reveals that the steady state probability

$$p = P(s_1) = \frac{p_{0,1}}{p_{0,1} + p_{1,0}}.$$

The covariance of the process $I_n$ can be calculated by

$$\begin{aligned}
\mathrm{Cov}(I_n, I_{n+1}) &= E(I_n - EI_n)(I_{n+1} - EI_{n+1}) = \\
&\quad (0 - p)(0 - p)qp_{0,0} + (0 - p)(1 - p)qp_{0,1} + \\
&\quad (1 - p)(0 - p)pp_{1,0} + (1 - p)(1 - p)pp_{1,1} = \\
&\quad p(p_{1,1} - p).
\end{aligned} \tag{5}$$

From (3) and (5) it follows that

$$R = \mathrm{ACF}(1) = \frac{p_{1,1} - p}{1 - p} = p_{0,0} - p_{1,0} = p_{1,1} - p_{0,1}. \tag{6}$$

From (6) it can be seen that the Gilbert model does not depend on the past if $p = p_{1,1} = p_{0,1}$. Furthermore it can be shown that for the Gilbert model the ACF has the following general form:

$$\mathrm{ACF}(k) = (-1)^k (p_{1,0} - p_{0,0})^k = (-1)^k (p_{0,1} - p_{1,1})^k, k > 0. \tag{7}$$

Since it is possible that longer dependencies exist in the observed packet losses, it makes sense to extend the Gilbert model to depend on more states of the past. When including $l$ packets from the past, the Markov chain state space grows to $2^l$ states, which soon exceeds a feasible model size. A simpler model is given by the so-called extended Gilbert model [3]. Here, only the size of the last *loss burst* is taken into account (Figure 2). The state $s_i$ denotes the event, that the current loss burst is *at least* $i$ packets long. The parameter $m$ defines how many lost packets of the past can be remembered. For computing the transition probabilities $p_{n,n+1}$ the following procedure can be applied. After observing the

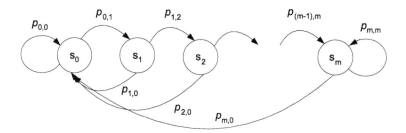

**Fig. 2.** Extended Gilbert loss model

packet arrival process, let $l(n)$ denote the number of times, a loss burst of length $0 \leq n < m$ *or larger* has been observed. Then

$$p_{n,n+1} = l(n+1)/l(n). \tag{8}$$

Once $m$ lost packets have been observed, $p_{m,m}$ denotes the probability for staying in state $s_m$, i.e., for continuing to lose packets. From this point on, however, the model behaves like the geometric model (1). Thus, the transition probabilities of the extended Gilbert model should reflect a behavior which is different to the geometric approach, whereas the last state and $p_{m,m}$ reflect a behavior that can either be neglected, or be approximated by a geometric model.

## 3 Video Quality

Digital video contains single pictures (frames) being compressed by some encoder following a video encoding (possibly proprietary) standard or scheme. Popular schemes include Microsoft WMV, H.263, and the well known MPEG-1, MPEG-2, and MPEG-4. While MPEG-2 is the basis of DVDs and digital television (DVB), the new standard MPEG-4 contains two different video encoding schemes, the Visual Layer (ISO 14496 Chapter 2) and the more advanced H.264 (ISO 14496 Chapter 10) encoder which has been defined recently. Both may be streamed via the Internet using the Real-Time Protocol (RTP) [4] above UDP/IP. In the experiments presented we focus on MPEG-4 Visual Layer codecs.

The quality of digital video as seen by the human eye may be affected by several causes. First, the higher the compression rate is, the more visible are compression artifacts. Second, if the video is streamed over a network, for instance, based on IP, packets might be delayed or lost due to congested routers or interrupted wireless connections. If a lost packet is sent anew from the sender, then the video presentation must be halted in order to wait for the missing packet. In case of live broadcasts or video conferencing, this is undesirable, while for video on demand, streaming buffers at the receiver can decrease the stall probability.

An *objective* video quality measure defines a distance metric between the original (uncompressed) video and a version of the video containing artifacts. The task of *subjective* video quality assessment is to show a disturbed video to a possibly large number of viewers and ask for a quality assessment on a given scale [2]. Additionally, after having carried out a number of subjective experiments, one can try to find objective measures that correlate well with the human judgements [8,9,10]. However, these metrics often rely on the fact that many video codecs divide the compressed frames into tiles of sizes $16 \times 16$ or $8 \times 8$. The higher the compression factor is, the more visible are the tiles. However, if the artifacts do not stem from tiling, then many objective metrics do not produce meaningful results. More basic metrics rely on a pixel-by-pixel comparison between original and disturbed frame, usually using the frame luminance component, i.e., a grey-scale version without color. Let $I(x, y, t)$ denote the luminance of a frame having the resolution $X \times Y$ and the time index $t$ at the position $(x, y)$, and $\tilde{I}(x, y, t)$ denote an impaired version of the same frame, then the mean square error is defined by

$$MSE(t) = \frac{1}{XY} \sum_{x=1}^{X} \sum_{y=1}^{Y} [I(x, y, t) - \tilde{I}(x, y, t)]^2,$$

and the peak signal to noise ratio (PSNR) is defined by

$$PSNR(t) = 10 \log_{10} \frac{L_{max}^2}{MSE(t)}. \tag{9}$$

Here, $L_{max}$ denotes the maximum luminance value. PSNR is a rather old metric stemming from analog television, where received Gaussian noise added to the TV signal is caught quite well. However, digital video usually is not affected by random Gaussian noise, but by other phenomena stemming from tiling and transformations like the Discrete Cosine Transform (DCT). It can be shown that a picture affected by Gaussian noise and one affected by tiling may on the one hand produce the same PSNR, but on the other hand, the effect of tiling is much more disturbing to the human eye than the one of Gaussian noise [6]. However, PSNR is a rather robust metric and correlates quite well with subjective experiments [5], and it works well even if the observed artifacts do not stem from video compression, but for instance from lost packets. In the latter case, more sophisticated metrics relying on the tiling effect would not work.

## 4    Deriving the WLAN Loss Model

We carried out a number of experiments for estimating the parameters for different versions of the extended Gilbert model. Here we measured the packet loss in a WLAN (IEEE 802.11b) infrastructure network between an access point and several mobile clients. Our clients are equippped with ORINOCO PCMCIA WLAN cards, which are also able to protocol the observed SNR. For the experiments we put the laptops to locations showing the SNRs 40 dB, 25 dB, 15 dB, and 11 dB (Figure 3), which resulted in network bitrates of 11 Mbs, 11 Mbs, 5 Mbs, and 1-2 Mbs. Locations with less than 11 dB produced an unstable network and

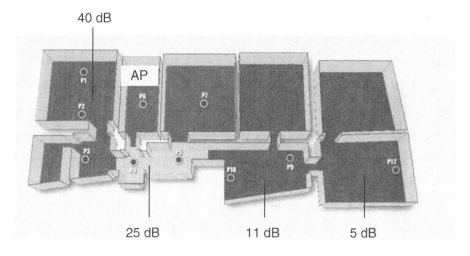

**Fig. 3.** Department signal-to-noise ratio areas

experiments usually where soon stopped because of connection losses. Following a specific pattern, in our experiments a server sends UDP packets to the mobile client. At the client, it is recorded whether a packet has been received or has been dropped. The used software is called CODIS Net.

The server sends its data according to a selected bitrate between 500 Kbps and 5.5 Mbps. The data is sent in bursts of equal size, at 20 bursts per second. If the bitrate is low enough, then each burst fits into just one packet. The packet size is limited to the parameter $MTU$ (Maximum Transfer Unit, i. e., maximum packet size), in this case 1450 bytes. If a burst does not fit into one UDP packet, then several packets are sent. This way, the pattern catches interdependencies of short time intervals (packets within a burst), and dependencies spanning longer time periods, i.e., from one burst to the next. If $b$ denotes the used bitrate in Kbps and $k$ bursts per second are sent, then the number of packets per burst $l$ is computed by

$$l = \frac{1024 \times b}{8 \times k \times MTU}. \tag{10}$$

Figure 4 shows the loss burst length distribution for 500 Kbps at the 11 dB location, the bitrate demanding three packets per burst according to (10). It can be seen that the loss burst length distribution decays quickly like a geometric distribution. This indicates a simple loss model, i.e., an extended Gilbert model with only a few states. Table 1 shows the parameters of different extended Gilbert models which have been computed according to the recorded data for 500 Kbps. A probability $p_{i,i}$ close to one together with a very small number of occurences of long bursts indicates that the model is overfit. Thus, in this case an extended Gilbert model of order two or three is sufficient. This coincides with the number of packets per burst $l = 3$, indicating that the dependencies in a burst are strong, whereas the dependencies between bursts are weak.

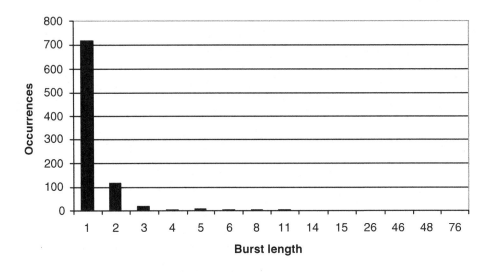

**Fig. 4.** Burst length distribution for 500 Kbps

**Table 1.** Parameters of different extended Gilbert models

| GB | 1 | 2 | 3 | 4 | 6 | 7 | 8 | 9 | 10 |
|---|---|---|---|---|---|---|---|---|---|
| $p_{0,1}$ | 0.022 | 0.022 | 0.022 | 0.022 | 0.022 | 0.022 | 0.022 | 0.022 | 0.022 |
| $p_{1,1}$ | 0.346 | | | | | | | | |
| $p_{1,2}$ | | 0.180 | 0.180 | 0.180 | 0.180 | 0.180 | 0.180 | 0.180 | 0.180 |
| $p_{2,2}$ | | 0.660 | | | | | | | |
| $p_{2,3}$ | | | 0.273 | 0.273 | 0.273 | 0.273 | 0.273 | 0.273 | 0.273 |
| $p_{3,3}$ | | | 0.860 | | | | | | |
| $p_{3,4}$ | | | | 0.605 | 0.605 | 0.605 | 0.605 | 0.605 | 0.605 |
| $p_{4,4}$ | | | | 0.902 | | | | | |
| $p_{4,5}$ | | | | | 0.808 | 0.808 | 0.808 | 0.808 | 0.808 |
| $p_{5,6}$ | | | | | 0.667 | 0.667 | 0.667 | 0.667 | 0.667 |
| $p_{6,6}$ | | | | | 0.935 | | | | |
| $p_{6,7}$ | | | | | | 0.714 | 0.714 | 0.714 | 0.714 |
| $p_{7,7}$ | | | | | | 0.951 | | | |
| $p_{7,8}$ | | | | | | | 1.0 | 1.0 | 1.0 |
| $p_{8,8}$ | | | | | | | 0.948 | | |
| $p_{8,9}$ | | | | | | | | 0.8 | 0.8 |
| $p_{9,9}$ | | | | | | | | 0.956 | |
| $p_{9,10}$ | | | | | | | | | 1.0 |
| $p_{10,11}$ | | | | | | | | | 0.954 |

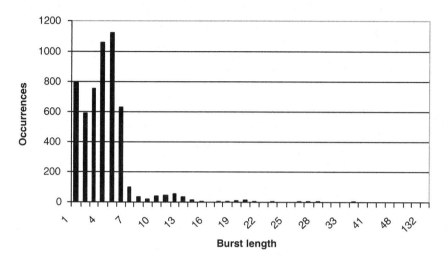

**Fig. 5.** Burst length distribution for 1500 Kbps

Figure 5 shows the loss burst length distribution for the 1500 Kbps case. Here each burst needs seven packets, and this is also reflected by the loss burst length distribution, indicating a model order of at most seven.

## 5   Effect of Packet Loss on Video Quality

In the previous section it was found that different packet patterns demand different loss models. In this section the effect of different loss models on the quality of streamed video is evaluated.

MPEG-4 video uses different frame types. An *intracoded frame* (I-frame) is like a JPEG picture and does not depend on other frames. A *predicted frame* (P-frame) only encodes the difference to the previous I or P-frame. A *bidirectionally predicted frame* (B-frame) only encodes the difference to the interpolation between the previous I or P-frame and the following I or P-frame. Thus, if an I-frame is damaged due to lost packets, all frames of the following *group of pictures* (GOP) are also affected, until the next I-frame is correctly received. If a P-frame is damaged due to a lost packet, then all following frames of the same GOP are affected too. Only if B-frames are damaged or dropped, the rest of the GOP is not affected. The structure of a GOP can be described by its frame types, like, for example, IPPPPPPPP or IBBPBBPBB. MPEG-4 allows to freely choose the structure as well as the GOP sizes. However, most encoders allow to specify *a maximum GOP size* that *must not be exceeded* (Max. I-frame interval), which typically is chosen between 12 and 300 frames. It must be noted that in *constant bitrate* (CBR) encoded videos there is a clear tradeoff between GOP length and picture quality. If the GOP length is small, then I-frames occur frequently. Thus damages due to packet losses quickly disappear again. On the other hand, I-frames need significantly more bits than P or B-frames. Thus, if many I-frames are to be encoded, then more compression artifacts are visible, thus lowering the subjectively perceived video quality.

For our experiments we used the MPEG-4 Visual Layer encoder DivX 5.1.1 Professional with two encoding runs, the encoded video scenes were taken from the Video Quality Experts Group (VQEG)[1], which provides standard television scenes in both PAL and NTSC resolution, each scene being about 8 seconds long. The material was first deinterlaced using an adaptive deinterlacer, then reduced in size to the standard CIF resolution, and finally encoded. As streaming server, Apple's Darwin has been used. The VQEG scenes have been used to create a test video of length 8:50 minutes. Since it is likely that an encoder places an I-frame after a scene cut, using the VQEG scenes, we artificially created single scenes which are longer than 8 seconds but do *not* show a scene cut. For this, we used each VQEG scene up to three times. First, the scene itself (8 seconds long), then the scene followed by the same scene but played in reverse (16 seconds long), then each scene, followed by itself played reverse, followed by the scene again (24 seconds long). The encoder parameters for encoding the resulting long video is shown in Table 2.

**Table 2.** MPEG-4 video encoding parameters

| Parameter | Values | Unit |
|---|---|---|
| Frame rate | 5, 10, 20, 25 | fps |
| Target rate | 64, 384, 768 | Kbps |
| Video bitrate | Target rate $\times 0.8-$ (assumed) Audio bitrate | Kbps |
| Max. I-frame interval | 15, 50, 100, 200, 300 | frames |
| B-frames allowed | yes, no | |

For our streaming experiments we used the streaming client CODIS RTSP (Figure 6). This client uses Java for the RTSP/RTP communication with the streaming server, and calls the open source codec XVID for decompressing MPEG-4 videos via the Java Native Interface (JNI). The client is able to artificially introduce packet losses due to a simple Gilbert loss model, or pre-recorded loss log files.

## 5.1    Player Freezes the Presentation

There are two possible ways for clients to react to lost packets. First, the rest of the affected GOP might not be shown to avoid the presentation of severely

---

[1] http://www.its.bldrdoc.gov/vqeg/

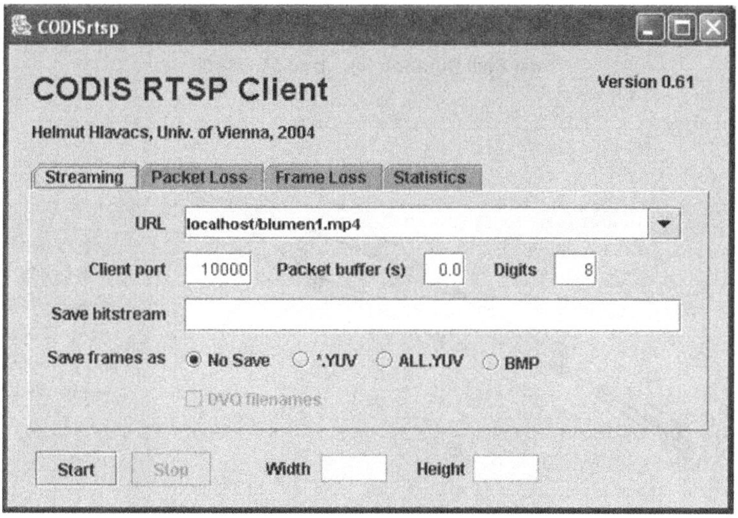

**Fig. 6.** CODIS RTSP client

damaged frames. In this scenario, every time a packet is lost in an I or P-frame, the player does not show the following frames until the next full I-frame has been received. This results in periodical video stalls, which freeze the presentation and may soon annoy human observers.

In the following experiments this behavior was assumed. Figure 7 shows the total amount of time (in seconds) the test video was frozen due to lost packets, when using a simple loss model without correlation. Here we used, as an example for medium loss (1%) and no correlation, the loss parameters $p = 0.01$ and $R = 0$. A clear linear behavior is present, and the results do not heavily depend on the target bitrate or the frame rate. This allows a good prediction of the video stalls to be expected under a given packet loss rate. Figure 8 shows the total stall duration depending on the used loss model for one particular target bitrate and frame rate. A clear dependence of the total stall duration on the correlation $R$ can be seen. The burstier the packet losses, the smaller the total stall duration is.

## 5.2 Player Shows Picture Artifacts

The second player behavior thinkable is to ignore packet losses and to continue showing the frames of an affected GOP even if the presented frames are heavily distorted. The metric for measuring the video quality is the PSNR, since it catches both compression artifacts and artifacts stemming from packet losses.

As a simple example, Figure 9 shows the PSNR of a popular 8 seconds long VQEG test scene ("Susie on the telephone") encoded with different parameters. Since this scene exhibits only little temporal activity, the overal video quality

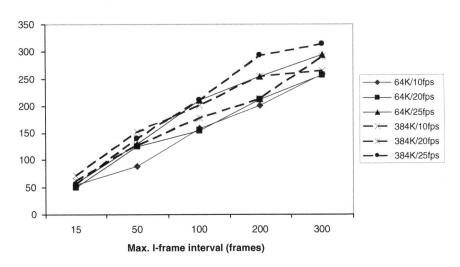

**Fig. 7.** Total video stall duration with fixed loss model

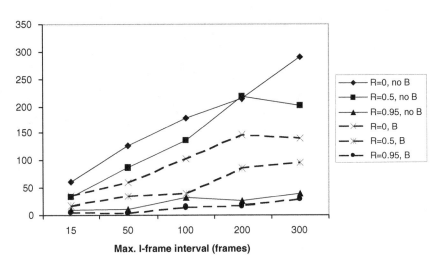

**Fig. 8.** Total video stall duration with different loss models

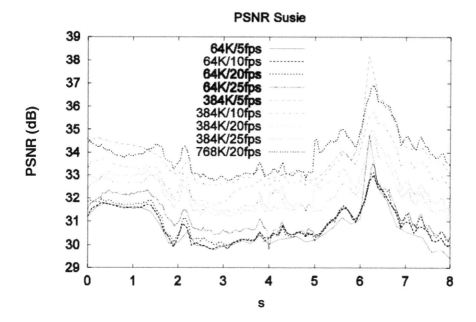

**Fig. 9.** Peak signal to noise ratio in dB of video "Susie on the telephone"

is good for all parameters (30-37 dB). Following subjective experiments, this quality would be judged as good, whereas a PSNR between 25 and 30 dB would be judged as medium, between 20 and 25 dB low, and below 20 dB as bad. Also, the differences between the videos remain constant at about 4 dB.

In order to obtain realistic loss models for the used video, we recorded the observed packet losses for this video at different locations in our department. Figure 10 shows the obtained packet loss probabilities $p$ and the correlations $R$ for the simple Gilbert model.

We used some of the obtained Gilbert model parameters to drop packets when streaming our 8:50 minutes long test video. As this video contains scenes with high temporal and spatial activity, the overal PSNR is much lower than the one of the simple "Susie on the telephone" scene. The effect of different loss model parameters on the overal video quality can be seen in Figure 11. Even for high packet losses the video quality stays quite stable, as long as the correlation is zero or positive. The effect of even moderate negative correlation is much more severe and drops the video quality into the low region.

## 6   Conclusion

In this paper we have evaluated the use of different loss models for modeling WLAN packet drops. It has been shown that the observed losses show a bursty behavior and a significant dependence on losses of the near past. Furthermore,

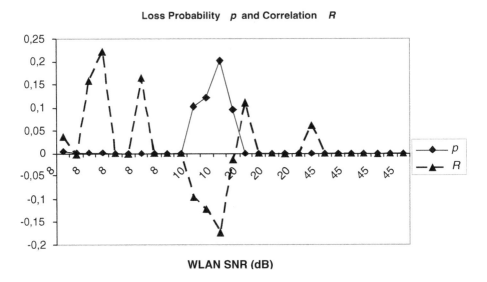

**Fig. 10.** Measured values for the Gilbert model

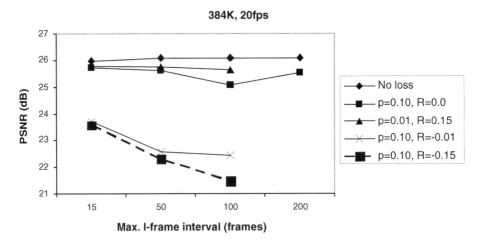

**Fig. 11.** Effect of different Gilbert models on the video quality

we have demonstrated the effect of different loss models on streaming video, for both players which freeze their presentations when facing packet losses, as well as for players which continue to show distorted frames. The observations indicate that the chosen loss model indeed has a severe effect on the perceived video quality and thus must be chosen with care. Due to their simplicity, extended Gilbert models seem to be good candidates for further evaluation of WLAN loss models.

In the future we will refine the model order estimation and mechnisms for choosing short and long term dependencies.

# References

1. E.N. Gilbert, Capacity of a burst-noise channel, Bell Syst. Tech. J. 39, (1960) 1253-1265.
2. ITU, Subjective video quality assessment methods for multimedia applications, ITU-T P.910, (1999).
3. H. Sanneck, G. Carle, A framework model for packet loss metrics based on loss runlengths, in Proceedings of the SPIE/ACM SIGMM Multimedia Computing and Networking Conference 2000 (MMCN 2000), pp. 177-187, San Jose, CA (2000).
4. H. Schulzrinne, S. Casner, R. Frederick, V. Jacobson, RTP: A Transport Protocol for Real-Time Applications, RFC 3550, IETF Network Working Group (2003).
5. Video Quality Experts Group, Final report from the Video Quality Experts Group on the validation of objetive models of video quality assessment (2000).
6. Z. Wang, H.R. Sheikh and A.C. Bovik, Objective Video Quality Assessment, in "The Handbook of Video Databases: Design and Applications", B. Furht and O. Marqure, ed., CRC Press (2003) 1041-1078.
7. C. Ware, T. Wysocki, J. Chicharo, On the Hidden Terminal Jamming Problem in IEEE 802.11 Mobile Ad Hoc Networks, ICC'2001 (2001).
8. S. Winkler, Quality metric design: A closer look. In Proc. SPIE Human Vision and Electronic Imaging Conference, vol. 3959, San Jose, California, January 22-28 (2000) 37-44.
9. A. Wörner, DVQ - An objective picture quality measurement not requiring a reference (NR). COMMITTEE T1 - TELECOMMUNICATIONS Committee Group T1A1.1, T1A1.1/2000-044, Charleston (2000).
10. S. Wolf, M. H. Pinson, A. A. Webster, G. W. Cermak, E. P. Tweedy, Objective and subjective measures of MPEG video quality. In Proc. 139th SMPTE Technical Conference, New York, NY (1997).

# Integrating MPLS and Policy Based Management Technologies in Mobile Environment

Mircea Axente-Stan[1] and Eugen Borcoci[2]

[1] Universitatea Politehnica Bucuresti (UPB)
mirceas@td.ornet.ro
[2] Universitatea Politehnica Bucuresti (UPB)
eugenbo@elcom.pub.ro

**Abstract.** Hierarchical architecture for Mobile IP (MIP), including both global mobility and local (micro) mobility management is a solution proposed in order to increase the efficiency and response time for fast local handoff processing. Multi-Protocol Label Switching (MPLS) is a technology of choice to facilitate traffic engineering and internetworking. Policy-Based Management (PBM) is a powerful approach, allowing flexible and scalable solutions for management, originally for IP based fixed networks. Extending and integrating MPLS and PBM into mobile environments, including the multi-domain heterogeneous networks is an active area for research. This paper proposes a variant of such an architecture integrating the MPLS and PBM in mobile environment (WLAN, 3G) while taking into account also micro/macro-mobility management and Quality of Service (QoS) control aspects.

## 1 Introduction

The Mobile IP (MIP) protocols proposed by IETF (MIPv4 and MIPv6) [4,6] offer a general framework to handle IP mobility, independent on wireless technology (WiFi or 3G), and they are simple and reliable solutions, but because of their generality these solutions have scalability and performance drawbacks when the mobile node is frequently changing its point of attachment. In order to minimize the delay during the handoff and reduce the overhead of control and data information, a new approach has been considered [8], with two levels of mobility management (MM). On the first MM level MIP is used to process macro-mobility events and to offer a general solution for inter-working. On the second level, a local or regional solution is used to handle micro-mobility events (Cellular IP, HAWAII, Regional Registration) [1,9,13].

This hierarchical architecture (with MIP on first level of MM and MIP extensions on second level of MM) can reduce service degradation during mobile node handoff, especially for real time services (e.g. voice, video). But natively the hierarchical IP cannot offer QoS support.

In recent years the MPLS networking technology emerged, offering a unified control mechanism and multiprotocol capabilities to run over mixed media infrastructures. MPLS defines signalling mechanisms to support both Class of Service (CoS)

G. Kotsis and O. Spaniol (Eds.): Mobile and Wireless Systems, LNCS 3427, pp. 166–175, 2005.

and QoS and also provides the means to relate these to the IP DiffServ markings of the originating IP traffic. MPLS can support constraint-based routing (CBR) and traffic engineering (TE) and can deliver the required QoS, to support Conversational, Streaming, and Interactive traffic. Hence, MPLS is more and more used as the technology of choice to facilitate traffic engineering (TE) and internetworking. The above mention advantages make attractive to use MPLS in wireless and mobile environment [7,14].

In order to obtain a gradual deployment, better scalability and QoS support for mobile environment, this paper proposes a variant of micro-mobility architecture built on top of an MPLS infrastructure, which will have a small number of entities aware of MIP signalling.

The next step in providing an efficient way of end-to-end QoS signalling in a mobile environment is to integrate into the management architecture the PBM paradigm. Thus one can get  a more flexible engineering of the resources and increase the possibility to offer controllable guarantees in scalable way.

The organization of the paper is structured as follows. In the section 2 we describe an overall architecture based on hierarchical approach, with micro-mobility management at MPLS level, focusing on interactions, between MIP and MPLS signalling. In section 3 we present some ideas on how we can combine the MPLS micro-mobility functions with policy-based management in order to provide QoS support for mobile nodes, and finally in section 4 we conclude our study and discuss possible directions of future work.

## 2    Mobility Management Architecture

The IP mobility management architecture proposed in this paper has as the starting point a hierarchical architecture [8]. In this approach MIP is supposed to handle inter-domain mobility management while MIP extensions on top of an MPLS infrastructure will handle intra-domain mobility [3,7,10,11].

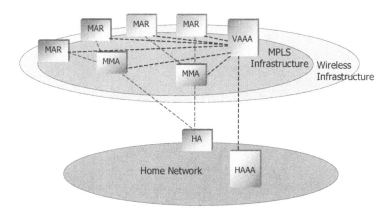

**Fig. 1.** Mobility Management Architecture

The figure 1 presents a high-level architecture showing the main entities involved in mobility management. The dashed lines show the horizontal interactions in the control plane between functional entities, as follows: MIP signalling, exchanged by MM aware elements: MAR, MMA, HA and AAA signalling, exchanged during authentication, authorisation and accounting process: MAR, MMA, AAAV, AAAH.

## 2.1    Functional Entities

The MPLS Access Router (MAR) is a Label Edge Router (LER) in MPLS domain and also plays the role of Foreign Agent (FA) for mobile domain. MAR will allow interactions between MPLS and MIP control plane and mapping functions in data plane. As an additional function, the MAR initiates the authentication process towards Authentication, Authorisation and Accounting (AAA) infrastructure.

The MPLS Mobility Agent (MMA) is a LER in MPLS domain and plays the role of Gateway Foreign Agent (GFA) for mobile domain. The MMA is second functional element that will allow interactions between MPLS and MIP control planes and mapping functions in data plane. The MMA will also keep binding information for each Mobile Node (MN) related to MPLS domain (MN, outgoing label).

The Authentication, Authorization and Accounting infrastructure (AAA) will offer standard AAA services and will dynamically allocate MMA for MNs using specific algorithm (e.g. round robin) that can also make use of current state of the network (e.g. network load).

## 2.2    MPLS Based Micro-mobility Management

By running MIP protocol transparently on top of MPLS infrastructure and having only few interaction points between mobility and MPLS control plane, the architecture will reduce the complexity and will offer a good flexibility. Moreover these interactions will allow taking advantages of all the advanced function offered by MPLS.

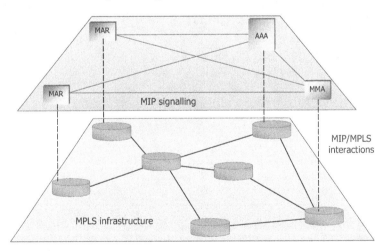

**Fig. 2.** Control Plane Interactions

Local mobility management will be done by managing MPLS tunnels between MMA and MAR. The change of mobile node point of attachment will require the change of Label Switched Paths (LSP) and thus reducing the handover delay by using label switching technology and data overhead by avoiding traditional IP in IP encapsulation. In the next two sections we describe the signalling process for Home Agent (HA) registration when the MN comes in the visited domain and local registration when the MN is moved from one MAR to another.

## 2.3    Registration Procedure with HA

Whenever a mobile node is powered up or enters into a visited domain, it has to execute the registration procedure with its Home Agent (HA). Upon successful registration the HA will update the binding information and will store it for registration lifetime.

The main steps during HA registration when the MN enter in a new domain are the following (see figure 3):

1. The MN receives (or can request) an *Advertising* message from one MAR which can offer its services to foreign MNs;
2. Based on information found in the *Advertising* message, the MN finds out that is away for its home network and starts the registration process, by forwarding the *Registration Request* to serving MAR;
3. When the MAR receives the *Registration Request*, it makes a local binding for MN and issue the authentication process with its local AAA infrastructure;
4. The visited AAA will then negotiate the security information with MN's home AAA. If the result of the negotiation is positive, the visited AAA will indicate to the initial MAR the identity of the MMA that will handle local mobility management for specified MN. The algorithm used for MMA allocation is out of scope of this paper (e.g. round robin or can be based on network load);
5. The MAR will forward the registration to MMA indicated by VAAA. Minimal information required in *Registration Request* must be the IP address, which identify the MN, the MAR address, IP address of HA, and security associations. The MMA will then send the registration message to HA;
6. Upon receiving the *Registration Request* message the HA updates its binding information with new routable IP address of MMA and send the *Registration Reply* message to MMA;
7. When the MMA receives the *Registration Reply* from HA, it will associate the MN to the same MPLS Forwarding Equivalence Class (FEC) as MAR address in its forwarding table if the label binding exists. Alternatively, it can send a label request message for MAR address and MAR will respond with label mapping message to MMA (here one of several MPLS procedures for label assignment can be followed);
8. The *Registration Reply* is forwarded to MAR and the end passed to MN.

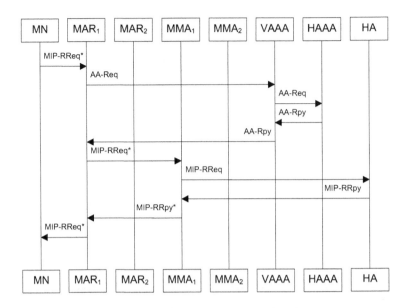

**Fig. 3.** Signalling messages for HA registration

**Note**: The asterisk sign indicate that the MIP messages should contain one or more MIP extension (e.g. for authentication and/or for local registration).

## 2.4    Local Registration

Each time the mobile node is changing its point of attachment but stays in the same domain, there is no need to execute the registration procedure towards HA. The registration can remain locally and the entities involved in regional registration are: the MMA, old MAR and new MAR. The MMA will handle the mobility management of mobile node in visited domain as long as the local registration lifetime doesn't expire.

The main steps during regional/local registration are the following (see figure 4):

1. The MN receives (or can request) an *Advertising* message from one MAR which can offer its services to foreign MNs;
2. Based on information found in the *Advertising* message, the MN finds out that it is located itself in the same domain and starts the local registration process, by forwarding the *Registration Request* to serving MAR and indicating the current MMA that serve the MN;
3. When the new MAR receives the *Registration Request*, it makes a local binding for MN and forwards the registration to MMA indicated in registration message;
4. Upon receiving the *Registration Request* message, the MMA updates the forwarding table for MN with the same FEC as for new MAR address, if the label binding exists. Alternatively, it can send a label request message for new MAR address and new MAR will respond with label mapping message to MMA.
5. The *Registration Reply* message is sent to new MAR and at the end then passed to MN.

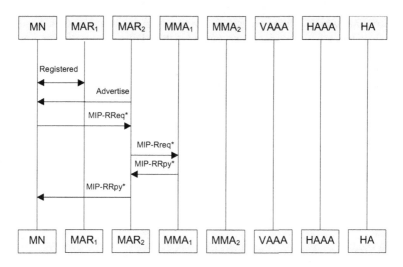

**Fig. 4.** Signalling messages for local registration

**Note**: The asterisk sign indicate that the MIP messages should contain one or more MIP extension (e.g. for authentication and/or for local registration).

## 3   Policy-Based Management for QoS Support

In previous section we have proposed a micro-mobility architecture that is scalable, will improve the handover procedure and can offer QoS support. In order to make use of QoS capabilities offered by MPLS infrastructure and to provide an efficient way of signalling end-to-end QoS, possible at the service level, in a mobile environment, we can enhance the proposed mobility management architecture with new functional entities, which will offer a policy-based framework. This framework will help us to properly use the network resources and to offer more than loose guarantees in scalable way.

The PBM is a powerful approach for network management, which defines high-level objectives of network, and system management based on a set of policies that can be enforced in the network [16]. The policies are a set of pre-defined rules (when a set of conditions are fulfilled then some defined actions will be triggered) that determine allocation and control of network resources. These conditions and actions can be established by the network administration with parameters that determine when the policies are to be implemented in the network [2,12,15].

The policies are usually defined based on the high-level business objectives of the network operator. Depending on the business model used, different service contracts SLA (Service Level Agreement) are agreed between the business entities, e.g. between User Customers and the Service Provider or between the providers themselves. PBM provides a high-abstraction view of a network to its operator, and among other advantages it helps the operator in the deployment of new IP QoS based services.

In the PBM architecture there is a policy server, which includes a central policy controller (CPC) and a set of policy decision points (PDP). The PDP's are responsible for determining which actions are applicable to which packets. The CPC has to ensure global consistency between decisions made by the PDP's. The policy actions are enforced and executed by the policy enforcement points (PEP). PEP's are typically co-located with packet forward components, such as border routers. PDP's interact with PEP's via special designed protocols like Common Open Policy Service. PDP's push configuration information down to the PEP's as well as respond to queries from the PEP's.

With the PBM system in a policy domain (PD), connections are maintained and admitted to different service classes based on assigned policy rules. By applying these rules, network routers can be determined to enforce admission control, traffic shaping, and scheduling mechanisms for different users under different traffic conditions. Usually, the rule parameters may include desired bandwidth, delay, duration, jitter, starting and finishing times, and some other limitations.

The MM architecture presented in this paper can be enhanced by adding functions of the generic $A^x$ architecture [5].

The $A^x$ framework is based on three basic concepts:

- Service separation; this extends the basic AAA architecture by separating user services from $A^x$ services;
- Service partitioning, allowing service diversification;
- Policy paradigm, all the provided services are implemented using policy framework by reusing existing work;

The architecture consists in different modules and services, which combine AAA and PBM requirements (see figure 5).

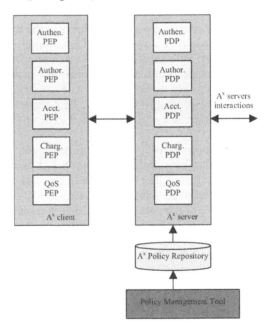

**Fig. 5.** A generic $A^x$ architecture

Because the AAA related services are well described in [5] we will take a closer look on QoS services and more precisely how and which network entities of MM architecture will interact with $A^x$ architecture entities.

The best way of explaining these interactions is to describe different scenarios in a gradual approach, from static configuration using top-down provisioning (from PDP to PEP, during initial registration phase), to dynamic interactions between PEP and PDP, triggered by QoS related events transported by signalling protocols (e.g. RSVP, SDP).

The refinement of PBM concepts applied to the proposed architecture is still for further study. In the following sections we give some examples of applying the static or dynamic PBM approach.

## 3.1    Static Approach

In a static approach, based on the HAAA response (see the figure 3) a local policy could indicate that all traffic coming from a certain MNs group should belong to a given QoS class (MPLS/DiffServ mapped).

During registration phase the AAAV server (e.g. QoS PDP) can provision a policy rule on the MAR (e.g. QoS PEP) where the MN is currently attached in order to mark all the traffic generated by a specific MN or group of MNs to a certain value (e.g. AF11).

**Fig. 6.** Interactions in static approach

The policy rule pushed by AAA server to MN's current MAR can be like follows:

```
if (RoamerNetworkId == NAI1)
then
   DSCP = AF11;
Endif
```

While preserving the best effort selected routes traffic of different MNs groups can be treated differently.

## 3.2    Signalled QoS with Best Effort Routes

As a next step, a more complex solution can offer dynamic behaviour. The routing inside the MPLS infrastructure is still assumed best effort. Based on a signalling protocol (e.g. Resource Reservation Protocol (RSVP)) the allocation of a certain QoS class for a flow could be dynamic e.g. per session or be determined by a service based local policy (SBLP).

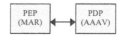

**Fig. 7.** Signalled QoS with best effort route

The PEP (MAR) forwards the signalling messages to PDP (AAA server). PDP response can indicate to PEP, installation of the following rule:

```
if signaled
     ((RoamerNetworkId == NAI1) &&
     (LatencyBound <= 100 msec))
then
     DSCP = EF;
Endif
```

### 3.3    Signalled QoS with Constraint-Based Routing

A further level of QoS guarantees can be obtained if constraint-based routing (CBR) is added to MPLS/DiffServ environment. This implies an interaction between AAAV, a SIP server and MAR. In the first phase the SIP server, acting as PEP for AAA services will negotiate the required credentials for the VoIP session during service invocation phase. When the negotiation phase is finished the PDP will push to QoS PEP (e.g. the MAR) the necessary rules in order to select the constrain-based route. The route selection through the MPLS infrastructure should be QoS constrained. Therefore different levels of QoS guarantees (loose, statistical, hard) can be obtained for each session.

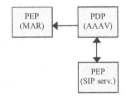

**Fig. 8.** Signalled QoS with constrain-based route

The PDP can push the following rule to the QoS PEP:
```
if signaled
     ((RoamerNetworkId == NAI1) &&
     (LatencyBound <= 100 msec) &&
     (Application = VoIP))
then
     DSCP = EF;
     ConstrainetRoute=Yes;
Endif
```

The rules installed on MAR can be modified by PDP as result of renegotiation between SIP server and AAAV.

# 4 Conclusion

In this paper, we have presented network architecture for MPLS-based micro-mobility, by integrating signalling and control mechanisms for MIP and MPLS. This integration provides the capability for QoS support, gradual evolution, and fast restoration and makes IP-in-IP tunnelling not necessary for data forwarding in MPLS domain. The architecture is well suited for fast handovers by reducing signalling overhead and latency (caused by wide-area mobility protocols), and also the transient packet loss associated with localized movement. By using AAA infrastructure allows for flexible registration points, and increase the reliability by eliminating single point of failure.

Integrating the proposed architecture in a policy based management framework can further add flexibility of the QoS management and allows the operators to make abstraction of the concrete wireless technology existent in the access part of the network.

In this paper, we have provided the framework for integrating mobility and policy-based management in mobile environment. The details of the protocol messages formats and its behaviour are under investigation. In addition, the algorithms behind the choice of MMA, using bandwidth availability, network status or a combination of other factors is open to further research.

# 5 References

1. A. Campbell, J. Gomez, Cellular IP, Internet Draft, December 1999;
2. B. Moore et al., Policy Core Information Model — Version 1 Specifications, RFC 3060, February 2001;
3. C. Perkins and P. Calhoun, AAA Keys for Mobile IP, Internet Draft, July 2001;
4. C. Perkins, IP Mobility Support, RFC3220, December 2001;
5. C. Rensing, M. Karsten, B. Stiller, AAA: A Survey and a Policy-Based Architecture and Framework, IEEE Network, Vol. 16, No. 6, 2002, pp. 22-27;
6. D. Johnson, C. Perkins, J. Arkko, Mobility Support in IPv6, Internet draft, July 2004;
7. E. Rosen, A. Viswanathan, R. Callon, Multiprotocol Label Switching Architecture, RFC 3031, January 2001;
8. E. Gustafsson, A. Jonsson and C. Perkins, Mobile IP Regional Tunnel Management, Internet Draft, October 2002;
9. E. Gustafsson, A. Jonsson, C. Perkins, Mobile IPv4 Regional Registration, Internet draft, October 2002;
10. F. Johansson, T. Johansson, Mobile IPv4 Extension for AAA Network Access Identifiers, Internet Draft, September 2003;
11. P. Calhoun and C. Perkins, DIAMETER Mobile IP Extensions, Internet Draft, June 2001;
12. R. Rajan, D.Verma, A policy framework for integrated and differentiated services in the Internet, IEEE Network, 13(5): 36–41, September/October 1999;
13. R. Ramjee, T. La Porta, IP micro-mobility support using HAWAII, Internet Draft, June 1999;
14. S.Vijayarangam and S.Ganesan, QoS Implementation For MPLS Based Wireless Networks ASEE Conference, April 2002, Oakland University, Michigan
15. Yavatkar, R., Pendarakis, D. and R. Guerin, A Framework for Policy-based Admission Control, RFC 2753, January 2000;
16. Internet Engineering Task Force: Policy Framework (policy) Working Group: URL: http://www.ietf.org/html.charters/policy-charter.html;

# A Reservation Scheme Satisfying Bandwidth QoS Constraints for Ad-Hoc Networks

Llorenç Cerdà[1], Michael Voorhaen[2], Rafael Guimarães[1],
José-M Barceló[1], Jorge García[1], and Chris Blondia[2]*

[1] Technical University of Catalonia
Computer Architecture Dept.
Jordi Girona 1-3, E-08034 Barcelona, Spain
{llorenc,rafael.guimaraes,joseb,jorge}@ac.upc.es

[2] University of Antwerp
Dept. Mathematics and Computer Science
Middelheimlaan 1, B-2020 Antwerpen, Belgium
{michael.voorhaen,chris.blondia}@ua.ac.be

**Abstract.** Achieving QoS (Quality of Service) in Mobile Ad-hoc NETworks (MANET) has been a research topic in the last years. In this paper we describe a QoS reservation mechanism for Routing Ad-hoc Networks. The mechanism is targeted for sources requiring a bandwidth allocation. The mechanism is based on the knowledge of the bandwidth requirements of the neighbors of a node and the interferent nodes in the cover area of each node. We describe as the protocol could be integrated in AODV and OLSR. We also give simulation results showing the advantages of our reservation scheme.

## 1 Introduction

MANETs (Mobile Ad-hoc NETworks) have characteristics such as flexibility, fast and easy deployment, robustness which make them an interesting technology for military, public safety, emergency and disaster applications. Providing QoS (Quality of Service) in a MANET is, however, a difficult task because: (i) the capacity of the physical links is variable depending on factors such as the distance, signal to noise ratio, interference, etc, (ii) the transmission media is shared between different nodes that have to be synchronized, (iii) MANET nodes are generally mobile and the network topology may change, and (iv) high signaling overhead due to the recovery of already hard-QoS reservations may be a problem due to the scarce transmission resources.

* This work was supported by the Ministry of Edu. of Spain under grant CICYT TIC-2001-0956-C04-01, by the Generalitat de Catalunya under grant CIRIT 2001-SGR-00226, by the Fund for Scientific Research Flanders under Scientific Research Community Broadband communication and multimedia services for mobile users, by DWTC Belgium under project IAP P5/11 MOTION (Mobile Multimedia Communication Systems and Networks), by IWT under project 020152–End-to-end QoS in IP based Mobile Networks, by the European NoE EuroNGI and by the European project WIDENS.

G. Kotsis and O. Spaniol (Eds.): Mobile and Wireless Systems, LNCS 3427, pp. 176–188, 2005.

The provisioning of QoS in a MANET involves the inter-working of several mechanisms spanning from the physical layer to the application layer. We center our work on the mechanisms related with the network layer: resource reservation, signaling and routing.

There are several QoS frameworks for MANETs proposed in the literature addressing some of the aspects for QoS support. Authors of [12] present a framework called FQMM (Flexible Quality of Service Model) that combines a reservation procedure for high priority traffic with a service differentiation for low-priority traffic. However, this hybrid provisioning scheme does not take into account the characteristics of MANETs and all the drawbacks of the IntServ and DiffServ remain. Other proposals are less general and address some of the aspects to be taken into account in a QoS framework for MANETs. INSIGNIA, see [4], is an in-band signaling protocol designed explicitly for MANETs which must be integrated with an ad-hoc routing protocol. CEDAR, see [10], is a protocol proposed to reduce the control overhead by defining a backbone and MMWN, see [9], is defined for cluster networks. A reservation scheme with AODV can be found in [13]. Another QoS approach based on measurements is presented in [3].

In this paper we treat the problem of achieving a reservation taking into account the available bandwidth in a coverage area and the traffic generated and forwarded by the neighbors and interferent MNs in that coverage area. Furthermore, we apply our reservation policy to AODV ([7]) and OLSR ([2]) routing protocols, although the reservation scheme can be applied to other ad-hoc routing protocols. The results show the feasibility of our scheme for guaranteeing the QoS requirements. Our reservation scheme works well for low mobility scenarios. Further analysis to optimize the reservation scheme under high mobility scenarios still is a current research topic.

## 2 Bandwidth QoS Constraint

Through this paper we shall assume the following:

- Without loss of generality, there are two traffic classes: with QoS and best effort.
- The MAC is able to isolate traffic classes such that QoS connections have priority over best effort, e.g. by using 802.11e.
- We use a *bandwidth reservation scheme* (e.g. peak rate allocation) subject to the following *QoS constraint*:

    *The occupancy of the wireless media by the QoS connections observed at any MN (i.e. transmitted or received by the MN antenna) is $\leq Q$ bps. I.e. the occupancy of the QoS traffic competing for the same shared media at any MN is $\leq Q$ bps.*

    The parameter $Q$ could be dimensioned such that delays are acceptable for QoS connections.
- A Call Admission Control (CAC) is used to block new QoS connections if the QoS constraint cannot be fulfilled.

We shall refer to the QoS traffic generated or in transit at $MN_i$ as the *bandwidth reservation* $(x_i)$ at a $MN_i$. I.e. if $r_{ij}$ is the amount of QoS traffic sent from $MN_i$ to $MN_j$, then:

$$x_i = \sum_{j \in \mathcal{N}_i} r_{ij} \tag{1}$$

Where $\mathcal{N}_i$ is the set of neighbor MNs of $MN_i$, i.e. $\{MN_j | j \in \mathcal{N}_i\}$ is the set of nodes in range with $MN_i$.

We define the *maximum available bandwidth* $MAB_i$ for QoS traffic at $MN_i$ as:

$$MAB_i = Q - x_i - \sum_{j \in \mathcal{N}_i} x_j \tag{2}$$

Therefore, the QoS constraint previously defined can be formulated as:

$$\text{QoS constraint: } MAB_i \geq 0, \forall i. \tag{3}$$

Note that the previous formulation of the QoS constraint would not be accurate for a MAC as 802.11 using RTS/CTS. This is because all nodes receiving not only RTS but also CTS are silent. Therefore, wireless media occupancy at a MN should be defined not only by the traffic transmitted by the neighbors, but also by the traffic received by them. Assume for instance the example shown in Fig. 1. In this figure there is only one ongoing QoS connection of $Q$ bps from $MN_1$ to $MN2$. Thus, using equations (1) and (2) we have: $x_1 = Q$, $x_2 = x_3 = x_4 = 0$, and: $MAB_1 = MAB_2 = 0$, $MAB_3 = MAB_4 = Q$. In case $MN_4$ accepts a reservation of $Q$ bps for $MN_3$, then $MAB_1 = MAB_2 = MAB_3 = MAB_4 = 0$, thus the QoS constraint is satisfied. However, $MN_3$ cannot receive packets from $MN_4$, since $MN_3$ is blocked by the CTS signals received from $MN_2$ (this is the well-known *exposed node problem* that occurs when using RTS/CTS).

Note also that even if $MAB_3 = Q$, $MN_3$ cannot accept new reservations due to the traffic constraint that $MN_2$ imposes on $MN_3$ (due to the well known *hidden node problem* that occurs in wireless networks). However, since our QoS constraint takes into account the traffic transmitted by the neighbors, it correctly captures this limitation. Assume for instance $MN_3$ accepting a reservation of $Q$ bps for $MN_4$. Then, the MNs would have: $x_1 = Q$, $x_2 = 0$, $x_3 = Q$, $x_4 = 0$, thus: $MAB_1 = 0$, $MAB_2 = -Q$, $MAB_3 = MAB_4 = 0$, so, the QoS constraint would not be satisfied.

## 3    Reservation Approach

We shall assume that connections requiring QoS use a reservation mechanism at the connection setup. This consists in the source sending a *Reservation Request* to the destination, which in turn sends back a *Reservation Reply* to the source if the reservation could be allocated.

Furthermore, we shall also assume that a *Call Admission Control* (CAC) is used to block new QoS connections if the QoS constraint cannot be fulfilled: i.e. a MN only accepts a Reservation Request if the QoS constraint can be satisfied.

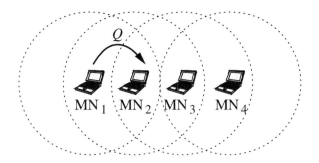

**Fig. 1.** Hidden node problem in QoS reservations

We define the *available bandwidth* $AB_i$ to allocate new reservations at $MN_i$ as:

$$AB_i = \min\{MAB_i, MAB_j\}, j \in \mathcal{N}_i \tag{4}$$

We shall use the notation $MN_i \rightarrow MN_j$ to denote two consecutive MNs belonging to the path to be reserved for a new QoS connection. Suppose that a new QoS connection of $r$ bps has to be established. We claim that if the path to be reserved does not follow unnecessary jumps (i.e. if $\cdots MN_i \rightarrow MN_j \rightarrow MN_k \cdots$, then $MN_i, MN_k \in \mathcal{N}_j, MN_l \notin \mathcal{N}_j, \forall l \neq i, j, k$), then, the QoS constraint given by (3) is satisfied if the following CAC conditions hold:

- If the QoS connection is generated at $MN_i$:
    - Accept if the destination is a neighbor and $AB_i \geq r$.
    - Accept if the destination is not a neighbor and $AB_i \geq 2r$.
- If the QoS connection is generated at another MN (transit traffic):
    - Accept if the destination is a neighbor and $AB_i \geq 2r$.
    - Accept if the destination is not a neighbor and $AB_i \geq 3r$.
- Otherwise the reservation request cannot be accommodated.

Note that this conditions should be fulfilled in every node along the path.

*Proof. Assume that the Reservation Request is accepted and use (2) and (4) to verify that the QoS constraint is satisfied.*                                                                               □

For instance, suppose the case when the new connection of $r$ bps is generated at $MN_1$ and the destination is not one of its neighbors (see Fig. 2). Assume that the CAC accepts this connection, and the next hop is the node $MN_2$ shown in the figure. Then, $x_1$ and $x_2$ will be increased by $r$. Thus, the $MAB$ of $MN_1$, $MN_2$ and all their common neighbors will be decreased by $2r$. Since $AB_i \geq 2r$, from (4), $MAB_i \geq 0, \forall i$.

The formerly described CAC may be further improved. Consider for instance that the node imposing the minimum $MAB$ in the previous example is a neighbor of $MN_1$ but not of $MN_2$. In this case, the $AB$ may be reduced by less than $2r$, thus the condition $AB_i \geq 2r$ may be too restrictive. However, in order to introduce this optimization, the nodes would not only need to know their neighbors, but also the coverage relation among them.

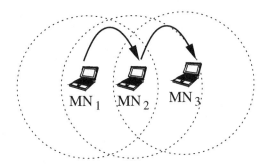

**Fig. 2.** Example of a connection generated at $MN_1$ with destination not a neighbor of $MN_1$

## 4   Implementation

The reservation scheme described in the previous sections requires that each $MN_i$ knows two quantities from their neighbors $\mathcal{N}_i$: their reservation ($x_j, j \in \mathcal{N}_i$) and their maximum available bandwidth ($MAB_i, j \in \mathcal{N}_i$). This could be implemented by means of each $MN_i$ broadcasting *HELLO packets* with $x_i$ and $MAB_i$.

In the following we describe how to integrate our reservation scheme in the AODV [7] and OLSR ad-hoc [2] routing protocols.

### 4.1   Integration in AODV

For the AODV protocol we propose the following modifications to implement the reservation scheme:

(i)   AODV HELLO messages are modified such that each $MN_i$ advertises $x_i$ and $MAB_i$ to their neighbors.
(ii)  Each $MN_i$ collects the QoS messages from their neighbors to compute $AB_i$ according to (4).
(iii) QoS Reservation Request and Reply messages are integrated in AODV as described in [6]: the bandwidth reservation is included in a Route Request (RREQ) message as an extension object. The RREQ QoS extensions include a session-ID to identify the flows together with the Source and Destination addresses.
(iv)  Upon receiving a RREQ, intermediate MNs apply the CAC algorithm described in Sect. 3. If the reservation is accepted, the RREQ is forwarded, and it is discarded otherwise. However, reservation is only done when the RREP is received (see Fig. 3). Opposite to AODV, if an intermediate MN has a route to a destination, this MN should not answer with a route reply to the sender, since the intermediate MN does not know whether further MNs can accomplish the bandwidth reservation. In order to avoid this situation the D flag of a RREQ is activated (see [7]) indicating that only the destination can send a RREP.

**Fig. 3.** Reservation procedure

## 4.2   Integration in OLSR

The modifications we propose for OLSR to implement the reservation scheme is some-how similar to what happens for AODV, as one may notice in the following steps:

(i)   OLSR HELLO messages are modified just like in AODV (see steps i and ii).
(ii)  We modified the OLSR TC messages such that they also advertise $AB_i$ next to advertising the MPR selectors. This way each node has knowledge of the network topology and the bandwidth available in the network.
(iii) In order to find a route that meets the QoS requirements, we modified the OLSR route selection algorithm to find a shortest hop path that has enough bandwidth to meet these requirements. Since the TC messages also advertise $AB_i$ the originating node has enough information to decide if enough resources are available.
(iv)  The reservation of the bandwidth at the intermediate nodes is done by adding the requested rate to the IP header (e.g. by using an IP option). This way an intermediate node which has not yet seen the flow will be able to allocate the bandwidth. The requested rate can be advertised for a certain amount of time, number of packets or until an ACK is received to say that the flow has been set up. This is done to make this approach robust to packet loss.

For the remainder of the paper we will call our OLSR implementation extended with the QoS signaling QOLSR. We wish to stress that our protocol has little in common with [1], only the idea of extending OLSR with QoS support. The signaling introduced in QOLSR has much in common with the INSIGNIA protocol [4], although the full feature set of INSIGNIA is not implemented since this was not necessary for the goal of this paper.

## 4.3   Flow Based Routing

Some words about flows: note these reservation schemes need a flow-id to identify ongoing QoS connections. IP look-ups are done using the pairs IP-address and Flow-id. These pairs must be unique. Using IPv6 it can be used the flow label specification described in [8]. Connections are identified by the 3-tuple Flow Label, Source and Destination Address fields. Packet classifiers use the former triplet to identify which flow a particular packet belongs to. Note that packets from different flows forwarded to the same destination may follow different paths.

## 5   Simulation Results

We have added our reservation scheme in the AODV protocol provided by the network simulator [11] and the OLSR implementation available in [5]. We shall refer as QAODV and QOLSR to our implementations. We have simulated the following scenario:

- MAC: 802.11 without RTS/CTS and link rate of 2 Mbps.
- CBR connections sending packets of size 500 bytes and rate 32 kbps.
- The QoS constraint for CBR connections is $Q = 250$ kbps.
- 40 MNs randomly placed over a square 1000x1000 meters.
- MN coverage of 300 meters.
- Each pair of nodes initiates a unidirectional QoS connection staggered 15s. Thus, 20 QoS connections are initiated (20 x 32 = 640 kbps).
- The simulation time is 600 s.
- The nodes don't move.

In the following we explain the results obtained using AODV/QAODV and OLSR/ QOLSR.

### 5.1   Simulation Results with AODV

Fig. 4 shows the evolution of the connections established with each protocol. Note that all connections are established with AODV but only 8 with QAODV (the others are blocked). Fig. 6 shows the distribution of the MNs and the connections that were successfully established. The figure also shows the coverage (300 meters) for one of the nodes.

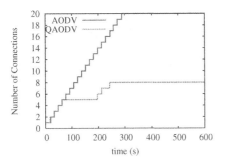

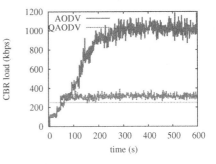

**Fig. 4.** Connection setup          **Fig. 5.** Maximum occupancy

Fig. 5 plots at each time $t$ the maximum CBR occupancy (as defined in section 2) observed by the most congested node at this moment. This occupancy is measured at each node counting the size of the frames carrying CBR packets that are seen by the node (including the collisions). This figure validates that the QoS constraint is satisfied, i.e. the maximum CBR occupancy is $\approx 250$ kbps. This value is exceeded a bit among other

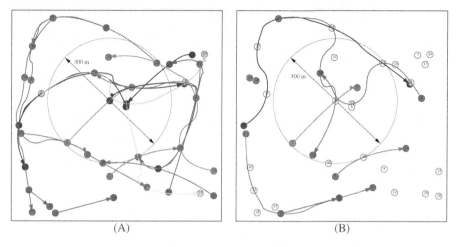

**Fig. 6.** Connections established using AODV (A) and QAODV (B)

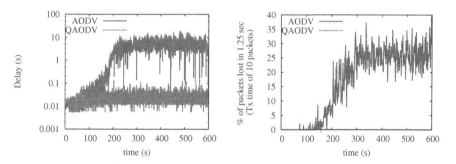

**Fig. 7.** Maximum delay          **Fig. 8.** Maximum loss

reasons, because of collisions and headers overhead (the 500 bytes packet size does not include the IP header, neither the 802.11 header, thus, the occupancy at the MAC is in fact $250 \times 572/500 = 286$ kbps). Thus, we conclude from Fig. 5 that the QoS constraint is satisfied.

Fig. 5 also shows that, using AODV, the MAC becomes congested at around 200 seconds (when only 14 of the 20 connections have started). This may be noticed by the fact that the CBR occupancy does not increase any more, although new connections are established. This is confirmed by Figs. 7 and 8. The first one depicts the maximum end-to-end delay of CBR packets, and the second one depicts the maximum percentage of packets lost by the connections, measured in intervals of 1.25 s (the transmission time of 10 packets).

It is also interesting to know how may connections are suffering from congestion. Figures 9-10 and 11 show respectively delay and loss-percentage Complementary Distribution Probability Functions (CDPF) for all the ongoing connections (loss CDPFs are not given for QAODV because no losses were detected with it).

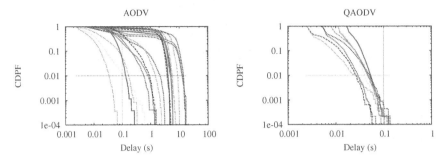

**Fig. 9.** CDPFs of the delay for all AODV con-    **Fig. 10.** CDPFs of the delay for all QAODV
nections                                            connections

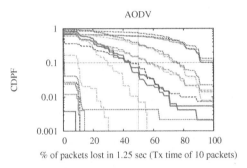

**Fig. 11.** CDPFs of packet loss for all AODV connections.

Fig. 9 shows that delays are huge for AODV: 11 of the 20 connections have delays higher than 2 s with probability higher than 30%. On the other hand, Fig. 10 shows that all connections with QAODV have delays higher than 60 ms with probability lower than 0.1%. Fig. 11 also shows that most of AODV connections suffer high loss rates (11 of the 20 connections have losses higher than 50% with probability higher than 5%). Thus, we conclude that most of the ongoing AODV connections are suffering from congestion.

## 5.2 Simulation Results with OLSR

The following paragraph describes the results obtained from the simulations using OLSR and QOLSR. Since OLSR is a proactive protocol we had to make sure that each node received the necessary topology information before the applications were started. We changed the parameters so that the simulation now took 700s. During the first 100 seconds no application was started, only OLSR routing messages were exchanged. This 100 second period gives OLSR ample time to exchange routing information between all nodes. We now compare the results of the last 600s of our simulation to those from AODV.

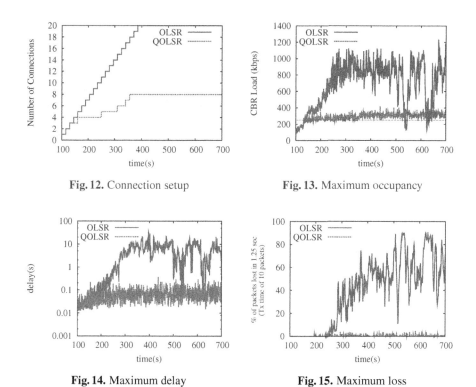

**Fig. 12.** Connection setup

**Fig. 13.** Maximum occupancy

**Fig. 14.** Maximum delay

**Fig. 15.** Maximum loss

Fig. 12 shows us that 8 connections are allowed to start, while the others are blocked by the CAC. However when observing the graph we notice that different applications are allowed to start by QAODV and QOLSR protocols. After carefully looking at the routes that were set up by both protocols we found that the route for some of the flows was chosen differently by them. In fact both protocols could choose between the same routes and both made an arbitrary choice (which is influenced by randomness e.g. the order of the links in the topology set of OLSR and the jitter introduced before re-broadcasting a RREQ in AODV). This different choice in routes caused that different applications were allowed to start.

Of course the previous paragraph does not prove that the CAC performed by both protocols behaves equally well since the result depends very much on the node placement and several random factors inherent to the scenario. To investigate any possible performance differences between the two protocols we ran the same simulation 400 times with both QAODV and QOLSR but each time using different node placements. Figures 20 and 21 show the results of these simulations.

As you can see QOADV allows on average 7 connections with a standard deviation of about 2 connections. QOLSR presents similar results, with an average of 7 to 8 connections and a standard deviation of 2 connections. It is interesting to notice that, although OLSR disseminates network topology using the multi-point relays (what causes only partial topology information to be spread), results are as good as in the case of AODV,

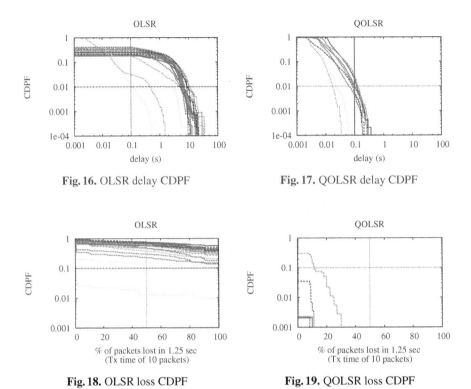

**Fig. 16.** OLSR delay CDPF

**Fig. 17.** QOLSR delay CDPF

**Fig. 18.** OLSR loss CDPF

**Fig. 19.** QOLSR loss CDPF

where this restriction is not present. In fact, repeating the experiment with QAODV using RTS/CTS, we obtained an average of 11 connections. The drawback of QAODV is that some nodes may not receive the broadcast because of collisions. This is more likely to happen without RTS/CTS, due to the hidden node problem. Thus, suboptimal paths may be chosen with QAODV, reducing the number of connections.

If we compare Fig. 5 to Fig. 13 we observe the following: QOLSR performs equally well as QAODV and both succeed in guaranteeing the QoS constraint. Secondly we also notice the drops in the occupancy measured with OLSR which did not occur with AODV. This occurs when the network gets congested and some of the broadcasts that are needed to advertise the topology information to the network get lost causing some nodes not to have full topology information. Since in this case these nodes might not have a route to the destination they will drop the packets before passing them to the MAC layer. After a while the MAC will get less congested and the topology information is advertised correctly.

We can see the same behavior in Fig. 14 where the delay drops at the same time the MAC gets less congested. Compared to QOADV (Fig. 7) we see that in QOLSR (Fig. 14) the packets incur a slightly higher delay which is confirmed by Fig. 17. Fig. 16 shows us that except for two flows all the others have a 10% chance of having a 10 s delay. With QOLSR on the other hand the majority of the flows have end-to-end delays

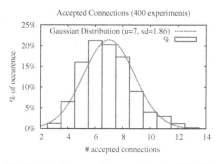
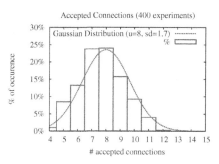

**Fig. 20.** % of accepted connections by QAODV    **Fig. 21.** % of accepted connections by QOLSR

higher than 100 ms with a probability lower than 1% (Fig. 17). The remaining flows show a better behavior than the two flows that behaved best with OLSR.

Fig. 15 shows us that QOLSR is not only successful in avoiding network congestion, but also in avoiding the packet losses that occur when the network becomes congested. Compared to QOLSR, OLSR behaves much worse since it loses up to 90% of the packets at some instances. Fig. 19 shows us that QOLSR has negligible losses just like QAODV.

# 6   Conclusions and Further Work

In this paper we have described a bandwidth reservation scheme for ad-hoc networks that satisfies the following QoS constraint: "The occupancy of the wireless media by the QoS connections observed at any mobile node (MN) is $\leq Q$ bps". Our reservation scheme only requires that MNs know the reservation and maximum available bandwidth of their neighbors. These quantities can be easily advertised by means of hello packets. We also give the CAC rules that MNs should apply to new connections requiring QoS.

We have described how to integrate our reservation scheme in the AODV and OLSR ad-hoc routing protocols and we have implemented them with the ns simulator. We have have simulated AODV and OLSR with and without our reservation scheme. The results obtained for both protocols are similar. The following items summarize our findings:

- Ad-hoc networks can easily become congested by QoS traffic (opposite to TCP, this kind of traffic typically doesn't have congestion control mechanisms).
- Congestion can easily extend to most of the network introducing high delays and losses, thus, damaging most of the connections having QoS requirements.
- Our reservation scheme provides a feasible way to avoid congestion, thus, guaranteeing QoS requirements to ongoing connections.
- Confronting our reservation scheme integrated in AODV and OLSR, we have observed that AODV allows on average almost the same number of connections than OLSR.

*Further work*: In the simulations carried out in this paper we have used static MNs (without movement). If MNs move, they may enter in coverage with new MNs, producing *QoS violation* (i.e. breaching the QoS constraint). A mechanism in needed to cope with this situation. For instance, the MNs receiving hello packets from a new MN such that a QoS violation occurs, may send a *Route Error* to some connections such that they look for another path that fulfills the QoS constraint. Other reasons may produce QoS violations, e.g. due to transient periods, or due to the establishment of a path having unnecessary jumps inside the coverage of another MN.

Another problem arises when a link is broken and a set of connections that traverse that node loose the reserve path to their destination. A reservation recovery must be initiated on the nodes whose flows have lost the QoS reservations. Furthermore, a mechanism to free the already reservations in the broken path is needed. This mechanism may use timers that free a reservation in a node if the interval of time after forwarding a packet belonging to a flow is higher than certain value.

# References

1. I. Gawedzki, A. Munaretto, K. Al Agha, and H. Badis. QOLSR: QoS with the OLSR protocol. http://qolsr.lri.fr/.
2. P. Jacquet, T. Clausen. RFC 3626: Optimized Link State Routing Protocol (OLSR), Oct 2003.
3. M. Kazantzidis, M. Gerla, and S. Lee. RFC 3697: Permissible throughput network for adaptative multimedia in AODV MANETs. In *IEEE ICC 2001*, 2001.
4. S. Lee, G. Ahn, and A. T. Campbell. Improving UDP and TCP performance in mobile ad hoc networks with INSIGNIA. In *IEEE Communications Magazine*, June 2001.
5. Naval Research Laboratory (NRL). NRLOLSR Implementation. http://pf.itd.nrl.navy.mil/projects.php?name=olsr.
6. C. Perkins and E. Belding-Royer. Quality of Service for Ad hoc On-Demand Distance Vector Routing (work in progress), Oct 2003. draft-perkins-manet-aodvqos-02.txt.
7. C. Perkins and S. Daas E. Belding-Royer. RFC 3561: Ad hoc On-Demand Distance Vector Routing, Jul 2003.
8. J. Rajahalme, A. Conta, B. Carpenter, and S. Deering. RFC 3697: IPv6 Flow Label Specification, March 2004.
9. R. Ramanathan and M. Streenstrup. Hierarchically-organized, multihop wireless networks for quality of service support. In *ACM Mobile Networks and Applications, Vol 3, $N^o 1$*, June 1998.
10. R. Sivakumar, P. Sinha, and V. Bharghavan. CEDAR: A COre-Extraction Distributed Ad Hoc Routing Algorithm. In *IEEE JSAC, Special Issue on Ad Hoc Networks, Vol 17, $N^o$ 8*, August 1999.
11. UCB/LBNL/VINT. The Network Simulator ns-2. http://www.isi.edu/nsnam/ns.
12. H. Xiao, W. G. Seah, A. Lo, and K. C. Chua. A flexible quality of service model for mobile ad hoc netowrks. In *Proceedings of the IEEE Vehicular Technology Conference, Tokio, Japan*, May 2000.
13. Q. Xue and A. Ganz. Ad hoc QoS on-demand routing (AQOR) in mobile ad hoc networks. *Journal of Parallel and Distributed Computing*, (63):154–165, 2003.

# Performance of Internet Access Solutions in Mobile Ad Hoc Networks

Ali Hamidian, Ulf Körner, and Anders Nilsson

Department of Communication Systems
Lund University, Sweden
Box 118, 221 00 Lund
{alexh, ulfk, andersn}@telecom.lth.se

**Abstract.** Although an autonomous mobile ad hoc network (MANET) is useful in many scenarios, a MANET connected to the Internet is more desirable. This interconnection is achieved by using gateways, which act as bridges between a MANET and the Internet. Before a mobile node can communicate with an Internet host it needs to find a route to a gateway. Thus, a gateway discovery mechanism is required. In this paper the MANET routing protocol Ad hoc On-Demand Distance Vector (AODV) is extended to achieve the interconnection between a MANET and the Internet. Moreover, the paper investigates and compares three approaches for gateway discovery. The question of whether the configuration phase with the gateway should be initiated by the gateway, by the mobile node or by mixing these two approaches is being discussed. We have implemented and simulated these three methods and we discuss the advantages and disadvantages of the three alternatives.

## 1 Introduction

A mobile ad hoc network (MANET) is an autonomous network that can be formed without need of any established infrastructure or centralized administration. It normally consists of mobile nodes, equipped with a wireless interface, that communicate with each other. Because these kinds of networks are very spontaneous and self-organizing, they are expected to be very useful. It is also highly likely that a user of the network will have the need to connect to the Internet.

The Internet Engineering Task Force (IETF) has proposed several routing protocols for MANETs, such as Ad hoc On-Demand Distance Vector (AODV) [10], Dynamic Source Routing (DSR) [6], Optimized Link State Routing Protocol (OLSR) [4] and Topology Dissemination Based on Reverse-Path Forwarding (TBRPF) [9]. However, these protocols were designed for communication within an autonomous MANET, so a routing protocol needs to be modified in order to achieve routing between a mobile device in a MANET and a host device in a wired network (e.g. the Internet). To achieve this network interconnection, gateways that understand not only the IP suite, but also the MANET protocol stack, are needed. Thus, a gateway acts as a bridge between a MANET and the Internet and all communication between the two networks must pass through any of the gateways.

G. Kotsis and O. Spaniol (Eds.): Mobile and Wireless Systems, LNCS 3427, pp. 189–201, 2005.
© Springer-Verlag Berlin Heidelberg 2005

The AODV routing protocol is one of the most developed and implemented routing protocols investigated by the IETF MANET working group. In this work AODV has been modified to achieve routing of packets towards a wired network [14]. Although AODV was used in this study, our approach can be applied to any reactive MANET routing protocol and with some modifications to proactive MANET routing protocols as well.

This paper evaluates three approaches for gateway discovery. An interesting question is whether the configuration phase with the gateway should be initiated by the gateway (proactive method), by the mobile node (reactive method) or by mixing these two approaches. We have implemented these three methods in Network Simulator 2 (ns-2) [8] and compare them by means of simulation. We also discuss the advantages and disadvantages of the three alternatives.

The remainder of this paper is organized as follows: Section 2 gives an overview of AODV and presents an Internet access solution for MANETs. Section 3 investigates three gateway discovery strategies. The simulation results are presented and discussed in Sect. 4. Finally, Sect. 5 concludes this paper and gives some directions for future work.

## 2  Protocol Description

As mentioned above, AODV was originally designed for routing packets within a MANET and not between a MANET and a wired network. In order to achieve routing across the network interconnection, the routing protocol needs to be modified. After giving an overview of AODV, we present a solution, which is referred to as AODV+ [13], where AODV is extended to provide Internet access for mobiles node in a MANET.

### 2.1  Ad Hoc On-Demand Distance Vector (AODV)

Ad hoc On-Demand Distance Vector (AODV) is a reactive MANET routing protocol [10], where the reactive property implies that a mobile node requests a route only when it needs one. Consequently, the node maintains a routing table containing route entries only to destinations it is currently communicating with. Each route entry contains a number of fields such as *Destination IP Address*, *Next Hop* (a neighbor node chosen to forward packets to the destination), *Hop Count* (the number of hops needed to reach the destination) and *Lifetime* (the expiration or deletion time of the route). AODV guarantees loop-free routes by using sequence numbers that indicate how fresh a route is.

**Route Discovery.** Whenever a node (source) determines that it needs a route to another node (destination) it broadcasts a *route request* (RREQ) message and sets a timer to wait for the reception of a *route reply* (RREP). A node that receives a RREQ creates a *reverse route entry* for the source in its routing table. Then it checks to determine whether it has received a RREQ with the same Originator IP Address and RREQ ID within the last PATH_DISCOVERY_TIME. If such a RREQ has been received, the node discards the newly received RREQ in order to prevent duplicated RREQs from being forwarded. If the RREQ is not discarded the node continues to process it as follows: If the node is either the destination or if it has an unexpired route to the destination it unicasts a RREP back to the source; otherwise it rebroadcasts the RREQ. If a RREP is generated, any intermediate node along the path back to the source creates a *forward route entry* for the destination in its routing table and forwards the RREP towards the source.

If the source does not receive any RREP before the RREQ timer expires, it broadcasts a new RREQ with an increased time to live (TTL) value. This technique is called *expanding ring search* and continues until either a RREP is received or a RREQ with the maximum TTL value is broadcasted. Broadcasting a RREQ with the maximum TTL value is referred to as a *network-wide search* since the RREQ is disseminated throughout the MANET. If a source performs a network-wide search without receiving any corresponding RREP, it may try again to find a route to the destination, up to a maximum of RREQ_RETRIES times after which the session is aborted.

**Route Maintenance.** When an active link breaks, the node upstream of the break invalidates all its routes that use the broken link. Then, the node broadcasts a *route error* (RERR) message that contains the IP address of each destination that has become unreachable due to the link break. Upon reception of such a RERR message, a node searches its routing table to see if it has any route(s) to the unreachable destination(s) (listed in the RERR message) that uses the originator of the RERR as the next hop. If such routes exist, they are invalidated and the node broadcasts a new RERR message. This process continues until the source receives a RERR message. The source then invalidates the listed routes as previously described and initiates a route discovery process if needed.

## 2.2   Internet Access for Mobile Ad Hoc Networks

Whenever a mobile node is about to communicate with a fixed wired node, it searches its routing table for a route towards the destination. If a route is found, the communication can be established. Otherwise, the mobile node starts a route discovery process by broadcasting a RREQ message as described above.

When an intermediate mobile node receives a RREQ message, it searches its routing table for a route towards the wired destination. If a route is found, the intermediate node would normally send a RREP back to the originator of the RREQ. But in that case, the source would think that the destination is a mobile node that can be reached via the intermediate node. It is important that the source knows that the destination is a fixed node and not a mobile node, because these are sometimes processed differently. In our solution, this problem has been solved by preventing the intermediate node to send a RREP back to the originator of the RREQ if the destination is a wired node. Instead, the intermediate node updates its routing table and rebroadcasts the received RREQ message. To determine whether the destination is a wired node or not, an intermediate node consults its routing table. If the next hop address of the destination is a default route (see Table 1), the destination is a wired node. Otherwise, the destination is a mobile node or a gateway.

Since neither the fixed node nor the mobile nodes in the MANET can reply to the RREQ, it is rebroadcasted until its TTL value reaches zero. When the timer of the RREQ expires, a new RREQ message is broadcasted with a larger TTL value. However, since the fixed node cannot receive the RREQ message (no matter how large the TTL value is) the source will never receive the RREP message it is waiting for. This problem has been solved by letting the source assume the destination is a fixed node if a network-wide search has been done without receiving any corresponding RREP. In that case, the source must find a route to a gateway (if it does not have one already, see Sect. 3) and send its data packets towards the gateway, which will forward them towards the fixed node.

It should be mentioned that when using the expanding ring search, a considerable route discovery delay will occur if the destination is a fixed node. Modifying the parameters involved in the expanding ring search technique (such as TTL_START and TTL_THRESHOLD) can decrease the route discovery delay if the destination is a fixed node. However, the modification can also result in increased routing overhead if the destination is a mobile node. The modification could for example be to increase TTL_START. Assuming the destination is a fixed node, increasing TTL_START would result in less number of broadcasted RREQs (and consequently less delay) before the source assumes that the destination is a fixed node. Thus, different approaches are preferable depending on whether a mobile node is to communicate mostly with the MANET or the Internet.

**Handover.** Due to the multihop nature of a MANET, there might be several reachable gateways for a mobile node at some point of time. If a mobile node receives gateway advertisements from more than one gateway, it has to decide which gateway to use for its connection to the Internet. In this solution a mobile node initiates a handover when it receives an advertisement from a gateway that is closer (in terms of number of hops) than the one it is currently registered with. Apart from the hop count, there are other potential criteria that could be used to determine whether a handover is needed or not; e.g. geographical distance, radio signal level, signal delay and direction of node movement [1]. However, the question of a suitable metric for route selection is a general routing issue in MANETs.

**Gateway Operation.** When a gateway receives a RREQ, it consults its routing table for the destination IP address specified in the RREQ message. If the address is not found, the gateway sends a RREP with an 'I' flag (RREP_I) back to the originator of the RREQ. On the other hand, if the gateway finds the destination in its routing table, it unicasts a RREP as normal, but may also optionally send a RREP_I back to the originator of the RREQ. This will provide the mobile node a default route although it has not requested it. If the mobile node is to communicate with the Internet later, the default route is already established, and another time consuming gateway discovery process can be avoided.

**Routing Table Management.** Another issue that must be taken into consideration is how the routing table should be updated after a network-wide search without receiving any corresponding RREP. Once the source has determined that the destination is a fixed node located on the Internet, it has to create a route entry for the fixed node in its routing table. If the route entry for the fixed destination would not be created in the routing table, the source would not find the address to the fixed node in its routing table when the next data packet would be generated and hence, the source would have to do another time consuming network-wide search.

Table 1 shows how the routing table of a mobile node should look like after creation of a route entry for a fixed node. The first entry tells the node that the destination is a fixed node since the next hop is specified by the default route. The second entry specifies which gateway the node has chosen for its Internet connection. The last entry gives information about the next hop towards the gateway.

**Table 1.** The routing table of a mobile node after creating a route entry for a fixed node

| Destination Address | Next Hop Address |
| --- | --- |
| Fixed node | Default |
| Default | Gateway |
| Gateway | IMN |

Another challenge is how to setup the routing table of an intermediate mobile node (IMN) chosen to forward data packets towards the gateway. Since the forward route entries are created for the gateway (the source of the RREP_I) and not for the fixed node, which is the final destination of the data packets, IMN will not find any valid route for the fixed node when it receives data packets from the source. Therefore, it would normally drop the data packets because it does not know how to forward them. In our solution, if IMN does not find a valid route to the destination and if the destination is a fixed node, it creates a (or updates the) route entry for the fixed node in its routing table and forwards the data packets towards the gateway.

# 3   Gateway Discovery

An interesting question to investigate is whether the configuration phase with the gateway should be initiated by the gateway (proactive method), by the mobile node (reactive method) or by mixing these two approaches (hybrid proactive/reactive method) has been discussed lately. In the following, the mechanisms of these three approaches are discussed.

## 3.1   Proactive Gateway Discovery

The proactive gateway discovery is initiated by the gateway itself. The gateway periodically broadcasts a *gateway advertisement* (GWADV) message with the period determined by ADVERTISEMENT_INTERVAL [13,5]. The advertisement period must be chosen with care so that the network is not flooded unnecessarily.

The mobile nodes that receive the advertisement, create a (or update the) route entry for the gateway and then rebroadcast the message. To assure that all mobile nodes within the MANET receive the advertisement, the number of retransmissions is determined by NET_DIAMETER defined by AODV. However, this will lead to enormously many unnecessary duplicated advertisements. A conceivable solution that prevents duplicated advertisements, is to introduce a "GWADV ID" field in the advertisement message format similar to the "RREQ ID" field in the RREQ message format (see Sect. 2.1).

It is worth mentioning that the mobile nodes randomize their rebroadcasting of the GWADV message in order to avoid synchronization and subsequent collisions with other nodes' rebroadcasts.

The advantage of this approach is that there is a chance for the mobile node to initiate a handover before it looses its Internet connection. The disadvantage is that since a control message is flooded through the whole MANET periodically, limited resources in a MANET, such as power and bandwidth, will be used a lot.

### 3.2    Reactive Gateway Discovery

The reactive gateway discovery is initiated by a mobile node that is to create or update a route to a gateway. The mobile node broadcasts a RREQ with an 'I' flag (RREQ_I) to the ALL_MANET_GW_MULTICAST [14] address, i.e. the IP address for the group of all gateways in a MANET. Thus, only the gateways are addressed by this message and only they process it. Intermediate mobile nodes that receive a RREQ_I are not allowed to answer it, so they just rebroadcast it. When a gateway receives a RREQ_I, it unicasts back a RREP_I which, among other things, contains the IP address of the gateway.

The advantage of this approach is that control messages are generated only when a mobile node needs information about reachable gateways. Hence, periodic flooding of the whole MANET, which has obvious disadvantages as discussed in 3.1, is prevented. The disadvantage of reactive gateway discovery is that a handover cannot be initiated before a mobile node looses its Internet connection. As a consequence, a situation can occur where a mobile node uses a gateway for its Internet connection although there are other gateways that are closer.

### 3.3    Hybrid Gateway Discovery

To minimize the disadvantages of the proactive and reactive strategies, they can be combined into a hybrid proactive/reactive method for gateway discovery. For mobile nodes in a certain range around a gateway, proactive gateway discovery is used while mobile nodes residing outside this range use reactive gateway discovery to obtain information about the gateway.

The gateway periodically broadcasts a GWADV message. Upon receipt of the message, the mobile nodes update their routing table and then rebroadcast the message. The maximum number of hops a GWADV can move through the MANET is determined by ADVERTISEMENT_ZONE. This value defines the range within which proactive gateway discovery is used. When a mobile node residing outside this range needs gateway information, it broadcasts a RREQ_I to the ALL_MANET_GW_MULTICAST address. Mobile nodes receiving the RREQ_I just rebroadcast it. When a gateway receives a RREQ_I, it sends a RREP_I towards the source.

Thus, the proactive gateway discovery method is used to handle the mobile nodes less or equal than ADVERTISEMENT_ZONE hops away from the gateway and the reactive gateway discovery method is used to handle the mobile nodes more than AD-VERTISEMENT_ZONE hops away from the gateway.

# 4 Performance Evaluation

In order to evaluate the performance of the three gateway discovery methods, the network simulator ns-2 has been used. First, the source code of AODV in ns-2 was extended to provide Internet access to mobile nodes. Then the three gateway discovery methods were implemented. This code, which is referred to as AODV+, has been contributed [13] to ns-2 and is free to be downloaded and used by everyone. The latest version of ns-2 (ns-2.27) has been used in this study.

## 4.1 Simulation Scenario

The studied scenario consists of 60 mobile nodes, two gateways, two routers and two hosts. The topology is a rectangular area with 1300 m length and 800 m width. A rectangular area was chosen in order to force the use of longer routes between nodes, compared to a square area with the same node density. The two gateways were placed on each side of the area; their x- and y-coordinates in meters are (200,500) and (1100,500). All simulations were run for 1000 seconds of simulation time. Since we were interested in studying the behaviour of the network in steady state, the first 100 seconds of the simulation were ignored.

Ten of the 60 mobile nodes are constant bit rate (CBR) traffic sources sending data packets with a size of 512 bytes, to one of the two hosts, chosen randomly. The sources are distributed randomly within the MANET. The transmission range of the mobile nodes is 250 meters.

A screenshot of the simulation scenario is shown in Fig. 1. The 60 small circles represent the mobile nodes. The two hexagonal nodes at each side of the figure are the gateways and the four square nodes are the two hosts and the two routers.

## 4.2 The Mobility Model

The mobile nodes move according to an improved version of the commonly used random waypoint model. It has been shown that the original random waypoint model can generate misleading results [7]. With the improved random waypoint model the mobile node speed reaches steady state after a quick warm-up period.

Each mobile node begins the simulation by selecting a random destination in the defined area and moves to that destination at a random speed. The random speed is distributed uniformly in the interval [1,19] m/s. Upon reaching the destination, the mobile node pauses for 10 seconds, selects another destination, and proceeds as described. This movement pattern is repeated for the duration of the simulation.

The gateways broadcast GWADVs every ADVERTISEMENT_INTERVAL=5 seconds when the proactive or hybrid discovery method is used (see Sect. 3.1 and 3.3).

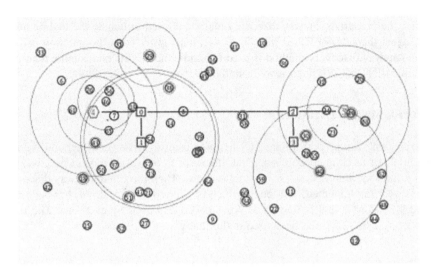

**Fig. 1.** Screenshot of the simulation scenario

ADVERTISEMENT_ZONE, which is set to three, is used for the hybrid gateway dis-covery method and defines the range within which proactive gateway discovery is used. Outside this range the reactive gateway discovery is used.

### 4.3   Performance Metrics

In comparing the gateway discovery approaches, the evaluation has been done accord-ing to the following three metrics:

- The packet delivery ratio is defined as the number of received data packets divided by the number of generated data packets.
- The end-to-end delay is defined as the time a data packet is received by the desti-nation minus the time the data packet is generated by the source.
- The overhead is defined as the amount of AODV messages in bytes divided by the sum of the AODV messages plus the data packets in bytes.

Each data point is an average value of ten runs with different randomly generated movement patterns.

### 4.4   Simulation Results

In all figures discussed in this section it should be noted that the term "traffic load" denotes only the data traffic that each source generates, which is ten times less than the total data traffic in the whole network. To that come also control packets sent by the data link and network layers.

Figure 2 shows the impact of the advertisement interval on the average end-to-end delay when the traffic load changes for the proactive gateway discovery method. It can be observed that the curve representing the advertisement interval of one second differs greatly from other curves representing higher advertisement intervals. The reason is that a very short interval leads to a lot of advertisements and thus a lot of overhead, which in turn means many collisions, retransmissions and route discoveries that increase the end-to-end delay.

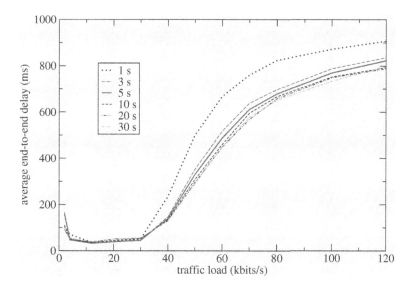

**Fig. 2.** The impact of advertisement interval

Figures 3, 4 and 5 show the packet delivery ratio, the average end-to-end delay and the AODV overhead respectively for the three gateway discovery methods when the traffic load changes.

Packet losses occur frequently due to many reasons, e.g. when a source sends packets along a path that recently has broken but the source has not been informed about that yet; or when a source has no other nodes within its transmission range (i.e. the node is isolated) for some time and its outgoing buffer is full. Since we have omitted the TCP protocol and its retransmission function from our model high packet losses may occur.

As Fig. 3 shows, the packet delivery ratio is high when the traffic load is light but decreases when the traffic increases. This result is expected but it can also be seen that increasing the traffic affects all three approaches pretty much the same way. One can also see that the delivery ratio is somewhat lower for very light loads (5 kbits/s/source) compared to light loads (20 kbits/s/source). The reason for this is that once a connection has been established, it is not fully used when the traffic is very light. Therefore, only a few number of packets are sent before the connection breaks and a new route must be discovered.

Figure 4 shows that the average end-to-end delay increases as expected when the load increases, since increased load means more collisions, retransmissions and route

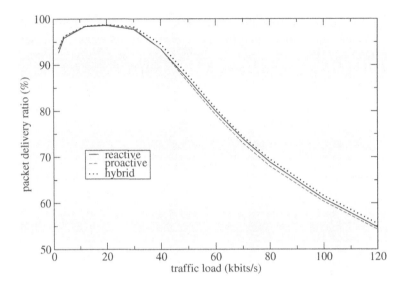

**Fig. 3.** Packet delivery ratio vs. traffic load

discoveries. We can also see that the difference between the different strategies is negligible.

One might have expected that the delivery ratio and the average end-to-end delay would have been different for the reactive method compared to e.g. the proactive. From one point of view, the reactive method should perform better since it generates less overhead, which should cause less number of collisions. On the other hand, the reactive method should perform worse because it does not send periodic advertisements, which would give shorter routes (in terms of number of hops) in the long term. Since a number of other aspects need to be taken into account, it is our belief that the given scenario and the assumptions made for the simulation have a significant impact on the results.

There are some problems with the ARP [1] implementation in ns-2, which is based on the BSD [2] implementation of ARP [12], that have negative impact on our results. Each node has an ARP queue that can hold only one packet for each neighbour while requesting the MAC address of the next hop. If other packets arrive to the queue before the MAC address is resolved, all but the last one will be dropped [2]. This can lead to loss of important messages from upper layers, such as the RREP or the RREP_I messages from AODV. Consequently, if the source does not receive any RREP or RREP_I before its timer expires, it has to reattempt its gateway discovery process where the reply could be lost again. Remember that this important message can be dropped by ARP on each hop between the gateway and the source where an address resolution process is started. In the worst case, the source will give up after some attempts and the session is aborted. Increasing the buffer size of ARP can prevent situations like this to occur.

---

[1] Address Resolution Protocol
[2] Berkeley Software Distribution

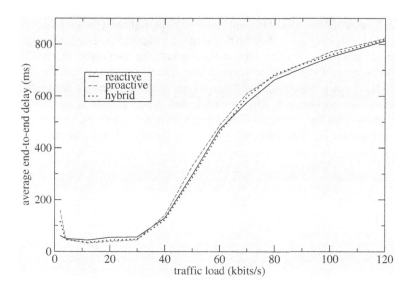

**Fig. 4.** Average end-to-end delay vs. traffic load

There is another problem, where ARP is involved, which cannot be solved by increasing the buffer size. Since there is no timer involved in the address resolution process, a retransmission will not occur until it is triggered by a new incoming packet. This can have a significant impact on the end-to-end delay. Suppose that a data packet is sent to ARP from the routing protocol. Because of some reason (e.g. collision) the address resolution fails. Before a new data packet is sent to ARP to trigger an ARP request retransmission, the routing protocol changes its route towards the destination (with a new next hop) and, hence, no MAC address resolution is needed for the old next hop anymore. So far there is no problem except that the old data packet remains in the ARP queue. If the node much later needs to resolve the MAC address of the old next hop and the ARP resolution succeeds, the data packet waiting in the queue will be sent to the next hop resulting in a very long end-to-end delay. Increasing the buffer size will in fact only make the problem even worse since then there are more than a single data packet that will be delivered to the next hop with a very long end-to-end delay.

Furthermore, the lack of retransmissions means that one single loss of an ARP request or an ARP reply means that the data (e.g. RREP_I) cannot be sent to the source, which will be forced to reattempt its gateway discovery process.

The first problem caused by ARP has been investigated in [3] which shows that increasing the ARP buffer size makes the situation much better (although another solution is preferred). The second problem is discussed in [11], which suggests a cross-layer feedback mechanism from MAC to ARP.

Another thing that affects the simulation results in a negative way is when sources become isolated from the MANET such that they cannot reach any gateway. Isolated sources result in decreased packet delivery ratio and increased end-to-end delay.

In Fig. 5 the AODV overhead is dominated by the periodically broadcasted GWADV messages. As the figure shows, the AODV overhead is significantly larger for the proactive approach than for the reactive approach, especially for light traffic loads. This is an expected result since the proactive approach periodically broadcasts gateway information no matter if the mobile nodes need them or not, while the reactive approach broadcasts gateway information only when a mobile node sends a request for it. Moreover, the figure shows that the overhead of the hybrid approach, which is a mixture of both the proactive and the reactive approach, is between the two other methods.

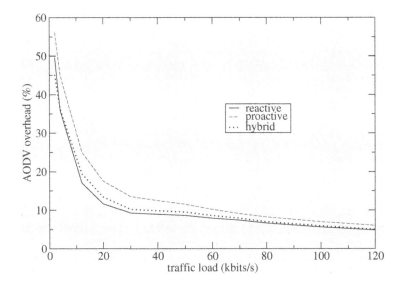

**Fig. 5.** AODV overhead vs. traffic load

## 5   Conclusion

We have presented a solution for Internet access for mobile nodes in a MANET. The MANET routing protocol AODV has been extended to route packets, between a wireless MANET and the wired Internet. To achieve this, some nodes must be able to communicate with the MANET and with the fixed Internet. As all communication between the wireless and the wired network must pass through these nodes, they are referred to as gateways. In this paper, three methods for detection of these gateways have been presented, implemented and compared. The three methods for gateway detection are referred to as reactive, proactive and hybrid gateway discovery. When it comes to end-to-end delay and packet delivery ratio, the three methods show surprisingly similar behaviour. The fact that the proactive method shows much higher overhead in terms of control packets than the other methods is more obvious.

In order to fully understand the reasons behind the large delays and the rather low packet delivery ratio that were found, the authors plan to do a more detailed study. This would provide a better understanding of which parts of the end-to-end path that contribute most to the discovered delays and packet losses.

# References

1. M. Bernard. *"Gateway Detection and Selection for Wireless Multihop Internet Access"*. Master's thesis. Olching, Germany, May 2002.
2. J. Broch, D. Maltz, D. B. Johnson, Y. Hu and J. Jetcheva. *"A Performance Comparison of Multi-Hop Wireless Ad Hoc Network Routing Protocols"*. In proceedings of the 4th ACM/IEEE International Conference on Mobile Computing and Networking (MobiCom '98), pages 85-97, October 1998.
3. C. Carter, S. Yi and R. Kravets. *"ARP Considered Harmful: Manycast Transactions in Ad Hoc Networks"*. Proceedings of the IEEE Wireless Communications and Networking Conference, 2003.
4. T. Clausen, P. Jacquet, A. Laouiti, P. Minet, P. Muhlethaler, A. Qayyum and L. Viennot. *"Optimized Link State Routing Protocol"*. Experimental RFC 3626.
5. A. Hamidian. *"A Study of Internet Connectivity for Mobile Ad Hoc Networks in NS 2"*. Master's thesis. Department of Communication Systems, Lund Institute of Technology, Lund University. January 2003.
6. D. B. Johnson, D. A. Maltz, Y. Hu and J. G. Jetcheva. *"The Dynamic Source Routing Protocol for Mobile Ad Hoc Networks (DSR)"*. IETF Internet Draft, April 2003. Work in progress.
7. J. Jungkeun, M. Liu and B. Noble. *"Random Waypoint Considered Harmful"*. IEEE INFOCOM 2003, San Francisco, April 2003.
8. S. McCanne and S. Floyd. *"The Network Simulator - ns-2"*. www.isi.edu/nsnam/ns/. K. Fall, K. Varadhan. *"The ns Manual"*.
9. R. Ogier, M. Lewis and F. Templin. *"Topology Dissemination Based on Reverse-Path Forwarding (TBRPF)"*. Experimental RFC 3684.
10. C. Perkins, E. M. Belding-Royer and S. Das. *"Ad hoc On-Demand Distance Vector (AODV) Routing"*. Experimental RFC 3561.
11. S. Perur, L. Wadia and S. Iyer. *"Improving the Performance of MANET Routing Protocols using Cross-Layer Feedback"*. www.it.iitb.ac.in/ srinath/pubs/cit03.pdf.
12. W. R. Stevens. *"TCP/IP Illustrated, Volume 1"*. Addison Wesely, 1994.
13. *"The Network Simulator: Contributed Code"*. www.isi.edu/nsnam/ns/ns-contributed.html.
14. R. Wakikawa, J. Malinen, C. Perkins, A. Nilsson and A. J. Tuominen. *"Global Connectivity for IPv6 Mobile Ad Hoc Networks"*, IETF Internet Draft, February 2003. Work in progress.

# On the Fractional Movement–Distance Based Scheme for PCS Location Management with Selective Paging

Vicente Casares-Giner and Pablo García-Escalle[*]

ITACA, ETSIT, Departamento de Comunicaciones
Universidad Politécnica de Valencia
Camino de Vera s/n, 46022 Valencia (Spain)
vcasares@dcom.upv.es, pgarciae@upvnet.upv.es

**Abstract.** In this paper we propose a fractional movement–distance based scheme. In our proposal, a mobile terminal stores in its local memory the identification of a set $X$ of cells within a distance $H$ (in terms of cells) from the cell where the last contact between the mobile terminal and the network occurred. When the mobile terminal visits a cells the following action is taken. If the identity of the visited cell is stored in the local memory of the mobile terminal, its movement counter is reset to zero. Otherwise its movement counter is increased by one unit. In this last case, if the counter has reached a given threshold $d_i$ the mobile terminal sends an update message with probability $q_i$ and with probability $1 - q_i$ the mobile terminal waits for the next decision which is taken in case of the next threshold $d_{i+1}$ being reached. A set of $N$ movement thresholds $\{d_i\}$ (integer numbers) with the corresponding set of $N$ probabilities $\{q_i\}$ has been used.

Furthermore, for delivering incoming calls we have considered two selective paging schemes that are combined with the proposed location update scheme. The tradeoff between our proposals on location update and paging has been analyzed by means of standard Markovian tools. Then, it has been shown that in some cases where selective paging is implemented, the optimal mean value of the set $\{d_i\}$, $\bar{d}$, is a real number, not necessarily integer. This optimal value minimizes the total location management cost per call arrival (location update plus paging cost) and outperforms the movement based scheme. However, the distance based scheme still offers a better performance. But, with few memory requirements for the mobile terminal (the set $X$), our proposed scheme is very close to the mentioned distance based scheme.

## 1 Introduction

Location management process plays an important role in Personal Communication Services (PCS) networks. In mobile communication systems the whereabouts of a mobile terminal (MT) must be known in order to correctly route

---

[*] The author was a visiting scholar at the Institut Mittag-Leffler, Royal Swedish Academy of Sciences, Djursholm (Sweden) during the final phase of this work.

G. Kotsis and O. Spaniol (Eds.): Mobile and Wireless Systems, LNCS 3427, pp. 202–218, 2005.
© Springer-Verlag Berlin Heidelberg 2005

its incoming calls. Mobility tracking is performed by a set of procedures whose main goal is to keep track of the MT's geographical position. In Global System for Mobile communications (GSM) terminology, these procedures are called location update and call delivery. First, the location of an MT must be reported to the database of the network and maintained up to date. The database entry of an MT is updated when the MT sends an update message to the network or when the MT successfully starts a call. Second, the call delivery procedure. It is decomposed in two sequential steps. The first step is the interrogation by which the last location information of the called MT is retrieved from the system databases, and constitutes an input for the second step, the paging. In the paging procedure, the MT is searched by sending polling messages through the cells that are geographically close to the last reported location of the called MT. The output of the paging procedure is the exact cell where the called MT is roaming.

There are many proposals to implement the location update (LU) procedure. For instance, in the existing cellular networks, a set of neighboring cells conforms a location area (LA). The sizes and borders of an LA are fixed. The MT sends an update message each time it enters into a new LA, and the location information is updated accordingly in the system database. This procedure belongs to the static (or global) location update schemes. They are global because all MTs send their update messages from the cells in the perimeter of the LAs. The first drawback of these schemes is that the associated signalling traffic is clearly unbalanced. Another drawback is that an MT roaming in the vecinities of the boundary between two LAs may send an excessive number of update messages as it moves back and forth between two LAs, [15], [10]. To overcome these deficiencies, three dynamic (or local) location update schemes that are MT dependent were proposed in [3]. Under these three schemes, update messages are sent based on the time elapsed, $T$ (the time threshold), the number of movements performed in terms of cells, $d$ (the movement threshold), and the distance traveled in terms of cells, $D$ (the distance threshold), respectively, since the last update message was sent. The mentioned distance is from the cell where the last contact with the fixed network occurred. In the sequel we will identify that cell as the center cell.

The comparative analysis carried out in [4] concludes that the distance based location update scheme outperforms both the movement based and the time based schemes. Nevertheless, the movement based scheme may be more practical and easier to implement than the distance based scheme, since the former does not require each MT to store information about the network topology, [1]. The movement based scheme combined with selective paging was analyzed in [1]. However, when the movement counter of the MT reaches threshold $d$, and at the same time the MT is revisiting the center cell, an unnecessary location update is performed. In [6], the authors presented a new proposal avoiding this situation: when the MT revisits the center cell, the movement counter is reset to zero. This strategy reduces the signalling traffic in update messages sent by the MT. However, as this fact results in fewer contacts with the network, the uncertainty on the MT's position increases and the paging cost increases slightly. But the net effect is a significant saving in the total cost of location update plus paging. The movement–distance based scheme, [7], is an extension of this idea. In this policy each MT stores in its local memory a set $X$ of cells (their identities) within a distance $H$, in terms of cells, from the center cell. When the MT visits a cell the following action is taken. If the identity of the visited cell is stored in the MT's local memory, its movement counter is reset to zero. Otherwise its movement counter is increased by one unit. In this last case, the MT verifies if a given threshold $d$ has been reached and if this is the case, an update message is sent to the network. After performing a location update, a new set $X$ of cells is transferred to the MT to be stored in its local memory.

Recently, a fractional movement based scheme for PCS location management has been proposed in [17]. It is similar to the Fractional Guard Channel scheme [16], and to the scheme in [12]. In [17] the sets of cells to be stored in the local memory of the MT is an empty set. The MT only needs a movement counter. Let $d$ be the movement counter threshold, an integer number. When an MT completes $d$ movements between cells it sends an update message with probability $p_0 = 1 - r$ $(r \in [0; 1])$. Otherwise the MT sends an update message when it completes $d + 1$ movements. Therefore the mean value of the movement threshold parameter is a real number given by $\overline{d} = d.p_0 + (d + 1)(1 - p_0) = d + (1 - p_0) = d + r$.

Motivated by the work in [7] and [17], we have addressed the study of a new location update scheme, that we call as the fractional movement–distance based scheme. It is combined with selective paging. Both, the new location update and the paging schemes are described in section 3. Before that, in section 2 we describe the geographical scenario and the mobility model used in our studies. In section 4 we present the analytical model used in the evaluation process. In sections 5 and 6, we derive explicit expressions for the location update and paging signalling cost per call arrival, respectively. In section 7 we discuss some examples that illustrate the performance of our proposal. Finally, the conclusions are summarized in section 8.

# 2    Geographical Scenario and Mobility Model

## 2.1    Cell Layout

Although our study can easily be generalized to square cells, hexagonal cells have been considered. All cells are regular hexagons and are the same size. Each cell is surrounded by rings of cells. The innermost ring (ring 0) consists of only one cell, the center cell. Ring 0 is surrounded by ring 1 which in turn is surrounded by ring 2, and so on. The mosaic graphs obtained are called, in general, mosaics $T$, [2]. Mosaic $T_m$, $m = 0$ corresponds to a single hexagon, and $m = 1$ corresponds to a cluster of 7 cells, see also mosaic $T_2$ in Fig. 1. Table 1 shows $K_n$, the number of cells in ring $n$ for mosaic $T_m$ $(0 \leq n \leq m)$, and $L_n$, the number of of cells in mosaic $T_n$.

**Fig. 1.** Mosaic graph $T_2$

**Table 1.** Number of cells in ring $n$ $(K_n)$ and accumulated values $(L_n)$ for mosaic graph $T_n$

| Mosaic | | Ring $n$ | | |
|---|---|---|---|---|
| | $n = 0$ | $n = 1$ | ... | $n = m$ |
| Mosaic $T_m$ $K_n$ | 1 | 6 | ... | $6m$ |
| $L_n$ | 1 | 7 | ... | $3m^2 + 3m + 1$ |

## 2.2 Mobility Model

In order to characterize the trajectory of a given $MT$ we need a mobility model. First, the cell dwell time[1] of an MT has been characterized with a generalized gamma distribution, [18], with probability density function (pdf) given by,

$$f(t; b_0, b_1, b_2) = \frac{b_2}{b_1^{b_0 b_2} \Gamma(b_0)} t^{b_0 b_2 - 1} e^{-(t/b_1)^{b_2}} = f(t); t, b_0, b_1, b_2 > 0, \qquad (1)$$

where,

- $\Gamma(b_0)$ is the gamma function, defined as $\Gamma(b_0) = \int_0^\infty x^{b_0-1} e^{-x} dx$ where $b_0$ is any real and positive number.
- the variables $b_0$, $b_1$ and $b_2$, are fixed according to [18]. In the cited article, the pdf of the cell dwell time is studied, and the suitable values of these variables are $b_0 = 2.31$, $b_1 = 1.22R$, and $b_2 = 1.72$, where $R$ is the equivalent cell radius (considering an average speed of 50 km/h and zero drift).

We denote its Laplace Transform (LT) as $f^*(s)$. Its mean value is given by,

$$-f^{*'}(0) = b_1 \frac{\Gamma(b_0 + 1/b_2)}{\Gamma(b_0)} = \frac{1}{\lambda_m} \qquad (2)$$

The variables $b_0$ and $b_2$ are fixed. Obviously there is a relation between $b_1$, $R$, and $\lambda_m$, only one of them needs to be fixed. Here we will use $\lambda_m$ as a parameter (the mobility parameter in a cell).

Second, we assume random walk mobility. When an MT leaves a cell, the probability $p$ to visit one of the six neighboring cells is proportional to the common perimeter between the left and the new visited cell. Therefore, in our case $p = 1/6$.

## 3 Our Proposal on Location Management

### 3.1 The Fractional Movement–Distance Based Location Update Procedure

In our proposal, each MT stores the non-empty set $X$ of cells within a distance $H$, in terms of cells, from the center cell. Starting at the center cell with its

---

[1] Also known as cell sojourn time or cell residence time

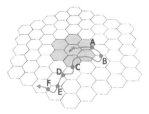

**Fig. 2.** Fractional movement–distance based strategy with $H = 1$, $d_0 = 1$, $d_1 = 2$, $d_2 = 3$ and $d_3 = 4$, for mosaic $T$.

movement counter set to zero, when the MT visits a cell the following action is taken. If the identity of the visited cell is stored in the MT's local memory, its movement counter is reset to zero. Otherwise its movement counter is increased by one unit. In the second case the MT verifies if the counter has reached a first fixed threshold $d_0$. If this is the case the MT sends an update message with probability $q_0$ and with probability $1 - q_0$ the MT waits for the next threshold $d_1$. When the movement counter reaches a second fixed threshold $d_1$, the MT sends an update message with probability $q_1$ and with probability $1 - q_1$ the MT waits for the next threshold $d_2$. And so on.

We have considered a set of $N$ integer movement thresholds: $d_0 < d_1 < ... < d_{N-1}$, with probabilities $q_0, q_1, ...$ and $q_{N-1} = 1$ respectively. Figure 2 illustrates an example where $H = 1$ (the number of cells in the set $X$ is equal to 7), $N = 4$, $d_0 = 1$, $d_1 = 2$, $d_2 = 3$ and $d_3 = 4$. Starting at the center cell, a movement path is shown along which no incoming calls are received. The movement counter starts counting at locations A and C. The MT sends an update message at locations A or C with probability $p_0 = q_0$, at locations B or D with probability $p_1 = (1 - q_0)q_1$, at location E with probability $p_2 = (1 - q_0)(1 - q_1)q_2$ and at location F with probability $p_3 = (1 - q_0)(1 - q_1)(1 - q_2)q_3$. We will also use the notation $D_i = H + d_i$ and the vectors $\boldsymbol{d} = [d_0, d_1, ..., d_{N-1}]$ and $\boldsymbol{p} = [p_0, p_1, ..., p_{N-1}]$. Clearly $\sum_{i=0}^{N-1} p_i = 1$. Note the MT is always within a distance $D_{N-1} - 1 = H + d_{N-1} - 1$ from the center cell. Also, notice that the standard hybrid movement–distance based scheme [7] is a particular case of our proposal. For instance, following the example, $H = 1$ and $d = 4$ for $\boldsymbol{p} = [p_0, p_1, p_2, p_3] = [0, 0, 0, 1]$. Then the MT will send an update message at location F with probability 1.

Notice that the mean value of the movement threshold parameter is given by $\overline{d} = \sum_{i=0}^{N-1} d_i p_i = \sum_{i=0}^{N-1} D_i p_i - H$. If $d_i = d_{i-1} + 1$ ($i \in \{1, ..., N-1\}$), then $\overline{d} = d_0 + \sum_{i=0}^{N-1} i p_i = d_0 + \overline{p}$. Clearly, with this policy the movement counter threshold is extended to real numbers.

### 3.2   Paging Procedures

Two different selective paging algorithms have been considered. First, a shortest–distance–first (SDF) selective paging based on [1]. We call the paging scheme A.

Before the paging procedure starts, the system must determine the paging sub-areas for the called MT. Note the MT is positively located in a mosaic $T_{D_{N-1}-1}$. Then, the area $T_{D_{N-1}-1}$ is split up into $l_A = \min(\eta, D_{N-1})$ subareas, where $\eta$ is the maximum allowable paging delay. $A_j$ denotes subarea $j$ ($j \in \{0, ..., l_A - 1\}$). Each subarea contains one or more rings of cells. Subarea $A_j$ contains all rings between $s_j^A$ to $e_j^A$, both of them included. These border rings are given by,

$$s_j^A = \begin{cases} 0; & j = 0. \\ \lfloor \frac{jD_{N-1}}{l_A} \rfloor; \forall j \in \{1, ..., l_A - 1\}. \end{cases} \quad \begin{array}{l} \forall j \in \{0, ..., l_A - 1\}, \\ e_j^A = \lfloor \frac{(j+1)D_{N-1}}{l_A} \rfloor - 1 \end{array} \quad (3)$$

After this partition is done, the system starts the paging procedure. First, the system simultaneously polls all cells in subarea $A_0$. If the MT is found in subarea $A_0$, the paging process ends. Otherwise, the system polls all cells in subarea $A_1$, and so on.

Second, an algorithm based on a probabilistic partitioning scheme (in line with [17]) has been considered. We call the paging scheme B. Mosaic $T_{D_N-1}$ is split up in $l_B = N$ subareas. $B_i$ denotes subarea $i$, $i \in \{0, 1, ..., l_B - 1\}$. Subarea $B_i$ contains all rings between $s_i^B$ to $e_i^B$, both of them included. These border rings are given by,

$$s_i^B = \begin{cases} 0; & i = 0. \\ H + d_{i-1}; \forall i \in \{1, ..., l_B - 1\}. \end{cases} \quad \begin{array}{l} \forall i \in \{0, 1, ..., l_B - 1\}, \\ e_i^B = H + d_i - 1 \end{array} \quad (4)$$

After this partition is done, the system starts an $N - i$ steps paging procedure with probability $p_i = \prod_{k=0}^{i-1}(1 - q_k)q_i$ ($i \in \{0, 1, ..., N - 1\}$). That is, with probability $p_i$, the system simultaneously polls all cells in subareas $\bigcup_{j=0}^{i} B_j$. If the MT is found in subareas $\bigcup_{j=0}^{i} B_j$, the paging process ends. Otherwise, the system polls all cells in subarea $B_{i+1}$, and so on.

## 4   Analytical Model

In this section we present an analytical model to evaluate the expected location update cost plus paging cost per call arrival. It is based on standard Markovian tools. To that purpose we establish several hypothesis referred to the incoming call arrival process and to the mobility model.

**Incoming Call Process** .- Although a general renewal point process could have been considered, [9], for the sake of simplicity we have assumed Poisson process with rate $\lambda_c$. Also, we assume the call duration is negligible compared with the interarrival time duration, such that the busy line effect does not occur [14] (i.e. there is no new phone call to an MT when it is in conversation). Then, the probability that there are $z$ boundary crossings between two call arrivals is of key importance. This probability, denoted as $\alpha(z, a, \theta)$, is given by, [1,13]

$$\alpha(z, a, \theta) = \begin{cases} 1 - (1 - a)/\theta; & z = 0, \\ (1 - a)^2 a^{z-1}/\theta; & z > 0, \end{cases} \quad (5)$$

where $a = f^*(\lambda_c)$, is given in terms of (1), its $LT$, and $\theta = \lambda_c/\lambda_m$ is the call-to-mobility ratio (CMR) defined in [11].

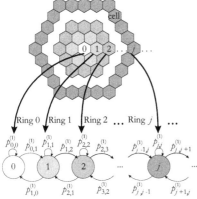

**Table 2.** Transition probabilities $p_{j,j-1}^{(1)}$ and $p_{j,j+1}^{(1)}$ from a cell in ring $j$ to a cell in rings $j-1$ and $j+1$ respectively, [1]

| Mosaic graph $T$ | | | | | | |
|---|---|---|---|---|---|---|
| $p_{0,1}^{(1)}$ | $p_{1,0}^{(1)}$ | $p_{1,2}^{(1)}$ | ... | $p_{j,j-1}^{(1)}$ | $p_{j,j+1}^{(1)}$ | ... |
| 1 | $\frac{1}{6}$ | $\frac{1}{2}$ | ... | $\frac{2j-1}{6j}$ | $\frac{2j+1}{6j}$ | ... |

**Fig. 3.** One dimensional Markov model

**An Approach to the Two Dimensional Mobility Model** .- For easier tractability we will map the two dimensional (2-D) mobility model presented in section 2 into a 1-D Markov model as Fig. 3 shows, [1]. Each ring of cells is merged into a single Markov state, so cell-ring $i$ is mapped into state $i$. The transition probability from a cell-ring $i$ (state $i$) to a cell-ring $j$ (state $j$) is denoted as $p_{i,j}^{(1)}$. The set $\{p_{i,j}^{(1)}\}$ can easily be derived having in mind the random walk mobility model and from geometric considerations -taking into account the common perimeter between cells in ring $i$ and cells in ring $j$-. Table 2 summarizes the set $\{p_{i,j}^{(1)}\}$.

**Splitting the Set of States** $H+1, H+2, ....$ .- In our scheme an MT stores in its local memory the identification of a set $X$ of cells within a distance $H$ (in terms of cells) from the center cell. It is equivalent to consider that the MT is aware of the visits to states $1, 2, ..., H$ -the set $X$ is mapped into the set of states $0, 1, 2, ...H$-. Then, the movement counter is reset to zero (an update message will never be sent) when visiting this set of states. On the contrary, when our MT is visiting states $H + 1, H + 2, ..$ its movement counter is increased by one unit per each visit to one of those states. In the last case and for mathematical tractability of the Markov chain we have assume that each time the MT leaves state $H$ towards state $H+1$ the following decision is taken "in-advance". The movement threshold is set to $d_i$ with probability $p_i = \prod_{k=0}^{i}(1 - q_k)q_i$, $(i = 0, 1, ..., N - 1)$ and this will be the threshold the MT will use in case of leaving state $H$ towards state $H + 1$, This is equivalent to say that the system will make a transition towards the branch of states $(*, i)$ with probability $p_i$, $(i = 0, 1, ..., N - 1)$. This new point of views is reflected in the Markov chain of Fig. 4 where the states $H + 1, H + 2, ...$ are split into states $(H + 1, i)$, $(H + 2, i)$ ,....

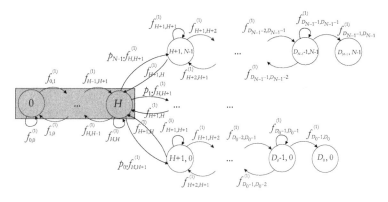

**Fig. 4.** Fractional movement–distance LU strategy

## 5   Location Update Cost

Each time the MT sends an update message or receives an incoming call, the location information of the system databases is updated and the non-empty set $X$ of cells stored in the local memory of the MT is updated, i.e a new set $X$ of $M$ cells (within a distance $H$ from the center cell) is transferred form the network to the MT (from Table 1, $M = L_H = 3H^2 + 3H + 1$). The center cell is the cell at which the MT sent its last update message or received its last incoming call.

Then, for a given number of movements, $z$, and considering the MT starts its movement in the center cell, we are interested in the average number of update messages sent by the MT between two consecutive call arrivals, $M_0(z, H, \boldsymbol{p}, \boldsymbol{d})$ ($\boldsymbol{p} = [p_0, p_1, ..., p_{N-1}]$ and $\boldsymbol{d} = [d_0, d_1, ..., d_{N-1}]$). In order to express the location update cost per call arrival, $C_{LU}(a, \theta, H, \boldsymbol{p}, \boldsymbol{d})$, $M_0(z, H, \boldsymbol{p}, \boldsymbol{d})$ must be weighted by the probability of $z$ movements between two consecutive call arrivals, $\alpha(z, a, \theta)$, (5),

$$C_{LU}(a, \theta, H, \boldsymbol{p}, \boldsymbol{d}) = \sum_{z=0}^{\infty} \alpha(z, a, \theta) M_0(z, H, \boldsymbol{p}, \boldsymbol{d}) = \frac{(1-a)^2}{\theta a} M_0^*(a, H, \boldsymbol{p}, \boldsymbol{d}) \quad (6)$$

where $M_0^*(a, H, \boldsymbol{p}, \boldsymbol{d}) = \sum_{z=D_0}^{\infty} a^z M_0(z, H, \boldsymbol{p}, \boldsymbol{d})$.

In the next lines, we conduct the analysis in terms of first passage, first return and taboo probabilities. We have followed the terminology in [8,5]. For instance, we call $f_{i,j}^{(n)}$ the probability of state $j$ being avoided at times $1, 2, .., n-1$ and entered at time $n$, given state $i$ is occupied initially. Obviously, $f_{i,j}^{(1)} = p_{i,j}^{(1)}$, see Fig. 4, Fig. 3 and Table 2.

### 5.1   Evaluation of $M_0^*(a, H, \boldsymbol{p}, \boldsymbol{d})$

Let $M_m(z, H, \boldsymbol{p}, \boldsymbol{d})$ be the expected number of update messages sent by the MT after $z$ movements, given the MT is initially in a cell in ring $m$ (i.e. state

$m$). Then, using the Markov chain of Fig. 3 or Fig. 4, the following recursive equations can be written for $M_m(z, H, \boldsymbol{p}, \boldsymbol{d})$ for $m = 0$:

$$M_0(z, H, \boldsymbol{p}, \boldsymbol{d}) = \begin{cases} 0; & z < D_0, \\ \displaystyle\sum_{l=0}^{1} f_{0,l}^{(1)} M_l(z-1, H, \boldsymbol{p}, \boldsymbol{d}); & D_0 \le z, \end{cases} \tag{7}$$

and for $m \in \{1, 2, ..., H-1\}$:

$$M_m(z, H, \boldsymbol{p}, \boldsymbol{d}) = \begin{cases} 0; & z < D_0 - m, \\ \displaystyle\sum_{l=m-1}^{m+1} f_{m,l}^{(1)} M_l(z-1, H, \boldsymbol{p}, \boldsymbol{d}); & D_0 - m \le z. \end{cases} \tag{8}$$

For $m = H$, first, we have to consider taboo probabilities. When the MT is initially in state $H$, the probability of the MT sending an update message given the movement threshold is set to $d_i$ is,

$$p_{\text{nab}}(H, d_i) = 1 - f_{H,H-1}^{(1)} - \sum_{n=1}^{d_i} {}_{H-1}f_{H,H}^{(n)} \tag{9}$$

In (9) $nab$ stand from no absorption, and the taboo probability ${}_{G}f_{i,j}^{(n)}$ is the probability that the Markov chain enters state $j$ for the first time at the $n^{\text{th}}$ step, having initially started from state $i$ and avoiding state $i$ and the set $G$ of states at times $1, 2, .., n-1$, [8,5]. From our 1-D Markov chain of Fig. 3 we have,

$$_{H-1}f_{H,H}^{(n)} = \begin{cases} p_{H,H}^{(1)}; & n = 1. \\ f_{H,H+1}^{(1)} f_{H+1,H}^{(n-1)}; & n > 1. \end{cases} \tag{10}$$

For $n > 1$, $f_{i,j}^{(n)}$ can be easily evaluated following the set of relationships given in [8,5]. Let $p_{i,j}^{(n)}$ denote the conditional probability that starting in state $i$, the Markov chain reaches state $j$ at the $n^{\text{th}}$ step (not necessarily for the first time). Then we have,

$$p_{i,j}^{(n)} = \sum_{k=1}^{n} f_{i,j}^{(k)} p_{j,j}^{(n-k)} \tag{11}$$

Second, having in mind the model of in Fig. 4, we can state the following equation for $M_H(z, H, \boldsymbol{p}, \boldsymbol{d})$,

$$M_H(z, H, \boldsymbol{p}, \boldsymbol{d}) =$$
$$\begin{cases} 0; & z < d_0, \\ \sum_{n=0}^{i} p_n \Big( f_{H,H-1}^{(1)} M_{H-1}(z-1, H, \boldsymbol{p}, \boldsymbol{d}) + \sum_{m=1}^{d_n} {}_{H-1}f_{H,H}^{(m)} M_H(z-m, H, \boldsymbol{p}, \boldsymbol{d}) + \\ \quad p_{\mathrm{nab}}(H, d_n)\big(1 + M_0(z - d_n, H, \boldsymbol{p}, \boldsymbol{d})\big) \Big) + \sum_{m=i+1}^{N-1} p_m f_{H,H-1}^{(1)} M_{H-1}(z-1, H, \boldsymbol{p}, \boldsymbol{d}); \\ \qquad\qquad \text{for } i \in \{0, ..., N-2\} \text{ and } d_i \le z < d_{i+1}, \\ \sum_{n=0}^{N-1} p_n \Big( f_{H,H-1}^{(1)} M_{H-1}(z-1, H, \boldsymbol{p}, \boldsymbol{d}) + \sum_{m=1}^{d_n} {}_{H-1}f_{H,H}^{(m)} M_H(z-m, H, \boldsymbol{p}, \boldsymbol{d}) + \\ \quad p_{\mathrm{nab}}(H, d_n)\big(1 + M_0(z - d_n, H, \boldsymbol{p}, \boldsymbol{d})\big) \Big); & d_{N-1} \le z. \end{cases}$$
$$(12)$$

Defining $M_m^*(a, H, \boldsymbol{p}, \boldsymbol{d}) = \sum_{z=D_0-m}^{\infty} a^z M_m(z, H, \boldsymbol{p}, \boldsymbol{d})$, $m \in \{0, 1, ..., H\}$, from (7) and (8), we can see that the following relationship is verified [7]

$$M_m^*(a, H, \boldsymbol{p}, \boldsymbol{d}) = F_m^*(a) M_0^*(a, H, \boldsymbol{p}, \boldsymbol{d}) \qquad (13)$$

where

$$F_m^*(a) = \begin{cases} 1; & m = 0 \\ \dfrac{1 - a f_{0,0}^{(1)}}{a f_{0,1}^{(1)}}; & m = 1 \\ \dfrac{1 - a f_{m-1,m-1}^{(1)}}{a f_{m-1,m}^{(1)}} F_{m-1}^*(a) - \dfrac{f_{m-1,m-2}^{(1)}}{f_{m-1,m}^{(1)}} F_{m-2}^*(a); & m \in \{2, ..., H\} \end{cases}$$
$$(14)$$

And finally from (12) we derive an expression for $M_H^*(a, H, \boldsymbol{p}, \boldsymbol{d}) = \sum_{z=D_0-H}^{\infty} a^z M_H(z, H, \boldsymbol{p}, \boldsymbol{d})$ in which we use (13) to get the following closed expression of $M_0^*(a, H, \boldsymbol{p}, \boldsymbol{d})$,

$$M_0^*(a, H, \boldsymbol{p}, \boldsymbol{d}) = \frac{\displaystyle\sum_{n=0}^{N-1} p_n p_{\mathrm{nab}}(H, d_n) a^{d_n}}{(1-a) \displaystyle\sum_{n=0}^{N-1} p_n J(a, H, d_n)} \qquad (15)$$

where $J(a, H, d_n)$ is given by,

$$J(a, H, d_n) = F_H^*(a)(1 - \sum_{m=1}^{d_n} {}_{H-1}f_{H,H}^{(m)} a^m) - F_{H-1}^*(a) a f_{H,H-1}^{(1)} - p_{\mathrm{nab}}(H, d_n) a^{d_n}$$
$$(16)$$

## 6   Terminal Paging Cost

Before the paging process starts, the area where the called MT is located is split in subareas. In order to evaluate the PG cost, we have to compute the number of cells, $N(Y_k)$, in subarea $Y_k$ ($Y \in \{A,B\}$ and $k \in \{0, ..., l_Y - 1\}$, $Y$ stands for the used paging scheme, scheme A or scheme B, see subsection 3.2) and the number of cells polled before the MT is successfully located, $w_k^Y$. Having in mind (3), (4) and Table 1, we can state for $Y \in \{A,B\}$,

$$N(Y_k) = \begin{cases} L_{e_0^Y}; & k = 0, \\ L_{e_k^Y} - L_{e_{k-1}^Y}; & k \in \{1, ..., l_Y - 1\}, \end{cases} \tag{17}$$

and

$$\forall k \in \{0, ..., l_Y - 1\} \quad w_k^Y = \sum_{m=0}^{k} N(Y_m) = L_{e_k^Y}. \tag{18}$$

Let $\pi_{0,i}^*(a, H, \boldsymbol{p}, \boldsymbol{d})$ be the probability the MT is located in cell in ring $i$ when a call arrival occurs, given the MT starts moving from the center cell, Fig. 3. Then, the probability the MT being located in subarea $Y_k$ when a call arrival occurs, $\rho_k^Y$ ($Y \in \{A,B\}$ and $k \in \{0, ..., l_Y - 1\}$), is given by,

$$\rho_k^Y = \sum_{i=s_k^Y}^{e_k^Y} \pi_{0,i}^*(a, H, \boldsymbol{p}, \boldsymbol{d}) \tag{19}$$

Then, for paging scheme A, the paging cost per call arrival, $C_{PG,\,A}(a, \theta, H, \boldsymbol{p}, \boldsymbol{d})$, is evaluated as

$$C_{PG,\,A}(a, \theta, H, \boldsymbol{p}, \boldsymbol{d}) = \sum_{k=0}^{l_A-1} w_k^A \rho_k^A = \sum_{k=0}^{l_A-1} L_{e_k^A} \left( \sum_{i=s_k^A}^{e_k^A} \pi_{0,i}^*(a, H, \boldsymbol{p}, \boldsymbol{d}) \right) \tag{20}$$

For paging scheme B, the paging cost per call arrival, $C_{PG,\,B}(a, \theta, H, \boldsymbol{p}, \boldsymbol{d})$, is evaluated as

$$C_{PG,\,B}(a, \theta, H, \boldsymbol{p}, \boldsymbol{d}) = \sum_{n=0}^{N-1} p_n \left( w_n^B \sum_{j=0}^{n} \rho_j^B + \sum_{k=n+1}^{N-1} w_k^B \rho_k^B \right) \tag{21}$$

$$= \sum_{n=0}^{N-1} p_n \left( L_{e_n^B} \sum_{j=0}^{n} \sum_{i=s_j^B}^{e_j^B} \pi_{0,i}^*(a, H, \boldsymbol{p}, \boldsymbol{d}) + \sum_{k=n+1}^{N-1} L_{e_k^B} \left( \sum_{i=s_k^B}^{e_k^B} \pi_{0,i}^*(a, H, \boldsymbol{p}, \boldsymbol{d}) \right) \right)$$

### 6.1   Evaluation of $\pi_{0,i}^*(a, H, \boldsymbol{p}, \boldsymbol{d})$

Let $\pi_{m,i}(z, H, \boldsymbol{p}, \boldsymbol{d})$ be the probability of the MT being in state $i$ after $z$ movements, given the MT is initially in state $m$ ($i$ and $m \in \{0, ..., D_{N-1} - 1\}$), see the Markov chain of Fig. 3 or Fig. 4. Then the following recursive equations can be written for $\pi_{m,i}(z, H, \boldsymbol{p}, \boldsymbol{d})$ for $m = 0$ and $i \in \{0, ..., D_{N-1} - 1\}$:

$$\pi_{0,i}(z, H, \boldsymbol{p}, \boldsymbol{d}) = \begin{cases} p_{0,i}^{(z)}; & z < D_0, \\ \sum_{l=0}^{1} f_{0,l}^{(1)} \pi_{l,i}(z - 1, H, \boldsymbol{p}, \boldsymbol{d}); & D_0 \leq z, \end{cases} \tag{22}$$

and for $m \in \{1, ..., H-1\}$ and $i \in \{0, ..., D_{N-1} - 1\}$:

$$\pi_{m,i}(z, H, \boldsymbol{p}, \boldsymbol{d}) = \begin{cases} p_{m,i}^{(z)}; & z < D_0 - m, \\ \sum_{l=m-1}^{m+1} f_{m,l}^{(1)} \pi_{l,i}(z-1, H, \boldsymbol{p}, \boldsymbol{d}); & D_0 - m \leq z. \end{cases} \quad (23)$$

For $m = H$, see the Markov chain of Fig. 3, we can state the following equation for $\pi_{H,i}(z, \boldsymbol{p}, \boldsymbol{d})$ ($i \in \{0, ..., D_{N-1} - 1\}$)

$$\pi_{H,i}(z, H, \boldsymbol{p}, \boldsymbol{d}) =$$

$$\begin{cases} \sum_{n=0}^{N-1} p_n p_{H,i}^{(z)}; & z < d_0, \\[2ex] \sum_{n=0}^{i} p_n \left( f_{H,H-1}^{(1)} \pi_{H-1,i}(z-1, H, \boldsymbol{p}, \boldsymbol{d}) + \sum_{j=1}^{d_n} {}_{H-1} f_{H,H}^{(j)} \pi_{H,i}(z-j, H, \boldsymbol{p}, \boldsymbol{d}) + \\ p_{\text{nab}}(H, d_n) \pi_0(z - d_n, H, \boldsymbol{p}, \boldsymbol{d}) \right) + \sum_{m=i+1}^{N-1} p_m p_{H,i}^{(z)}; \ (i \in \{0, ..., N-2\}) \ d_i \leq z < d_{i+1}, \\[2ex] \sum_{n=0}^{N-1} p_n \left( f_{H,H-1}^{(1)} \pi_{H-1,i}(z-1, H, \boldsymbol{p}, \boldsymbol{d}) + \sum_{j=1}^{d_n} {}_{H-1} f_{H,H}^{(j)} \pi_{H,i}(z-j, H, \boldsymbol{p}, \boldsymbol{d}) + \\ p_{\text{nab}}(H, d_n) \pi_0(z - d_n, H, \boldsymbol{p}, \boldsymbol{d}) \right); & d_{N-1} \leq z. \end{cases}$$
$$(24)$$

From (22) and (23), we derive an expression for the probability of the MT being in state $i$ when a call arrival occurs, given the MT starts moving from state $m$, $\pi_{m,i}^*(a, H, \boldsymbol{p}, \boldsymbol{d}) = \sum_{z=0}^{\infty} \alpha(z, a, \theta) \, \pi_{m,i}(z, H, \boldsymbol{p}, \boldsymbol{d})$, for $m \in \{0, ..., H-1\}$ and $\forall i \in \{0, ..., D_{N-1} - 1\}$,

$$\pi_{m,i}^*(a, H, \boldsymbol{p}, \boldsymbol{d}) = \begin{cases} b_{0,i} + \sum_{l=0}^{1} f_{0,l}^{(1)} a \pi_{l,i}^*(a, H, \boldsymbol{p}, \boldsymbol{d}); & m = 0, \\ b_{m,i} + \sum_{l=m-1}^{m+1} f_{m,l}^{(1)} a \pi_{l,i}^*(a, H, \boldsymbol{p}, \boldsymbol{d}); & m \in \{1, ..., H-1\}, \end{cases} \quad (25)$$

where

$$b_{m,i} = \alpha(0) p_{m,i}^{(0)} + [\alpha(1) - a\alpha(0)] p_{m,i}^{(1)} \quad (26)$$

Working on (25), we can state, [7]

$$\pi_{m,i}^*(a, H, \boldsymbol{p}, \boldsymbol{d}) = F_m^*(a) \pi_{0,i}^*(a, H, \boldsymbol{p}, \boldsymbol{d}) + G_{m,i}^*(a) \quad (27)$$

where $F_m^*(a)$ has been given in (14) and

$$G_{m,i}^*(a) = \begin{cases} 0; & m = 0 \\ -\dfrac{b_{0,i}}{a f_{0,1}^{(1)}}; & m = 1 \\ \dfrac{1 - a f_{m-1,m-1}^{(1)}}{a f_{m-1,m}^{(1)}} G_{m-1,i}^*(a) - \dfrac{f_{m-1,m-2}^{(1)}}{f_{m-1,m}^{(1)}} G_{m-2,i}^*(a) - \dfrac{b_{m-1,i}}{a f_{m-1,m}^{(1)}}; & m \in \{2, ..., H\} \end{cases}$$
$$(28)$$

Finally from (24) we derive an expression for $\pi_{H,i}^*(a, H, \boldsymbol{p}, \boldsymbol{d}) = \sum_{z=0}^{\infty} \alpha(z, a, \theta)$ $\pi_{H,i}(z, H, \boldsymbol{p}, \boldsymbol{d})$ in which we use (27) to get a closed expression of $\pi_{0,i}^*(a, H, \boldsymbol{p}, \boldsymbol{d})$ for $i \in \{0, ..., D_{N-1} - 1\}$,

$$
\pi_{0,i}^*(a, H, \boldsymbol{p}, \boldsymbol{d}) = \frac{\sum_{n=0}^{N-1} p_n I_i(a, H, d_n)}{\sum_{n=0}^{N-1} p_n J(a, H, d_n)} \tag{29}
$$

where $J(a, H, d_n)$ is given by (16), and

$$
\begin{aligned}
I_i(a, H, d_n) = & \sum_{z=0}^{d_n-1} \alpha(z) p_{H,i}^{(z)} + \left(\alpha(d_n) - \alpha(0)a^{d_n}\right) \left(p_{\mathrm{nab}}(H, d_n) p_{0,i}^{(0)} +_{H-1} f_{H,H}^{(d_n)} p_{H,i}^{(0)}\right) \\
& - a f_{H,H-1}^{(1)} \sum_{z=0}^{d_n-2} \alpha(z) p_{H-1,i}^{(z)} - \sum_{m=1}^{d_n-1} {}_{H-1} f_{H,H}^{(m)} a^m \sum_{z=0}^{d_n-1-m} \alpha(z) p_{H,i}^{(z)} \\
& - G_{H,i}^*(a) \left(1 - \sum_{m=1}^{d_n} {}_{H-1} f_{H,H}^{(m)} a^m\right) + G_{H-1,i}^*(a) a f_{H,H-1}^{(1)} \tag{30}
\end{aligned}
$$

## 7   Performance Evaluation and Numerical Results

With the analytical models presented in sections 5 and 6 we can compute the total cost per call arrival, $C_T$. It is defined as:

$$
C_T(a, \theta, H, \boldsymbol{p}, \boldsymbol{d}) = U C_{LU}(a, \theta, H, \boldsymbol{p}, \boldsymbol{d}) + V C_{PG, Y}(a, \theta, H, \boldsymbol{p}, \boldsymbol{d}) \tag{31}
$$

where $U$ and $V$ are the cost of an update message and the cost for polling a cell respectively. $Y \in \{A, B\}$ indicates the paging scheme used, scheme A or scheme B. $U$ and $V$ are independent of the location of the MT. $U$ includes the cost of transferring from the network to the MT the set $X$ of $M$ new identifiers corresponding to the cells within a distance $H$ from the new center cell. The costs $U$ and $V$ are set to 5 and 1 respectively, in all the graphs, as in previous studies such as [12].

This cost is evaluated for several set of parameters. The parameters include not only $U$ and $V$, but also the vectors $\boldsymbol{d}$ and $\boldsymbol{p}$ (all the movement thresholds and the corresponding probabilities), the parameter $H$, the probability $a = f^*(\lambda_c)$, $\theta = \lambda_c / \lambda_m$ (CMR), and the maximum paging delay, $\eta$.

In general, in our proposed location update schemes, as the size of the set $X$ increases, fewer update messages are sent by the MT, when compared with the original movement–based scheme. As a result of fewer contacts with the network, it is expected an increase of the uncertainty of the MT position. Hence, we have a tradeoff between the reduction of the location update cost and the growth of the paging cost.

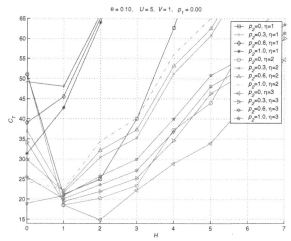

**Fig. 5.** $C_T$ vs $H$, when SDF paging, scheme A, is used. $CMR = 0.1$. $\boldsymbol{d} = [d_0\ d_1\ d_2] = [1,\ 2,\ 3]$. $p_1 = 0$ and $p_0 + p_2 = 1$. $U = 5$ and $V = 1$

Figures 5 and 6 show the total cost $C_T$ when SDF paging (scheme A) is implemented. For both figures we set $N = 3$, $\boldsymbol{d} = [d_0,\ d_1,\ d_2] = [1,\ 2,\ 3]$ and $CMR = 0.1$. In Fig. 5, $p_1 = 0$, and in Fig. 6, $p_1 = 0.5$. In these figures, for each set of parameters we have a minimum total cost for a given $H$ value, $H^*$. When $H > H^*$, as $H$ increases the paging cost predominates and the total cost, $C_T$, grows. When $H < H^*$, as $H$ decreases the location update cost predominates and the total cost, $C_T$, also grows. Note also the paging cost decreases as the maximum paging delay, $\eta$ increases. Fig. 5, (respectively fig. 6), shows the best performance for $H = H^* = 2$, $\eta = 3$ and $\boldsymbol{p} = [1, 0, 0] \Rightarrow \overline{d} = 1$, (respectively $H = H^* = 1$, $\eta = 3$ and $\boldsymbol{p} = [0.5, 0.5, 0] \Rightarrow \overline{d} = 1.5$, a real number). Observe in Fig. 5, for $\eta = 1$ and $\eta = 2$ the lowest total cost is achieved for $H = H^* = 1$, $d_0 = 1$, and $p_0 = 1$, and for $\eta = 3$ the best performance is obtained for $H = H^* = 2$, $d_0 = 1$, and $p_0 = 1$ (we have the distance–based scheme when $d_0 = 1$ and $p_0 = q_0 = 1$, [4]).

Next we compare Fig. 7, for $H = 2$ and Fig. 8, for $H = 1$, when $CMR = 0.1$ and $\eta = 3$. Fig. 7 confirms the distance–based scheme offers the best performance, $C_T = 14.89$ ($d_0 = 1$, $p_0 = q_0 = 1$, $H = H^* = 2$). In Fig. 8, the point $(p_0 = q_0 = 0$, $p_1 = (1 - q_0)q_1 = 1)$ give us, $C_T = 15.82$. The total cost at this point is $6.2\% = (15.82\text{-}14.89)/14.89$ higher than the total cost when the distance scheme is used ($H = 2$, $d_0 = 1$, $p_0 = 1$). This percentage would be the price to be payed if we want to reduce the signaling load on the air interface due to the transfer of cell identifiers from the network to the MT. For $H = 2$, 19 cell identifiers need to be transferred, but for $H = 1$ this amount is reduced to 7 cell identifiers, a $63\%$ of reduction (see Table 1, $63\% = (L_2\text{-}L_1)/L_2 = (19\text{-}7)/19$).

In Fig. 9 and 10, $H = 0$, the MT stores in its local memory the identity of a single cell. The probabilistic PG scheme (in line with [17]) is used. Figure 9

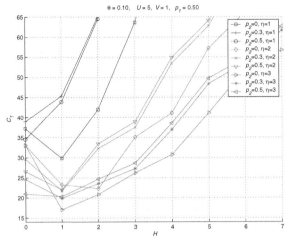

**Fig. 6.** $C_T$ vs $H$, when SDF paging, scheme A, is used. $CMR = 0.1$. $\boldsymbol{d} = [d_0\ d_1\ d_2] = [1,\ 2,\ 3]$. $p_1 = 0.5$ and $p_0 + p_2 = 0.5$. $U = 5$ and $V = 1$

shows $C_T$ vs $\theta$ when only one threshold is used, [6,7]. The minimum cost in this figure has also been drawn for $H = 0$, (solid line without any symbol) and, as can be observed, two thresholds are needed ($N = 2$, $d_0$ and $d_1 = d_0 + 1$) for some range of $\theta$. Figure 10 shows the suitable values for $D_0$ and $p_1$ ($p_0 = 1 - p_1$) which give the minimum cost, $C_T$, of Fig. 9. Observe $D^* = H + d^* = D_0 + p_1$ as $d^* = d_0 + p_1$. As we can see, the suitable value for the movement counter threshold, $d^*$, is a real number, not necessarily integer. Therefore, with a single register at the MT, [6], our fractional movement-distance based scheme, can improve the original fractional movement based scheme, [17].

## 8    Conclusions

In this paper, a general framework on fractional movement–distance location update has been provided. Our results show that among the location update schemes proposed, the distance based scheme provides the best performance from the signalling point of view. Some suboptimal schemes are also suitable since they slightly increase the optimal cost (6%) but they reduce considerably the amount of memory needed to be transferred from the network to the mobile terminal (63%). When the amount of memory in the MT is reduced to a single register, the interest of providing a finer grained threshold value has also been shown, and a precise probabilistic paging scheme has been provided (in line with [17]). We believe the implementation of our proposal is easy in real cellular systems.

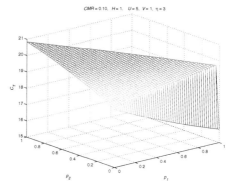
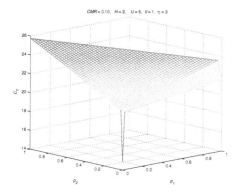

**Fig. 7.** $C_T$ vs $(p_1, p_2)$, when SDF paging, scheme A, is used, $\eta = 3$. $CMR = 0.1$, $H = 2$ and $\boldsymbol{d} = [d_0\ d_1\ d_2] = [1\ 2\ 3]$. $U = 5$ and $V = 1$

**Fig. 8.** $C_T$ vs $(p_1, p_2)$, when SDF paging, scheme A, is used, $\eta = 3$. $CMR = 0.1$, $H = 1$ and $\boldsymbol{d} = [d_0\ d_1\ d_2] = [1\ 2\ 3]$. $U = 5$ and $V = 1$

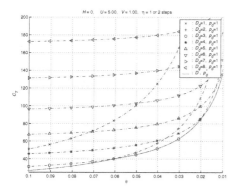
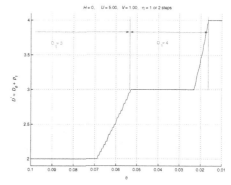

**Fig. 9.** $C_T$ vs $\theta$ when the probabilistic PG scheme is used. $H = 0$. $U = 5$ and $V = 1$

**Fig. 10.** Suitable values for $D_0$ and $p_1$ vs $\theta$ in order to reach the minimum total cost, $C_T$ (see Fig. 9). The probabilistic PG scheme is used. $H = 0$. $U = 5$ and $V = 1$

# 9 Acknowledgments

Thanks are given to *Ministerio de Ciencia y Tecnología* (MCyT) and to *Secretaría de Estado de Educación y Universidades* (Spain) for financial support under projects number *TIC2001-0956-C04-04* and *TIC2003-08272*, and *PR2004-0580*.

# References

1. I. F. Akyildiz, J. S.M. Ho and Y.-B. Lin, "Movement based location update and selective paging for PCS networks", IEEE/ACM Transactions on Networking, Vol. 4, n. 4, pp. 629-638, August 1996.

2. E. Alonso, K. S. Meier-Hellstern, G. Pollini, "Influence of cell geometry on handover and registration rates in cellular and universal personal telecommunication networks", Proceedings of the $8^{th}$ International Teletraffic Congress (ITC), Specialists Seminar on Universal Personal Telecommunications pp. 261- 270, October 12- 14, 1992. Santa Margherita Ligure, Genova (Italy).

3. A. Bar-Noy, I. Kessler, M. Sidi, "Mobile users: To update or not to update", Proceedings of the INFOCOM'94 pp. 570-576, June 14-16, 1994, Toronto, Ontario (Canada).

4. A. Bar-Noy, I. Kessler, Mo. Sidi, "Mobile users: To update or not to update", ACM-Baltzer Journal of Wireless Networks, Vol. 1, n.2, pp.175-186, July 1995.

5. U. N. Bhat,"Elements of applied stochastic processes", John Wiley, 1984.

6. V. Casares-Giner, J. Mataix-Oltra, "On movement based mobility tracking strategy - An enhanced version", IEEE Communications Letters, Vol. 2, n. 2, pp. 45-47, February 1998.

7. V. Casares-Giner, P. García-Escalle, "An hybrid movement–distance based location update strategy for mobility tracking", Proceedings of the European Wireless'04, pp. 121-127, February 24-27, 2004, Barcelona (Spain).

8. D. R. Cox and H.D.Miller,"The theory of stochastic process", Chapman-Hall, (Science Paperbacks) 1972.

9. Y. Fang, "Movement based mobility management and trade off analysis for wireless mobile networks", IEEE Transactions on Computers, Vol. 52, n. 6, pp. 791-803, June 2003.

10. P. García-Escalle, V. Casares-Giner, J. Mataix-Oltra, "Reducing location update and paging cost in a PCS network", IEEE Transactions on Wireless Communications, Vol. 1, n. 1, pp. 200-209, January 2002.

11. R. Jain, Y.-B. Lin, C.N. Lo and S. Mohan, "A caching strategy to reduce network impacts of PCS", IEEE Journal on Selected Areas in Communications, Vol. 12, n. 8 pp 1434-1445, August 1994.

12. J. Li, Y. Pan, X. Jia, "Analysis of dynamic location management for PCS networks", IEEE Transactions on Vehicular Technology, Vol. 51, n. 5, pp. 1109-1119. September 2002.

13. Y.-B. Lin, "Reducing location update cost in PCN", IEEE/ACM Transactions on Networking, Vol. 5, n. 1, pp. 25-33, February 1997.

14. Y.-B. Lin and W. Chen, "Impact of busy lines and mobility on cell blocking in PCS networks", International Journal of Communication Systems, Vol. 9, pp. 35-45, 1996

15. S. Okasaka, S. Onoe, S. Yasuda, A. Maebara, "A new location updating method for digital cellular systems", Proceedings of the $41^{st}$ Vehicular Technology Conference'91, pp. 345-350, May 19-22, 1991, St. Louis Missouri, (USA).

16. R. Ramjee, D. Towsley, R. Nagarajan, "On optimal call admission control in cellular networks", Wireless Networks, Vol. 3, n.1, pp. 29-41, March 1997.

17. Y. Xiao, "Optimal fractional movement based scheme for PCS location management", IEEE Communications Letters, Vol. 7, n. 2, pp. 67-69, February 2003.

18. M.M. Zonoozi and P. Dassanayake, "User mobility modeling and characterization of mobility patterns", IEEE Journal Selected Areas Communications, Vol. 15, n. 7, pp. 1239-1252, September 1997.

# Enabling Mobile Peer-to-Peer Networking

Jens O. Oberender[1], Frank-Uwe Andersen[3], Hermann de Meer[1],
Ivan Dedinski[1], Tobias Hoßfeld[2], Cornelia Kappler[3], Andreas Mäder[2], and
Kurt Tutschku[2]

[1] University of Passau, Chair of Computer Networks and
Computer Communications. Innstraße 33, 94032 Passau, Germany.
`[oberender|demeer|dedinski]@fmi.uni-passau.de`
[2] University of Würzburg, Department of Distributed Systems.
Am Hubland, 97074 Würzburg, Germany.
`[maeder|hossfeld|tutschku]@informatik.uni-wuerzburg.de`
[3] SIEMENS AG.
Siemensdamm 62, 13623 Berlin, Germany.
`[frank-uwe.andersen|cornelia.kappler]@siemens.com`

**Abstract.** In this paper we present a P2P file-sharing architecture optimized for mobile networks. We discuss the applicability of current P2P techniques for resource access and mediation in the context of 2.5G/3G mobile networks. We investigate a mobile P2P architecture that is able to reconcile the decentralized operation of P2P file sharing with the interests of network operators, e. g. control and performance. The architecture is based on the popular eDonkey protocol and is enhanced by additional caching entities and a crawler.

## 1   Introduction

P2P file sharing systems account for a high percentage of the traffic volume in the fixed Internet, having exceeded http (WWW) or email traffic [2] [8]. The increasing availability of mobile data networks such as GPRS and UMTS in conjunction with attractive pricing schemes makes P2P file sharing an interesting application also in the mobile context. But the operation of P2P systems in mobile environments encounters several problems, such as a relatively narrow and expensive air interface, highly varying online states (presence) of the subscribers, a hierarchical network structure (GPRS), and limited device capabilities.

P2P is a distributed application architecture where equal entities, denoted as peers, voluntarily share resources, e.g. files or CPU cycles, via direct, end-to-end exchanges. In order to share resources, P2P applications need to support two fundamental coordination and control functions: *Resource mediation* mechanisms, i.e. functions to locate resources or entities, and *resource control* mechanisms, i.e. functions to permit, prioritize, and schedule the access to resources. *Pure P2P* architectures are implementing both mechanisms in a fully decentralized manner [3], while *Hybrid P2P* systems utilize central entities that collect mediation data. An example for a Hybrid P2P system is the eDonkey filesharing protocol, where the index servers collect and distribute file location information about all peers.

The desire of mobile network operators is to add value to the P2P data flows and to turn P2P into a service they can charge for. When creating such services operators retain control on traffic and content. However the basic P2P user experience and connectivity should be preserved. In this paper, which is an extension of [1], we describe such a service and analyze its impact on the network usage by means of a simulation.

This paper is structured as follows. In Sec. 2, we analyze the requirements and objectives of mobile P2P systems. We also analyze the problems of mobile P2P file sharing systems, and map out possible solutions. In Sec. 3, we present our proposed mobile P2P architecture. We identify key concepts (Sec. 3.1), describe our extension of the eDonkey architecture (Sec. 3.2) and introduce the Cache Peer (Sec. 3.3), the enhanced Indexing Server (Sec. 3.4) and the Crawler (Sec. 3.5). Sec. 3.6 identifies caching parameters and introduces caching strategies for mobile networks. In order to evaluate the system performance, we define a simulation model. Sec. 4 outlines the restrictions imposed by mobile networks and concludes the cache strategy which fits best for P2P traffic. Sec. 5 presents the numerical evaluated cache strategies. Finally, Sec. 6 summarizes the efforts achieved so far and gives an outlook.

## 2  Requirements and Objectives of Mobile P2P Systems

Mobile wireless communication systems are in many aspects different from the fixed Internet. For the access to IP-based applications like WAP, Web or E-Mail, a great variety of access technologies such as GPRS, EDGE or the UMTS packet switched data services exists. Mobile access technologies differ in terms of the air interface, QoS-capabilities, available bit rates and underlying transport mechanisms in the core network. In the following, we consider some of these aspects and their implications for a P2P system.

The **Air Interface** is commonly seen as the bottleneck in mobile communication systems. Although 3G systems like UMTS provide bit rates up to 2 Mbps in TDD mode and up to 10 Mbps with the HSDPA technology (High Speed Downlink Packet Access), the cost of data transmissions over the air interface is generally higher than in fixed networks. This is even more true for 2G and 2.5G systems like GSM/GPRS with a theoretical maximum bit rate of 171 kbps and typically achievable bit rates between 28 and 50 kbps. Furthermore, the mean round-trip times are significantly higher than in wired systems due to the higher protocol overhead and complex error correction schemes, leading to a lower performance of especially TCP [7]. These results are also confirmed by our measurements of eDonkey via GPRS [4].

The two main restrictions of the air interface, a relatively low effective bandwidth and high latencies, make it essential to reduce the signalling overhead as much as possible to achieve an acceptable performance. Direct traffic between peers should be avoided as much as possible, since all mobile-to-mobile

UTRAN/GERAN          PS-domain

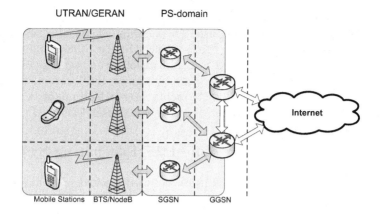

Mobile Stations    BTS/NodeB          SGSN          GGSN

**Fig. 1.** Simplified scheme of core network for packet data transport

transmissions use twice the amount of air interface resources if compared to mobile-to-fixed-network transmissions.

Furthermore, the limitations of the transmission power and battery capacity cause the uplink bandwidth to be significantly more expensive in terms of network resource usage than the downlink. So the use of uploads from mobile devices must be more efficient when asked for. Battery consumption will be a long-lasting issue for mobile devices. Therefore, mobile user equipment will continue to have a lower online time if compared to non-mobile Internet devices, on which the majority of the P2P applications runs today. Reduced online time of the peers will greatly affect the download time and thus the user experience of P2P systems.

In general, the **Core Network** of a mobile communication system is designed hierarchically. For GPRS or UMTS, the data traffic stream of each mobile traverses along core network, from the UMTS Terrestrial Radio Access Network (UTRAN) through the packet-switched domain and back. At the GGSN, the mobile hosts get assigned an IP address. Therefore, the GGSN is both the interface to the Internet and to other mobiles in the mobile domain, making it also the point in the core network where all packet traffic is concentrated, see Fig. 1. Note that generally in the core network several GGSNs exist, each serving as a gateway for a large portion of the mobile network. This hierarchical, very centralized topology is in strong contrast to the flat, mesh-like overlay network topologies of most P2P systems.

One of the most important **Operational Requirements** of mobile network operators is to maintain control over the network and the ability to charge for provided services. Furthermore, operators would like to keep traffic in their own domain to avoid cost due to inter-domain traffic. This is true for both mobile and fixed-line operators. If mobile P2P is integrated into the service structure, it is therefore necessary to provide means for controlling and for charging. On the one hand, the control mechanisms for a mobile P2P system must be carefully chosen in order to avoid the total degeneration towards a centralized system.

Control mechanisms should not tamper fundamental P2P concepts such as decentralization. The business model used for charging should also comply with P2P applications, e.g. reward users for sharing. On the other hand, a mobile P2P system can benefit from the existing infrastructure and services of a mobile communication system. The network providers know the location, the online status and the service agreement of the mobile user, which might be useful to avoid signalling overhead and to increase the quality of service.

# 3    An Architecture for Mobile P2P Filesharing-Systems

P2P filesharing systems extensively utilize network resources. As an optimization the architecture is adapted to that of the underlying network. The major challenge of mobile networks is their hierarchical infrastructure. This must be reflected in an architecture for mobile P2P systems. We designed a caching mechanism that efficiently maps filesharing onto mobile infrastructures.

## 3.1    eDonkey Features

To meet the requirements of operator-managed services with P2P-based content distribution, a hybrid P2P architecture has been selected. The chosen architecture is based on the eDonkey P2P file sharing protocol, because of its popularity and its proven robustness. It is classified as a hybrid P2P filesharing network, as data exchange is achieved decentrally between peers while mediation is provided by centralized index servers.

The eDonkey protocol introduced the **multi-source download protocol**, which is an integral part to the scalability of P2P file-sharing. It means, that the download process for one resource may utilize multiple sources. Coordination between several sources is somewhat hard, since files could be tampered or even renamed. The multi-source download protocol relies on the MD5 Hash-IDs. All copies of a resource carry the unique Hash-ID with them and so a requester can be sure that he downloads fragments of the very same file and version. Then the fragments can be afterwards compiled into the original resource.

The eDonkey protocol addresses the free-rider problem using **fragment sharing**. Any resource fragment is shared after completion check. Thus all peers provide fragments during their download. This increases the number of early available sources and the resource access load is distributed over the community.

The fragment sharing concept forces downloaders of a resource to share completed fragments with others. Multi-source downloading scenarios culminate into fully-connected graphs[4]. The original eDonkey architecture achieves source convergence centrally, i.e. by asking a super peer. Thus a bunch of peers, called a **horde**, exists that currently access the same resource. EMule introduced *source exchange*, a decentral approach to distribute sources. Because the peers communicate with each other, they can easily notify the list of sharing peers. This behaviour makes frequent request to the super peer unnecessary.

---

[4] unless the maximum number of connections is exceeded

To apply a file-sharing protocol on **mobile networks**, some minor issues had to be solved. Mobile Internet devices have an IP stack and thus can in principle be fully integrated into the Internet. However, security mechanisms like firewalling, NAT boxing and VPN interfere with basic P2P operations. P2P applications can handle firewalled connections as long as there is either one partner with open ports. The eDonkey/eMule terminus *HighID* denominates a peer in case foreign hosts can initiate communications with that peer. Firewalled peers need to establish the connection themselves, other peers may reply message but cannot initiate transmissions. These are marked with *LowID* indicating that these peers need actively connection establishment. P2P networks can handle firewalled connections as long as either one peer of a direct communication allows incoming connections. Rigid firewalling can be overcome using VPN, which we have also tested. While the mobile peer software can be updated, such a restriction would abandon connections to Internet peers that run current software releases.

### 3.2   Extended eDonkey Architecture

Our enhancements to the eDonkey architecture comprise three parts: Modifications to the *index server*, a *cache peer* and a *crawler*. The index server monitors the file popularity and exports the collected data to the cache peer. The cache peer stores popular information at the network core. The crawling peers support the index server with resources that are unknown in the mobile operator domain. Extended signalling includes information from the mobile network domain, e.g. presence information. The architecture components shown in Fig. 2 will be described in detail in this Section.

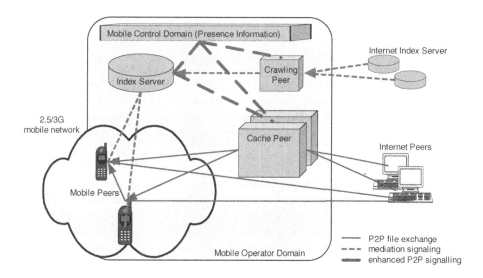

**Fig. 2.** Mobile P2P Architecture Overview

With centralized mediation we can gain information on popular files and cache these at the network core. This improves the overall performance, because network-edge-stored resources cause higher cost as they generate double traffic (from network edge to GGSN and then to network edge again) compared to a resource transfer from the network core. We assume here that networks of different providers are interconnected and exchange IP traffic, e. g. of a centrally operated cache peer.

Beneficial **caching for P2P** has two ingredients: identifying popular resources, and forcing peers to use the cached instance. First, to *identify popular resources* in a hybrid P2P network, information at the indexing server can be utilized. During download each peer frequently requests new sources from the indexing server; it signals the resource ID and receives a list of sharing peers. Because the indexing server can distinguish between requesting peers, it can derive statistics, which resources are heavily accessed. While the number of interested peers is incorporated, the current allocation and bandwidth remain unknown.

Second, to gain the full benefit of mobile services, the mobile peers must be encouraged to *access the cached instance* but no other. The standard peer software is designed to connect to any available source[5], thus gaining multiple waiting slots and improving chances of an early resource access. Modifications in the indexing server hide other sources as soon as a cache copy has been recorded. *Shrinking the source peer set* at the indexing server does not apply to peers that have requested sources earlier. Acquiring sources is done by merging any source candidates, there is no option for removing them. Outdated source IPs are deselected if they do not respond to ping messages.

A fixed-network cache peer can allow a significantly larger number of simultaneous uploads than any mobile peer. Because of the larger upload capacity, waiting queues are shorter and a faster response can be achieved. This is why we believe, that most often peers will receive fragments from the cached instances at the network-core rather than from network-edge peers. Our simulations show that this can reduce network traffic on the mobile backbone and shorten the download time for a file (cf. Sec. 5).

The proposed P2P components offer a value-added service. All components are optional, i. e. an operator could offer a mobile P2P service utilizing just the index server, crawler and proxy to enforce the use of local resources. Our current development of integrated features in this architecture is still ongoing.

### 3.3    Cache Peer

Peers access and share resources. In a way one could see them as a cache, because information that has been downloaded to the peer is also shared with the community. For caching an autonomous control is indispensable: a cache peer needs to decide, which resources should be cached. In our solution this decision will be determined using information provided from the indexing server. We did not investigate legal issues in our project.

---

[5] Restricted number of connected to sources from 150 up

The cache peer is a specialised peer that stores popular files at the network core to reduce the amount of expensive air-interface usage. The cache peer owes its name to the fact that we recommend to implement it as an ordinary peer. It interfaces with both the mobile domain controller and the indexing server. These negotiate what resources should be stored at the network-core. In our implementation the cache peer receives the list of popular resources from the indexing server to adopt its caching strategy. Based on this, it decides whether to fetch or to drop a cached resource.

If the access characteristic measured at the index servers signals multiple downloads of a popular file, caching is initiated. For downloading of files, the cache peer uses the same mechanism as an arbitrary peer. At that moment, resource access control is partly shifted from the network-edge towards the network-core. This signalling of chunk completion is required as it switches the super peer behaviour; from then on, all other sources except the cache peer will be hidden from further source requests. New downloads from peers on the mobile infrastructure are prevented.

### 3.4   Enhanced Index Server

The eDonkey protocol belongs to the hybrid class of P2P systems using weakly centralized resource mediation, which is provided by several index servers. The index servers provide two essential services: name search and to answering source requests. In name search a peer asks for all resources that match a given string. Secondly, when peers start to download a certain resource, they ask for peers that currently share this resource.

In our solution we recommend using a single index server that administrates all resources known inside the mobile domain. Thus popular resources can be identified and then caching can be initiated. Two extensions can deliver sufficient information to bring the caching mechanism in place. First, we log source requests by resource ID. All peers that are connected to this index server frequently ask for any new source that has been discovered lately. In reverse, from this message we gain a list of resources that are actively downloading by now.

Second, we alter the response messages of resource requests. If the cache peer is contained in the result, all other sources are rejected. Note, that the cache peer publishes the first resource fragment and this will block all other sources with possibly other fragments. However the cache peer will download only complete resources and therefore should soon reach a state where the full resource is available.

### 3.5   Crawler

The eDonkey community offers a large variety of resources. If the primary index server does not return enough query hits, the software automatically connects to other available index servers. For the mobile context this weakly-decentralized mediation behavior is undesirable, since the mobile domain index server cannot keep track of popular files. Besides, other index servers cannot distinguish cache peers and therefore cannot hide other sources.

To maximize the benefits of the modified eDonkey architecture, mobile peers must connect to one of the enhanced index servers. The crawler entity is used for coordination between index servers of the mobile domain with any external index servers (other operators or Internet). The index server requests unknown resources from the crawler, which fetches mediation data from the Internet index servers. Thus, any resource available inside the global eDonkey community can be located and accessed.

## 3.6   Caching Strategies for Mobile P2P File-Sharing Systems

The cache peer is a central element in the current mobile P2P architecture. In order to realize the objectives of the cache (minimized external and air-to-air traffic, reachability of files despite the absence of their providing mobile peers, etc.), a specially optimized caching strategy is needed. It has to take into account the characteristics of the mobile network and of the file-sharing protocol in use.

Depending on the type of storage units to be cached, one can divide the caching mechanisms in file-based and chunk-based strategies. For file-based strategies, the granularity of the cache is a single file. However, the file-based strategies are not flexible enough if only small pieces of a big file are needed, as the not required parts of the file also occupy memory capacity of the cache. A chunk-based caching strategy works on chunks which are also the natural data exchange units in many P2P networks, like eDonkey. This granularity fits well to P2P traffic, as most of the files are not downloaded completely. The users usually search through many files until they find exactly the file they need. For each promising target file, only some chunks or chunk portions (typically at the beginning and the end) are downloaded. The user may decide, whether the resource is suited for his needs. Otherwise the user will cancel the download. A file based cache strategy cannot handle such download behavior effectively, while a chunk based strategy handles this automatically, since only requested chunks are cached.

In general, the chunk-based strategy leads to a better system performance than a file-based one due to the smaller granularity, the better adaptation to the user behavior, and the better utilization of the cache capacity. But in current GPRS networks we assume most of the exchanged files to be smaller than an eDonkey chunk of 9 MB, cf. Section 5. Thus, we do not differ between a file-based and a chunk-based strategy in the following. Moreover, a file based strategy would not have the additional overhead for fragmenting and defragmenting files.

Our cache strategy consists of two aspects: *Cache population strategy* and *cache replacement strategy*. The latter is used when the cache population conditions for a new file $f$ are fulfilled and the file size $s_f$ exceeds the available capacity of the cache. Here a certain ranking $X_f(i)$ to the stored files is applied. Depending on the strategy, the value $X_f(i)$ may include the number $Q_f(i)$ of file requests at the index server and the amount of uploaded traffic $V_f(i)$ of the cache for file $f$ during the time interval $[(i-1)\Delta t; i\Delta t] =_{def} t_i$. If a file is inserted into the cache during the time interval $t_i$, the file $f$ with the minimal ranking value $X_f(i-1)$ of the prior interval $t_{i-1}$ is replaced.

RANDOM, FIFO, LRU (Least Recently Used), LFU (Least Frequently Used), LSB (Least Sent Bytes) are standard replacement strategies [9] that do not require any special application level knowledge about future caching events. E.g. the ranking value is $X_f(i) = Q_f(i)$ for LFU and $X_f(i) = V_f(i)$ for LSB, respectively. In the following sections we propose a cache strategy which is adapted onto P2P traffic in mobile telecommunication systems and incorporates the occurring restrictions of mobile P2P. This strategy is referred to as *Intelligent Memory Usage* (IMU).

**IMU – Cache Population Strategy** The basic concept for inserting a file $f$ into the cache is that the number of file requests exceeds a given threshold $\Theta$ at time $t \in t_i$, i.e. $Q_f(i-1) > \Theta$. If a file is inserted during the time interval $t_i$, it is not replaced during this period. The idea behind this is that we assume that the file is only inserted into the cache, because this increases the system performance during the current time interval $t_i$; otherwise $\Theta$ was badly chosen. The measurement values $X_f(i)$ are used in the following time interval $t_{i+1}$ to decide which file is a replacement candidate.

Another condition for inserting a file $f$ into the cache has to be fulfilled in order to ensure that $f$ does not replace a more useful file with respect to the key aspects of the cache. This is done by checking if $Q_f(i) > Q_m(i)$ for the file $m$ with the minimal replacement value $X_m(i-1)$.

**IMU – Cache Replacement Strategy** One major problem of the standard cache strategies is that they do not take into account the lengths of the files they cache. For example, a FIFO strategy always removes the last file in its caching queue. If a new file of length 5 kB has to be cached, it is obviously not necessary to remove a file of length 1 GB when there are files of length 6 kB already in the cache. However, if the huge file is the last in the FIFO queue, it is removed.

One way to consider the file sizes in the replacement decision is to use a slightly modified LRU strategy. The kick-out criteria should not be directly related with the last access time for a file, like in the standard LRU. The amount $V_f(i)$ of traffic generated by this file during $t_i$ describes in a more correct way the importance of the file, because minimizing of the traffic to external peers is a key aspect of the cache.

The size of a file on the other hand means additional costs for the cache peer, i.e. huge files use more storage resources. It would be reasonable to remove big files first, if they produce the same traffic as small files. This dependency is taken into account if the ranking value includes the factor $\left(\frac{V_f(i)}{s_f}\right)^\alpha$. $\alpha$ is the *weighting factor* and determines how strong it influences the ranking with respect to the number of file requests. $s_f$ denotes the compressed file size because eDonkey compresses files before transmitting.

The number $Q_f(i)$ of file requests during time interval $t_i$ is another measure indicating the popularity of a file. The more requests are seen at the index server, the more popular the file is. Hence, we define the initial ranking value of IMU for a file $f$ which is inserted during $t_{i_0}$ by

$$X_f(i_0) = \Gamma_f(i_0) \text{ with } \Gamma_f(i) = \left(\frac{V_f(i)}{s_f}\right)^\alpha \cdot Q_f(i). \qquad (1)$$

Since the file $f$ is then not replaced during $t_{i_0}$, we are able to include historical values for the following time intervals. This avoids too fast reacting on very frequent changes of the file requests and smooths the variation over time. The parameter $\beta$ is called the *aging factor*. We propose the following ranking value of IMU for $i > i_0$:

$$X_f(i) = \frac{\beta X_f(i-1) + \Gamma_f(i)}{2} \qquad (2)$$

## 4   Simulation Model

In the literature, many papers about caches and their performance exist. Even for P2P networks, cache replacement policies are investigated, e.g. in [10,6,5]. However, in this work we propose the IMU strategy especially adapted on P2P traffic in mobile networks which is evaluated by means of the simulation.

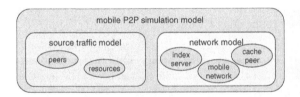

**Fig. 3.** Components of the mobile P2P simulation model

The mobile P2P simulation model consists of the source traffic model and the network model. The latter describes the restrictions of the P2P system because of the mobile network architecture. The source traffic model of a P2P specific system comprises the resources, i.e. the provided files, and the behavior of a peer, among other things the characteristics of a mobile subscriber. Figure 3 illustrates the components of the mobile P2P simulation model.

### 4.1   Peer and Resource Model

The resource model depicts the provided files and their popularity determining the file request arrival rate. In P2P networks, there is a large number $N_{files}$ of files available. Typically, only a small number $N_{pop}$ of very popular files generate a huge amount of traffic [11]. In our simulation, the request arrivals follow a Poisson process with rate $\lambda_f$ for each file $f$.

We assume that there are mobile specific content types, like ring tones (MIDI or mp3) or digital images, which are shared in mobile P2P. The file sizes for different content types have been measured at the University of Würzburg. We fitted the cumulative distribution function for the file size with a lognormal distribution which we applied in the simulation. Table 1 shows the measured parameters.

In order to reflect the highly fluctuating connection status of a mobile peer, we describe a mobile peer by an ON/OFF-process. This means that a peer is either in the ON state, i.e., the peer is present in the mobile domain and is connected to the P2P network, or in the OFF state, i.e., the peer is not connected to the P2P network. In addition, the ON period and OFF period are determined by exponential distributions with means $L_{ON}$ and $L_{OFF}$. Therefore, the transition rates between these two states are $\frac{1}{L_{ON}}$ and $\frac{1}{L_{ON}}$. During the ON period, the peer participates in the P2P network by providing its own files and requesting for other files. With probability $p_{new}$, a peer entering the ON state shares a new file.

Another mobile specific aspect is the small memory capacity of a mobile peer. If a newly requested file exceeds this capacity, the oldest files which are shared longest are deleted (FIFO) until sufficient memory is available for storing the new file. Additionally to the mobile peers, we also consider Internet peers. The main difference between both is the access type. In our simulations presented here, we use a ratio of 2:1 between GPRS and DSL users.

In the eDonkey application, we have an upload list reflecting the simultaneously served peers and a waiting list which contains all requesting peers. The upload bandwidth is equally split among the requesting peers in the upload list. Thus, the received bandwidth is very easy to calculate in a system where the bottleneck is the receiver upload bandwidth and not the possible download bandwidth. This is not valid in a mobile telecommunication system. Here, the problem is that not only the upload bandwidth of the peers but also the download bandwidth is a limiting factor due to the small bandwidth of mobile peers.

While the upload list is limited in order to guarantee a minimal download bandwidth, the waiting list is unlimited. A newly arriving file request joins the end of the waiting list; this also holds after downloading a download unit. It has to be noted that in eDonkey, a file is structured into chunks of 9.5 Mb and each chunk is downloaded in smaller pieces of fixed size, the so-called 'download units'. Immediately after downloading an entire chunk, it is provided as source of the file in the P2P network.

### 4.2   Mobile P2P Network Model

We consider GPRS, since we have performed measurements of eDonkey over GPRS (without our proposed mobile network elements) in parallel to the sim-

**Table 1.** Measurement of the file sizes for mobile P2P specific contents

|  | ring tone | game | image | mp3-audio |
|---|---|---|---|---|
| mean [kB] | 8.5762 | 37.9288 | 420.2075 | 4829.3306 |
| standard deviation [kB] | 9.3479 | 26.5833 | 21.3963 | 2305.5083 |

ulation, cf. [4]. We assume that a peer always utilizes its full capacity in uplink and downlink direction. It is interesting to see that, starting with the GPRS data service, asymmetric data paths are introduced by 3GPP standards that may also change over time (due to real time cell effects). Another characteristic of the air interface which affects the performance of a mobile user is the significantly high round trip time (RTT), which is also depending on the number of subscribers in a cell. We consider the data transfer of eDonkey via TCP whose throughput is then slowed down.

In the eDonkey network, a user has to be connected to an index server for participating in the network. Thus, the index server immediately notices when a peer goes online. We additionally assume that the index server discovers instantaneously when a peer goes offline due to not replied hello-packets. Therefore, the user presence information is always known to the index server and all files in the network and their corresponding sources are also known.

Each peer searching for a file asks for sources at the index server, which sends 200 sources at maximum to the requesting peer. We have limited the number of sources according to the original eDonkey source code because the searching peer requests the file at every sharing peer. Hence, the requesting peer joins the waiting list of each sharing peer. The waiting time before entering the upload list is increased and the overall throughput and the effective download bandwidth of all peers in the upload queue of sharing peers is decreased. This problem is overcome by limiting the number of retrieved sources. The index server returns uniform randomly 200 sources in order to distribute the emerging load equally within the network.

If the cache peer shares the file requested by a peer, the cache peer is always returned as first element of the source list. It is also possible to select in the simulation that the cache peer is the only returned source and all other sources are hidden.

The cache peer is assumed to be attached to the network with a link with almost infinite capacity. In this case, we have selected a 4 Gbps link, so that we can rule out a bottleneck in the interconnection of the cache peer with the downloading peers. The number of parallel upload connections from the cache is limited to 400, i.e. 400 mobile subscribers may download from the cache with 21.44 Mbps.

### 4.3 Abstract Model

The goal of the abstract simulation is to answer which cache replacement strategy fits best for the mobile P2P network. In contrast to the detailed simulation, we only use a subset of the parameters for the abstract simulation resulting in a much smaller computing time. The distinctive feature of the P2P network which plays an important role for the investigation of the cache is the file request arrival process. The popular files are requested very often; there are also a lot of less popular files which also generate many requests in total. Thus, the file request arrival process has to be simulated in detail, while the used transport mechanism

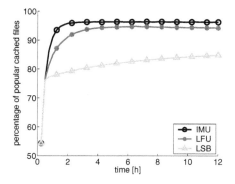 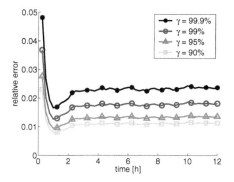

**Fig. 4.** Percentage of popular cached files     **Fig. 5.** Relative error of the results

or eDonkey's complex upload queue mechanism can be neglected for evaluating the performance of different cache strategies.

# 5   Numerical Results

In this section, we evaluate different cache strategies (LFU, LSB, IMU) by application of the abstract simulation. The target value which we use is the percentage $\Psi$ of popular files which are stored in the cache. This value directly relates to the byte-hit-rate, the request-hit-rate, and the amount of traffic which is kept within the mobile domain. The latter aspect is very important for a provider. The more popular files are stored in the cache the more data is sent from the cache to the requesting peers with the maximal available download bandwidth of the peers and the more file requests are successfully served.

Afterwards, the influence of the proposed strategy on the mobile P2P network is demonstrated quantitatively by means of the detailed simulation. We consider the upload data volume and different interactions between cache peer and index server.

## 5.1   Comparison of the Cache Strategies

We simulate 100 popular mp3-files and start with 50% of them in the cache. The cache peer is dimensioned as large as the sum of the popular files' sizes. Thus, $\Psi$ may reach 100%. The used parameters of IMU are $\alpha = 1, \beta = 0.5, \Delta t = 15$min, $\Theta = 4$. Figure 4 shows the percentage of popular cached files for each time period $\Delta t$. It seems to be astonishing that LFU is nearly as effective as the recommended IMU strategy, but the reason is the independent and identically distributed (iid) size for every file. Thus, the file request arrival rate is the main indicator for the file's popularity and LFU delivers good results. For a scenario with a more complex file size distribution, e.g. several large files, the LFU cannot return as good results as IMU, because a large, popular file may not be cached, although it produces more traffic. In this case, LSB may outstrip LFU.

In the regarded scenario, LSB comes off badly, although the transferred data volume is directly proportional to the number of file requests. Hence, LSB should perform as well as LFU. But this is only valid if the time interval during which the measurements are taken is large enough for a download of a file to finish within this period. Figure 4 shows that IMU achieves the best results, because the transmitted data volume and the number of the file requests are considered. About 95% of the popular files are detected within a short time frame. Furthermore, IMU is a good base for estimating whether a file is really popular or not, because temporarily high or low measurement values during the last time interval are weighted by the historical values. Thus, the popularity of a file in the next time frame can be estimated by the actual measured value and the curve progression from past.

Figure 5 shows the relative error for different levels of significance $\gamma$. It is defined as the half-width of the confidence interval normalized by the mean value. We performed 1,000 simulation runs and obtained a relative error below 5% even for $\gamma = 99.99\%$. The peak at the beginning results from the random initialization of the cache.

## 5.2    Influence of the Proposed Strategy

The following numerical values focus on a single popular file and its influence on the transferred data volume on the upstream, while the file disperses in the P2P network. In a first step, we begin to pick out a single chunk file, i.e. a file whose file size is less than the chunk size of 9 MB, because the probability that a file is smaller than 9 MB is more than 90%.

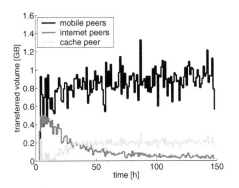
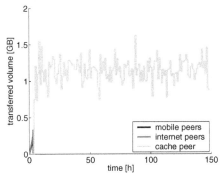

**Fig. 6.** Uploaded data volume of mobile and Internet peers and of the cache peer

**Fig. 7.** Uploaded data volume with the cache peer as exclusively returned source

Figure 6 shows the data volume characteristic for a file of size 3MB with an initial diffusion of 0.1%, i.e. at the beginning of the simulation 0.1% share this file. On the y-axis, the totally transmitted data volume in uplink direction of mobile and Internet peers and the cache peer within a time interval of 1 hour is plotted. At this point, we have to refer back on Section 4.2. The index server returns randomly 200 sources of all sources to the searching peer. The latter requests download units of this file at every returned peer, independent of the access speed of the providing peer. Obviously, 2/3 of the returned peers are mobile peers. With each mobile peer that successfully finishes its download, the probability for retrieving a mobile peer by the index server increases. Therefore, the data volume transmitted from the Internet peers decreases because the number of mobile, providing peers prevails the Internet peers.

The upload rate of the cache peer oscillates about 0.2 Gigabit per hour. This is because of the bottleneck in the downlink of the mobile peers. The downlink like the uplink has fair shared bandwidth. So the bandwidth is shared in similar parts for each uploading peer, as long as the uploading peer can provide this amount of data. With too many active downlink connections at a specific peer, the cache peer is not able to bring its high bandwidth capacity to bear.

Figure 7 shows the same scenario, but the index server answers source queries for the file only with the cache peer, as soon as the cache peer provides the file. Neither the mobile peers nor the Internet peers upload data, after the upload from the cache peers has started. As we can see, this modification is required in order to utilize the cache peer completely.

Summarizing, the index server should answer a file request not only with the sources but also with the available upload bandwidth in order to minimize the download time. In this case, the cache peer is always preferred. The simulation results are given in Table 2. Another point is that the user behavior should be adapted in mobile P2P environment. E.g. in the case of downloading 8 files, one from the cache peer and the other from other mobile peers, the downlink bandwidth is equally split between all data connections. In this case, the upload bandwidth of the cache peer cannot be utilized. Thus, it would be more appropriate only to download 2 or 3 files in parallel. Although the throughput is the same in both cases, the time for a single file download is much lower in the latter case.

**Table 2.** Percentage of traffic kept in the mobile network and the byte-hit-rate

| *cache peer...* | as single source | among other sources |
|---|---|---|
| traffic within mobile network | 99.68% | 89.06% |
| byte-hit-rate | 99.18% | 15.26% |

# 6  Conclusions

Current access and mediation control mechanisms has been discussed for applicability in the mobile context and as a result the eDonkey file sharing system has been enhanced by caching peers and crawlers. The new architecture for a mobile P2P service has been implemented for GPRS (2.5G) networks and has also been tested with UMTS. With the eDonkey index server, the three components adapt the resulting overlay network to the core structure in 2.5G/3G networks and especially to the needs of mobile operators and subscribers, thus improving the P2P performance.

Users remain in charge of access control, while network operators gain control on mediation of resources. This influence allows for keeping some P2P traffic inside the operator's network. Popular content will be cached at a central instance to reduce traffic. This also remedies bandwidth shortages caused from repetition of data transfers, which are observed in today's access networks, Unlike other mechanisms that oppress P2P traffic, this architecture offers a network-supported service that allows peers to cooperate with the global community.

The simulation model for mobile P2P architectures includes the proposed IMU cache strategy and the numerical results show good adaption outperforming standard cache strategies, like LFU or LSB. In future work, we will investigate more influence factors, like the mobile subscriber behavior or the mobile access type.

# References

1. Andersen, F.U., de Meer, H., Dedinski, I., Kappler, C., Mäder, A., Oberender, J.O., Tutschku, K.: An Architecture Concept for Mobile P2P File Sharing Services. In Dadam, P., Reichert, M., eds.: GI Jahrestagung (2). Volume 51 of LNI., GI (2004) 229–233
2. Azzouna, N.B., Clerot, F., Fricker, C., Guillemin, F.: Modeling ADSL traffic on an IP backbone link. In: Annals of Telecommunications, Traffic engineering and routing. (2004) 1260–1314
3. Barkai, D.: Peer-to-Peer Computing. Intel Press, Hillsborow, OR (2001)
4. Hoßfeld, T., Tutschku, K., Andersen, F.U.: Mapping of File-Sharing onto Mobile Environments: Feasibility and Performance of eDonkey with GPRS. Technical Report 338, University of Würzburg (2004)
5. Iyer, S., Rowstron, A., Druschel, P.: SQUIRREL: A Decentralized, Peer-to-Peer Web Cache. In: Twenty-First ACM Symposium on Principles of Distributed Computing, Monterey, CA (2002)
6. Leibowitz, N., Bergman, A., Ben-Shaul, R., Shavit, A.: Are file swapping networks cacheable? Characterizing P2P traffic. In: 7th Int. WWW Caching Workshop, Boulder, CO (2002)
7. Meyer, M.: TCP performance over GPRS. In: First Wireless Communications and Networking Conference (IEEE WCNC), New Orleans, MS (1999) 1248–1252
8. Sen, S., Wang, J.: Analyzing peer-to-peer traffic across large networks. IEEE/ACM Trans. Netw. **12** (2004) 219–232
9. Tanenbaum, A.: Modern Operating Systems. 2 edn. Prentice Hall (2004)
10. Wierzbicki, A., Leibowitz, N., Ripeanu, M., Wozniak, R.: Cache Replacement Policies Revisited The Case of P2P Traffic. European Transactions on Telecommunications, Special Issue on P2P Networking and P2P Services **15** (2004)
11. Wierzbicki, A., Leibowitz, N., Ripeanu, M., Wozniak, R.: Cache Replacement Policies For P2P File Sharing Protocols. European Transactions on Telecommunications **15** (2004) 559–569

# A Family of Encounter-Based Broadcast Protocols for Mobile Ad-Hoc Networks

D.E. Cooper, P. Ezhilchelvan, and I. Mitrani

School of Computing Science, University of Newcastle
Newcastle upon Tyne, NE1 7RU, U.K.
[d.e.cooper, paul.ezhilchelvan, isi.mitrani]@ncl.ac.uk

**Abstract.** A family of message propagation protocols for highly mobile ad-hoc networks is defined, and is studied analytically and by simulation. The coverage of a message (the fraction of nodes that receive it), can be made arbitrarily close to 1, at a moderate cost of extra message traffic. Under certain simplifying assumptions, it is shown that a high coverage is achieved by making a total of $O(n \ln n)$ broadcasts, where $n$ is the number of nodes, and the time to propagate a message is $O(\ln n)$. The effect of various parameters on the protocol performance is examined.

**Keywords:** Ad-hoc networks, message propagation, broadcasting.

## 1 Introduction

Recent advances in the technologies of mobile devices and wireless communication have given rise to an increasingly popular form of networking, called Mobile Ad-hoc networking. A Mobile Ad-hoc network (MANET) consists of small, versatile and powerful mobile computing devices (nodes). It is typically formed at short notice and does not make use of any fixed networking infrastructure. A distinguishing feature of a MANET is that the nodes are not just the sources of message traffic but also engage in forwarding messages to final destinations; given that the nodes can be highly mobile, a MANET is a dynamic network characterized by frequent and hard-to-predict topological changes.

An application of a mobile network usually involves user collaboration towards achieving a common goal, in situations where access to base stations is unavailable or unreliable (e.g., command and control or disaster relief). The success of such collaborative undertakings depends to a large extent on the provision of reliable multicast [5]. That is, a message originating at any node should reach all other nodes within a reasonably period of time. Unfortunately, both the nature of the devices (limited memory and power), and their mobility, imply that a guaranteed reliable multicast is normally harder to achieve in a MANET. Our objective, therefore, is to devise and evaluate multicast protocols which aim to maximize the probability of delivering a message to all nodes, while keeping the propagation time as low as possible.

G. Kotsis and O. Spaniol (Eds.): Mobile and Wireless Systems, LNCS 3427, pp. 235–248, 2005.

Existing work in this area has concentrated on minimizing the number of broadcasts carried out while propagating a message. Several protocols have been proposed, where the nodes maintain pro-actively, or construct on demand, distributed state information about the network topology. That state information is then used for the purpose of improving coverage with small overhead (see [3,10,4,1]). When the degree of mobility is low, these protocols perform well, but when it is high, the network state information can become out-of-date quickly and the coverage achieved (i.e., the fraction of nodes that receive a message) can be poor [9,11].

A topology-independent and stateless protocol that seems to work better in highly mobile networks is 'flooding'. Every node broadcasts every message once, either immediately upon receipt or after a random interval (for a study of basic flooding, see Ho et al [6]; an optimized version was examined in Ni et al [8]). The coverage achieved by flooding depends not only on the mobility pattern, but also on the 'density' of nodes (usually defined as the average number of nodes within a disc of radius equal to the wireless range). When the density is low, the flooding coverage tends to be poor.

We propose, and study, a family of protocols which preserve the topology-independent nature of flooding, while being able to achieve coverage levels arbitrarily close to 1, for any node density. Of course a specific high coverage cannot be guaranteed in any given instance, but can be expected with high probability. These protocols are based on a notion of 'encounter', and are controlled by an 'encounter threshold' parameter. The cost paid for a high coverage is an increase in the message traffic, since messages are broadcast more than once by each node. Under certain simplifying assumptions, analysis shows that to achieve a coverage close to 1 in a network with $n$ nodes, the total average number of broadcasts per message is on the order of $O(n \ln n)$. This is a moderate increase on the $O(n)$ broadcasts carried out in flooding. The propagation time of a message is on the order of $O(\ln n)$. Various aspects of the protocols' performance are examined by simulation (such an investigation, using a less realistic simulator, was presented in [2]).

The estimate of the necessary threshold provided by the analytical model is deliberately pessimistic. Because of that, it is worth introducing schemes for reducing the number of unnecessary broadcasts during the propagation of a message. One such scheme, *Random Assessment Delay* (RAD), is investigated by simulation.

The model, and the message propagation protocols, are described in section 2. Some analytical results concerning the propagation time and the number of broadcasts are obtained in section 3. The outcomes of a number of simulation experiments are presented in section 4, while section 5 summarizes the results obtained and outlines avenues of further enquiry.

## 2   The Model

The system under consideration consists of $n$ mobile nodes which move within a given terrain. The nodes communicate with each other using wireless technology, but without any fixed network infrastructure support. That is, the nodes themselves are the sources as well as the forwarders of the message traffic, and thus form a mobile ad-hoc network. Each node has a unique identifier (MAC or IP address). It is assumed that nodes do not fail; however, due to their mobility, they may become disconnected, and reconnected, as they move out of and into each others wireless range. Thus, the structure of the network can change with time in an unpredictable manner. For simplicity, assume that the wireless ranges of all nodes are equal and remain constant during the period of interest.

The movement of each node is governed by some 'mobility pattern', which controls its current speed and direction. It is assumed that the $n$ nodes are statistically identical, i.e. the rules of their mobility patterns are the same, and any random variables involved have the same distributions for all nodes.

We shall define a protocol whose principal objective is to deliver a message, originating at any node, to all other nodes with high probability. A secondary objective is to minimize, as far as possible, the memory requirements at each node. In fact, what will be defined is not a single protocol, but a family of protocols depending on an integer parameter, $\tau$.

Node $i$ ($i = 1, 2, \ldots, n$) advertises its presence by broadcasting, at regular intervals, a signal carrying its identifier and saying, essentially, 'hello, this is node $i$'. It also listens for similar signals from other nodes and maintains a list, $\{j_1, j_2, \ldots, j_k\}$, of the nodes, other than itself, that it can hear. That list is called the 'current neighbourhood' of node $i$. At any moment in time, any current neighbourhood may be empty, or it may contain any number of other nodes.

The current neighbourhood of node $i$ changes when a node which was in it, say $j_1$, moves out of range, or when a node which was not in it, say $j_{k+1}$, moves into range. The latter event is called an 'encounter'; that is, node $i$ is said to encounter node $j_{k+1}$. Note that, since 'hello' signals are not assumed to be synchronized among the nodes, if node $i$ encounters node $j$, node $j$ does not necessarily encounter node $i$ at the same time. Also note that, if node $j$ leaves the current neighbourhood of node $i$ and at some later point enters it again, then that entry constitutes an encounter. Nodes do not maintain a history of their current neighbourhoods, in order to keep their memory requirements low.

Now consider a message propagation protocol where each node behaves as follows:

- 1. Upon receiving or originating a new message, $m$, store it, together with an associated counter, $c(m)$, which is set to zero. Add the sending node to the current neighbourhood, unless already present. If the current neighbourhood contains nodes other than the sending one, broadcast $m$ and increment $c(m)$ by 1.

- 2. At every encounter thereafter, if $c(m) < \tau$, broadcast $m$ and increment $c(m)$ by 1.
- 3. When $c(m) = \tau$, remove $m$ from memory (but keep its sequence number in order to remember that it has been handled).

Thus, every node receiving a message broadcasts it at $\tau$ consecutive encounters (one of which may be the message arrival), and then discards it. There are no acknowledgements. The integer $\tau$ is called the 'encounter threshold'. The above protocol, with encounter threshold $\tau$, will be referred to as '$\tau$-propagation'.

When $\tau = 1$, the 1-propagation protocol behaves like flooding (except that the broadcast is delayed until the next encounter if the current neigbourhood contains only the sender). At the other extreme, if $\tau = \infty$, we have an $\infty$-propagation protocol whereby messages are kept forever and broadcast at every encounter. Assuming that the mobility pattern is such that every node eventually encounters every other node, $\infty$-propagation achieves coverage 1. Of course, $\infty$-propagation is not a practical option, but we shall see in section 3 that it can provide some useful insights.

It should be pointed out that $\tau$-propagation trades memory capacity and probability of reaching all nodes against message traffic. Because past histories are not kept and exchanged, messages may be sent again to nodes who have already received them. By increasing the value of $\tau$, the coverage can be made to approach 1, at the cost of having to store more messages for longer periods, and making more broadcasts.

In this paper, we place greater emphasis on evaluating the ability of $\tau$-propagation to achieve high coverage, than on minimizing the message traffic overheads. That is why we assume the following:

- The overheads of collision resolution are negligible.
- Hello signals are sent and monitored at the MAC level; the information necessary to maintain the neighbourhood list is obtained at no extra cost to the higher level protocol.
- Encounters last long enough for a message to be received, i.e. the processing and propagation times of hello and broadcast messages are small enough for the encountered node to remain in the range of the encountering node.

The performance measures of interest are:

- (i) The average response time of $\tau$-propagation, defined as the interval between the arrival (origin) of a message and the moment when no node can propagate it further.
- (ii) The average propagation time of a message, defined as the interval between its arrival and the moment when either all nodes have received it, or no node can propagate it further.
- (iii) The coverage of a message, i.e. the fraction of nodes that have received it by the end of its propagation time.

All of these performance measures are stated in terms of averages. However, each simulation experiment is repeated 50 times with different random number streams. Thus, observing a coverage of 1 implies that *all 50 runs* achieved a coverage of 1.

It is important to be able to choose the value of $\tau$ so as to achieve high coverage, without unduly increasing the response and propagation times. This question will be addressed in the following sections.

## 3   Analytical Approximation

Consider an idealized system with $n$ mobile nodes who never cease to propagate the messages they receive ($\infty$-propagation). Let $T$ be the random variable representing a message propagation time, i.e., the interval between the origin of a message at some node, and the first instant thereafter at which all nodes have received it. If messages are not discarded, and every node eventually encounters every other node, $T$ is finite with probability 1. It is then of interest to estimate its average value, $E(T)$. That quantity will also be used in choosing a suitable value for $\tau$, when designing a practicable $\tau$-propagation protocol.

An estimate for $E(T)$ will be obtained under the following simplifying assumptions:

- (a) Each node experiences encounters at intervals which are exponentially distributed with mean $\xi$.
- (b) At each encounter, a node meets one other node (in other words, the intervals between hello signals are infinitesimal).
- (c) The node encountered is equally likely to be any of the other nodes; that is, the probability that node $i$ will next encounter node $j$, $j \neq i$, is equal to $1/(n-1)$, regardless of past history.

Assumption (a) can be justified by remarking that the interval until the next encounter experienced by a given node — say node 1 — is the smallest of the intervals until its next encounters with node 2, node 3, ..., node $n$. It is known (e.g., see [7]) that, under weak assumptions, the interval until the first of many random occurrences is approximately exponentially distributed. The value of $\xi$ depends on the density of nodes, on the speed with which they move, and on the mobility pattern. It may be difficult to determine $\xi$ analytically, but in practice it can be estimated by monitoring the system and taking measurements.

Assumption (b) is deliberately pessimistic, in order to give the estimate the character of an upper bound. If a node encounters more than one other node at the same time, then the propagation will proceed faster. In fact, it will be seen in the experiments that at high densities this assumption is *very* pessimistic.

Assumption (c) is loosely based on the fact that all nodes are statistically identical, and move independently of each other. If the starting positions of the nodes are uniformly distributed, the assumption is justifiable at the first encounter, although it may well be violated in subsequent ones. However, this assumption provides the simplification necessary for analytical tractability. Its effect on the performance measures will be evaluated in the simulation experiments.

Let $X = \{X(t) ; t \geq 0\}$ be the Markov process whose state at any given time is the number of nodes that have already received the message. The initial state of $X$ is $X(0) = 1$ (only the originating node has received it). This is a pessimistic simplification; the original neighbourhood may in fact contain other nodes, in which case $X(0)$ would be greater than 1 and the propagation would be faster.

The random variable $T$ is the first passage time of $X$ from state 1 to state $n$.

Suppose that $X$ is in state $k$, i.e. $k$ nodes have received the message and $n - k$ have not. If any of the former $k$ nodes encounters any of the latter $n - k$, the process will jump to state $k + 1$. Since each node experiences encounters at rate $1/\xi$, and the probability of encountering any other node is $1/(n - 1)$, the transition rate of $X$ from state $k$ to state $k + 1$, $r_{k,k+1}$, is equal to

$$r_k = \left[\frac{k}{\xi}\right] \left[\frac{n - k}{n - 1}\right] . \tag{1}$$

In other words, the average time that $X$ remains in state $k$ is

$$\frac{1}{r_k} = \frac{(n - 1)\xi}{k(n - k)} . \tag{2}$$

Hence, the average first passage time from state 1 to state $n$ is given by

$$E(T) = (n - 1)\xi \sum_{k=1}^{n-1} \frac{1}{k(n - k)} . \tag{3}$$

This last expression can be simplified by rewriting the terms under the summation sign in the form

$$\frac{1}{k(n - k)} = \frac{1}{n} \left[\frac{1}{k} + \frac{1}{n - k}\right] .$$

The two resulting sums are in fact identical. Therefore,

$$E(T) = \frac{2(n - 1)\xi}{n} \sum_{k=1}^{n-1} \frac{1}{k} = \frac{2(n - 1)\xi H_{n-1}}{n} , \tag{4}$$

where $H_n$ is the $n$th harmonic number. When $n$ is large, the latter is approximately equal to

$$H_n \approx \ln n + \gamma ,$$

where $\gamma = 0.5772...$ is Euler-Mascheroni's number. Also, when $n$ is large, $(n - 1)/n \approx 1$ and $\ln(n - 1) \approx \ln n$.

We have thus arrived at the following estimate, valid under assumptions (a), (b) and (c):

**Proposition 1.** *In a large mobile network where messages are not discarded, the average propagation period for a message is approximately equal to*

$$E(T) \approx 2\xi(\ln n + \gamma) \,. \tag{5}$$

An immediate corollary of Proposition 1 is that, during the propagation period $T$, the originating node experiences an average of $2(\ln n + \gamma)$ encounters. Other nodes, who receive the message later on, tend to experience fewer encounters. Thus, choosing the encounter threshold, $\tau$, to have the value

$$\tau = 2\lceil \ln n + \gamma \rceil \,, \tag{6}$$

should ensure that, when the protocol terminates, most nodes will have received the message. This suggestion will be tested experimentally.

**Note 1.** An attractive aspect of equation (6) is that the only parameter appearing in it is the number of nodes, $n$. The mobility pattern and the node density do not matter, because assumptions (a), (b) and (c) were deliberately chosen to be pessimistic. In practice, lower thresholds than those provided by (6) will be satisfactory, especially at higher densities. This will be illustrated by the simulation experiments.

**Note 2.** Since, under $\tau$-propagation, every node that receives a message broadcasts it $\tau$ times, the total number of broadcasts per message is on the order of $O(n\tau)$. Hence, if $\tau$ is chosen according to (6), the total number of broadcasts per message is on the order of $O(n \ln n)$.

## 4    Experimental Results

A number of experiments were carried out, using the Glomosim simulation package. The objectives were two-fold: First, to evaluate the effect of various parameters on the performance of $\tau$-propagation, as measured by (a) the coverage achieved, and (b) the response and propagation times. The second objective was to investigate some schemes for reducing the protocol overheads, measured by the average number of *redundant broadcast per node*. A broadcast is considered to be redundant if all of its targets have already received the message).

The following factors were kept fixed:

The terrain is a square of dimensions $(1000\ m) \times (1000\ m)$.

The number of nodes is 64.

The wireless range of all nodes is either $50\ m$ or $180\ m$. These two ranges correspond to node densities of 0.5 and 6.5 respectively.

The node speed is 2 m/sec.

The mobility pattern is 'Random Waypoint': Initially, the nodes are distributed uniformly on the square; thereafter, each node chooses a random destination (also uniformly distributed on the square) and moves towards it at a given speed; upon reaching the destination, the node pauses for a given interval ($1\ ms$ in our case), selects a new random destination and so on.

Each run starts at time 0 with a message originating at node 1, and terminates when no node can propagate the message further. For each set of parameter values, the simulation ran 50 times, with different random number seeds, and the performance observations were averaged.

## RAD Enhanced Encounter Propagation

One technique that is used to reduce redundant broadcasts is Random Assessment Delay (RAD). Having decided to broadcast a message, either as an originator or at an encounter epoch, a node waits for a random period of time, called the 'RAD interval'. An encounter which occurs during a RAD interval does not generate a new RAD interval. If, during a RAD interval, a node hears another broadcast of the same message, then the broadcast it had planned is canceled (see [11]). The idea is that if several nodes in a given neighbourhood are in possession of the message and decide to broadcast it, one of them will do so first (the one with the shortest RAD interval), and then the others can keep quiet.

Remember that, under the $\tau$-propagation protocol described in section 2, a node ceases to broadcast message $m$ when the number of encounters, recorded in $c(m)$, reaches the value $\tau$. Now, the addition of RAD may affect the way $c(m)$ is incremented. During a RAD interval associated with message $m$, the node counts the number of broadcasts of $m$ that it hears. Denote that number by $r$. If $r = 0$ at the end of the RAD interval, then the node broadcasts $m$ and increments $c(m)$ by 1. If $r > 0$, there are two possibilities:

1. Do not broadcast $m$ and increase $c(m)$ by 1;
2. Do not broadcast $m$ and increase $c(m)$ by $r$.

These two policies were simulated, but their effects on both performance and overheads turned out to be very similar. Therefore, only the results obtained with policy 1 are displayed.

Figures 1 and 2 show the coverage achieved as a function of the encounter threshold, $\tau$, for node densities 0.5 and 6.5, respectively. The different graphs in each figure correspond to different distributions of the RAD interval. More precisely, the RAD interval is distributed uniformly on $(0, RAD)$, for different values of $RAD$. Thus, the case $RAD = 0$ corresponds to the original protocol, without the enhancement.

The figures quantify the extent to which the coverage can be improved by increasing $\tau$: at low densities, where flooding performs poorly ($\tau = 0$), the improvement is very considerable; at high densities, flooding performs well and the gain of increasing $\tau$ is correspondingly smaller.

Consider the analytical predictions concerning $\tau$. For the assumed terrain area and wireless range, the densities 0.5 and 6.5. For the case of 64 nodes, the encounter threshold given by equation (6) is $\tau = 10$, and the figures indicate that it does, indeed, achieve coverages close to 1. In fact, when the density is high, the threshold provided by equation (6) is rather conservative. This is because, for those densities, assumption (b) in section 3 is too pessimistic.

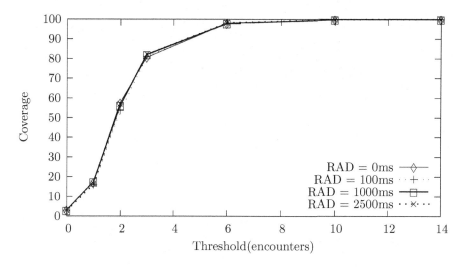

**Fig. 1.** Coverage vs Encounter Threshold; Density $= 0.5$

At the low density of 0.5, the introduction of RAD has no appreciable effect on the coverage. This is not surprising, since an encounter rarely involves more than one other node and so the RAD counter $r$ is usually 0. At the high density of 6.5 and low threshold values, some coverage is lost by RAD because nodes who could usefully broadcast have in fact decided to stop too early.

The gains achieved by the RAD enhancement are shown in figures 3 and 4. At the low density of 0.5, a reduction of about 35% in redundant broadcasts per node can be achieved, without loss of coverage. Increasing the average RAD interval generally leads to bigger reductions, but the incremental gains become lower (the largest gain is achieved in moving from $RAD = 0$ to $RAD = 100$).

At the high density of 6.5, the picture is similar, but now there is a genuine trade-off between coverage and redundancy at low thresholds. At high thresholds, the reduction in redundancy is again achieved without loss of coverage.

Figures 5 and 6 show the average response time and the average propagation time as functions of $\tau$, for the same two densities, 0.5 and 6.5. Remember that the propagation time is the period until all nodes receive the message (or the protocol terminates, if earlier), whereas the response time is the period until the protocol terminates. A noteworthy aspect of these figures is that, while the response time tends to keep growing with $\tau$ (as expected), the propagation time increases up to a point, and then decreases. To explain that behaviour, note that when the threshold is low, the coverage is less than 1 and therefore the propagation time is equal to the response time. When the threshold is large, a coverage of 1 is reached and the propagation completes, before nodes have stopped broadcasting. Moreover, further increases in $\tau$ tend to speed up the propagation, but prolong the response time.

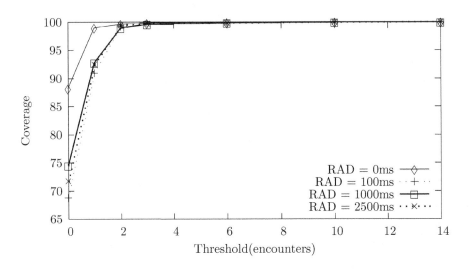

**Fig. 2.** Coverage vs Encounter Threshold; Density = 6.5

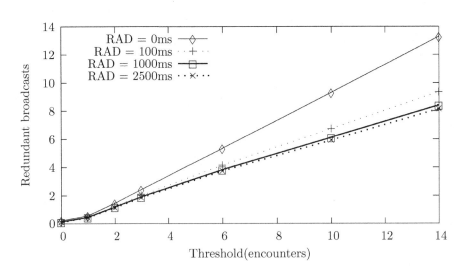

**Fig. 3.** Redundant broadcasts vs Encounter Threshold; Density = 0.5

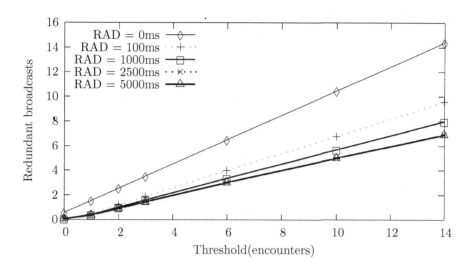

**Fig. 4.** Redundant broadcasts vs Encounter Threshold; Density = 6.5

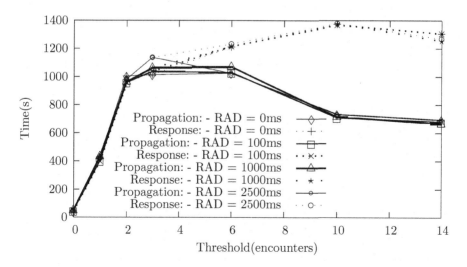

**Fig. 5.** Response/Propagation Time vs Encounter Threshold; Density =0.5

Increasing the average RAD interval does, of course, lead to longer average response and propagation times. However, the effect is negligible at low density, and becomes significant at high density mainly for the response time, and only when the threshold is low.

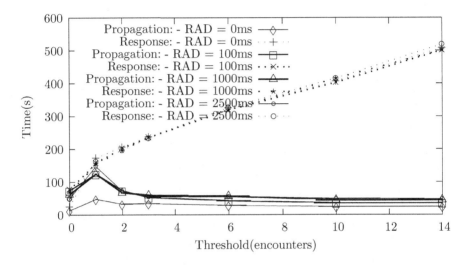

**Fig. 6.** Response/Propagation Time vs Encounter Threshold; Density =6.5

The process of propagating a message among the nodes in a network where the speed and threshold ($\tau = 14$) are fixed, while the density is varied in the range $0.5 - 6.5$, is illustrated in figure 7. For the purpose of this figure only, the wireless range was kept at 50 $m$, and the density was changed by varying the number of nodes between 64 and 828; a different simulator was used. The graphs show how the rate of propagation changes as more and more nodes are covered. At high densities, it takes longer to cover the last 5% of the nodes than the first 95%. This phenomenon is due to the fact that some nodes on the periphery of the terrain can be relatively more difficult to reach than the others. It is less pronounced at lower densities, but is still in evidence: the last 20% of the nodes take about as long to cover as the first 80%.

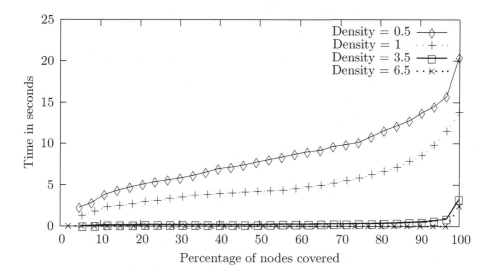

**Fig. 7.** Process of propagation: speed $= 60 \ ms^{-1}$; $\tau = 14$

## 5   Conclusions

The main contributions of this paper can be summarized as follows:

- 1. Introduction of the $\tau$-propagation family (section 2).
- 2. Mobility-independent estimate for the value of $\tau$ that achieves high coverage (equation (6)).
- 3. Quantitative performance results obtained by experimentation (section 4).

A more adaptable family of propagation protocols may be designed by introducing a FIFO buffer for messages. Messages would be kept in the buffer, and re-broadcast, until either they are displaced by new messages or they reach an encounter threshold. The number of times a message is broadcast by a node would then change dynamically in response to changing conditions. That number could also be adjusted by keeping track of repeated receptions of the same message. A time-out interval can be introduced, to force the discarding of a message if the node does not experience a sufficient number of encounters. The encounter threshold may be adjusted dynamically, as a function of the number of nodes already encountered, and possibly as a function of the mobility pattern. All these are worthy topics for future research.

It should be pointed out that the Random Waypoint mobility model is particularly favourable to the assumption that each node is equally likely to be encountered. Other mobility models are more likely to violate that assumption. That is why it is important to investigate the behaviour of models with more pronounced locality properties, such as 'Manhattan Grid' and 'Drunken Walk'.

**Acknowledgement**

This work was carried out as part of the research project PACE (Protocols for Ad-hoc Collaborative Environments), funded by the UK Engineering and Physical Sciences Research Council. We are also grateful to Einar Vollset, for some helpful discussions.

# References

1. C. Chiang and M. Gerla, "On-Demand Multicast in Mobile Networks", Procs., *IEEE ICMP*, pp. 260-270, Austin, 1998.
2. D.E. Cooper, P. Ezhilchelvan and I. Mitrani, "High Coverage Broadcasting for Mobile Ad Hoc Networks", *Procs., Networking'04*, Athens, 2004.
3. J. Garcia-Luna-Aceves and E. Madruga, "A Multicast Routing Protocol for Ad-hoc Networks", Procs., *Infocom*, pp.784-792, New York, 1999.
4. T. Gopalsamy, M. Shinghal, D. Panda and P. Sadayappan, "A Reliable Multicast Algorithm for Mobile Ad-hoc Networks", Procs., *ICDCS*, Vienna, 2002.
5. V. Hadzilacos and S. Tueg, "Fault-Tolerant Broadcasts and Related Problems", in *Distributed Systems* (Ed. S. Mullender), Addison-Wesley, 1993.
6. C. Ho, K. Obraczka, G. Tsudik and K. Viswanath, "Flooding for Reliable Multicast in Multihop Ad-hoc Networks", Procs., *Discrete Algorithms and Methods for Mobile Computing (DIAL-M)*, pp. 64-71, Seattle, 1999.
7. I. Mitrani, *Probabilistic Modelling*, Cambridge University Press, 1998.
8. S. Ni, Y. Tseng, Y. Chen and J. Sheu, "The Broadcast Storm Problem in a Mobile Ad-hoc Network", Procs., *ACM Int. Conf. on Mobile Computing and Networking (MOBICOM)*, pp. 151-162, Seattle, 1999.
9. E. Pagani and G.P. Rossi, "Reliable Broadcast in Mobile Multihop Packet Networks", Procs., *ACM Int. Conf. on Mobile Computing and Networking (MOBICOM)*, pp. 34-42, Budapest, 1997.
10. P. Sinha, R. Sivakumar and V. Bharagavan, "MCEDAR: Multicast Core Extraction Distributed Ad-hoc Networking", Procs., *Wireless Communications and Networking Conference (WCNC)*, pp. 1313-1317, New Orleans, 1999.
11. B. Williams and T. Camp, "Comparison of Broadcasting Techniques for Mobile Ad-hoc Networks", Procs., *ACM Int. Symp. on Mobile Ad-hoc Networking and Computing (MOBIHOC)*, Lausanne, 2002.

# Author Index